US Policy
TOWARD
Africa

ADST-DACOR Diplomats and Diplomacy Series
Series Editor MARGERY BOICHEL THOMPSON

Since 1776, extraordinary men and women have represented the United States abroad under widely varying circumstances. What they did and how and why they did it remain little known to their compatriots. In 1995, the Association for Diplomatic Studies and Training (ADST) and DACOR, an organization of foreign affairs professionals, created the Diplomats and Diplomacy book series to increase public knowledge and appreciation of the professionalism of US diplomats and their involvement in world history. In this seventieth volume in the series, Career Ambassador Herman "Hank" Cohen provides a comprehensive survey of how every US administration, from Roosevelt to Trump, interacted with African states.

For a list of selected ADST series titles, see page 280.

US Policy
TOWARD
Africa

Eight Decades of Realpolitik

Herman J. Cohen

LYNNE
RIENNER
PUBLISHERS

BOULDER
LONDON

The opinions and characterizations in this book are those of the author and do not necessarily represent official positions of the US government, the Association for Diplomatic Studies and Training, or DACOR.

Published in the United States of America in 2020 by
Lynne Rienner Publishers, Inc.
1800 30th Street, Boulder, Colorado 80301
www.rienner.com

and in the United Kingdom by
Lynne Rienner Publishers, Inc.
Gray's Inn House, 127 Clerkenwell Road, London EC1 5DB

Library of Congress Cataloging-in-Publication Data
Names: Cohen, Herman J., author.
Title: US policy toward Africa: eight decades of realpolitik / Herman J.
    Cohen.
Other titles: ADST-DACOR diplomats and diplomacy series.
Description: Boulder, Colorado: Lynne Rienner Publishers, Inc., 2020. |
    Series: ADST-DACOR diplomats and diplomacy series | Includes
    bibliographical references and index.
Identifiers: LCCN 2019033985 | ISBN 9781626378698 (hardcover) | ISBN
    9781626378704 (paperback)
Subjects: LCSH: United States—Foreign relations—Africa. | United
    States—Foreign relations—20th century. | United States—Foreign
    relations—21st century. | Africa—Foreign relations—United States.
Classification: LCC JZ1480.A56 C64 2020 | DDC 327.7306—dc23
LC record available at https://lccn.loc.gov/2019033985

British Cataloguing in Publication Data
A Cataloguing in Publication record for this book
is available from the British Library.

Printed and bound in the United States of America

The paper used in this publication meets the requirements
of the American National Standard for Permanence of
Paper for Printed Library Materials Z39.48-1992.

5 4 3 2 1

Contents

Preface   vii

1 The United States and Africa: A Historical Perspective   1

2 Franklin D. Roosevelt: 1941–1945   5

3 Harry S. Truman: 1945–1953   15

4 Dwight D. Eisenhower: 1953–1961   31

5 John F. Kennedy: 1961–1963   47

6 Lyndon B. Johnson: 1963–1969   61

7 Richard M. Nixon: 1969–1974   85

8 Gerald Ford: 1974–1977   99

9 Jimmy Carter: 1977–1981   113

10 Ronald Reagan: 1981–1989   133

11 George H. W. Bush: 1989–1993   147

12 William J. Clinton: 1993–2001   175

13 George W. Bush: 2001–2009   199

14 Barack H. Obama: 2009–2017   211

15 Donald J. Trump: 2017–2019   227

16 Reflections on Successes and Failures   235

Notes   251
Bibliography   263
Index   265
About the Book   279
Related ADST Series Titles   280

Preface

I entered the US Foreign Service in 1955. The Cold War was at its height, as I had witnessed firsthand during the two preceding years commanding a US Army infantry platoon in Germany. Although little oxygen was available for other foreign policy issues, I was able to discover newly emerging Africa.

Our mentors in the entry-level training course emphasized the growing complexity of international relations and strongly recommended career specialization. Gone were the days when a career Foreign Service officer could envision serving successively in Brazil, Finland, Japan, and South Africa. Specialization had become a requirement, either in a geographic region or in a sector such as economics or political-military relations.

Having done undergraduate research in the economics of developing countries, I decided to look at Africa. The British and the French were busy preparing about forty African colonies for independence. The United States faced the challenge of opening diplomatic relations with most of these new nations. The prospect of applying the economic development theory I had formulated through research intrigued me, so I decided to specialize in United States–Africa relations.

My career specialization in Africa led me to service in five African countries: Uganda, Zimbabwe, Zambia, Congo (Kinshasa), and Senegal, this last as US ambassador. During assignments in Washington, I served as director for Central Africa, assistant secretary of state for Africa, and senior director for Africa on the National Security Council.

My career advanced in parallel with the initial decades of African independence, when I played influential roles, at various levels, in the formulation and implementation of US policy during seven administrations.

That experience, I believe, placed me in a unique position to describe and analyze the evolution of US policy during independent Africa's youth and early middle age.

After my retirement from the Foreign Service in 1994, I continued to be involved with African issues. From 1994 to 1999, I served as a senior adviser to the Global Coalition for Africa (GCA), under contract to the World Bank. The GCA was an intergovernmental forum designed to encourage African governments to adopt economic growth policies. After leaving the GCA, I established a consulting firm in support of US corporations doing business in Africa or seeking business opportunities there. These activities outside the US government enhanced my ability to analyze US policy toward Africa.

It would have been extremely more difficult to write this book without the support of the State Department's Office of the Historian, which reviews and declassifies official national security documents. I was able to access these documents covering the years through the end of the Carter administration. I have nothing but the highest praise for the way the office organizes and presents documents that originate in 150 US embassies and in several agencies, including the State Department, Defense Department, National Security Council, and intelligence agencies. I enjoyed reading the reporting cables, memoranda of conversation, and analytical papers of many of my Foreign Service colleagues and friends, not to mention rereading my own output.

I want to express special appreciation to the late ambassadors Frank Carlucci and David Newsom, as well as former secretary of state James Baker and the late president George H. W. Bush for the confidence they placed in me as a senior specialist in US policy toward Africa. Working under the guidance of these four leaders was consistently rewarding. Among the colleagues who worked with me over the years, I want to give special recognition to Ambassador Jeffrey Davidow, my alter ego and principal deputy assistant secretary of state for Africa, and to Alison Rosenberg, who was my deputy director for Africa on the National Security Council during the administration of President Ronald Reagan. I valued their frank advice, wise counsel, and fresh ideas.

Twenty-five years after my retirement from the Foreign Service, as I look at the younger generation of Foreign Service officers currently specializing in US policy toward Africa, with their advanced degrees in African studies and knowledge of esoteric African languages, I feel confident that US policy remains in excellent hands.

—*Herman J. Cohen*

1

The United States and Africa: A Historical Perspective

The United States has been a colonial power, but never in Africa. That was a significant factor in the unfolding of positive US-Africa post–World War II relations. During the nineteenth century, between 1800 and 1885, there was a massive movement into Africa on the part of the Western European powers: France, Great Britain, Germany, Portugal, Belgium, and Spain. This so-called scramble for Africa resulted in the creation of fifty-four colonial dependencies. By the turn of the twentieth century, there were only two independent African nations: Ethiopia and Liberia. Approximately 90 percent of the African continent had been colonized.

What is striking about this aspect of African history is the absence of the United States. During the early years of the nineteenth century, the United States had a blue water navy. Its many East Coast ports were engaged in significant commerce with West Africa, including the slave trade and whaling. During the presidency of Thomas Jefferson, the United States fought and won the Barbary Wars against North African pirates based in Tunisia, Algeria, and Libya who had been engaged in predatory attacks on commercial shipping and coastal European communities for over a century.

So why did the United States refrain from establishing colonies in Africa? The answer lies in the Louisiana Purchase, the transaction through which President Thomas Jefferson negotiated the acquisition of France's vast lands west of the Mississippi River in 1803 for $15 million.

1

The territory contained 828,000 square miles, including the Port of New Orleans. The result of this significant enlargement of US territory was that the United States began to look westward for land and opportunity. Any possible interest in colonizing Africa disappeared. In addition, American Christian missionaries who ventured into West Africa during the first half of the nineteenth century suffered heavily from disease in what they called "the white man's grave."

The absence of US colonies in Africa did not prevent US companies from engaging in trade with Africa. US trade with Africa was sufficiently important for the US government to establish consulates and commercial agencies throughout the continent—in Port Louis (Mauritius) in 1794, Cape Town (South Africa) in 1799, Bathurst (Gambia) in 1834, and Luanda (Angola) in 1850, and by 1862 there were twenty-five consuls and commercial agents in Africa. US companies were interested mainly in importing ivory, palm oil, and hides.[1]

The US Navy was also active in patrolling in Africa's Atlantic waters. In the Webster-Ashburton Treaty of 1842 between the United States and the United Kingdom, the United States agreed to cooperate in the suppression of the slave trade, despite the fact that slavery continued to be legal in the United States. That commitment required the United States to maintain active naval patrols along the African coast.[2]

Toward the end of the nineteenth century, the United States fought a war with Spain that resulted in the acquisition of Spanish territories that became US colonies, notably the Philippine Islands and Guam in the western Pacific Ocean and Puerto Rico in the Caribbean Sea. Later the United States also acquired the Panama Canal Zone from Colombia by supporting the local Panamanian independence movement, as a prelude to the construction of the Atlantic-to-Pacific canal, and annexed the independent kingdom of Hawaii as being vital to US economic and naval interests. At the end of World War II, therefore, the United States could not claim to be unblemished from colonialism. Nevertheless, US policy in the postwar atmosphere was decidedly anticolonial.[3]

The US ideological turn against colonialism began with President Woodrow Wilson in 1918. In April 1917, the United States entered World War I against Germany on the side of France and England. Since Wilson had won reelection in 1916 with the slogan "He kept us out of war," he needed to develop an ideological justification for taking the United States into the war. This took the form of his famous "Fourteen Points," which presented an agenda for the postwar future in which all disputes would be settled peacefully and transparently, with democracy serving as the necessary unifying element.

Within this document, President Wilson also addressed colonialism. His fifth point called for the "impartial adjustment of all colonial claims under the strict observance of the principle that the interests of the populations concerned must have equal weight with the equitable claims of the government whose title is to be determined." He also called for granting autonomy to the European territories under Turkish rule and to the peoples in the Austro-Hungarian Empire. He made no mention of African territories, but the basic implication of autonomy for colonial peoples was clear.[4]

Woodrow Wilson's "Fourteen Points" were far ahead of their time. While the US contribution to the war effort against Germany was crucial to the Allied victory, Wilson's formula for postwar peace, harmony, and democracy was totally ignored in the peace arrangements. But one senior US official in Wilson's wartime government, Franklin D. Roosevelt, took his president's "fourteen points" seriously and worked hard to implement them when he became president during World War II.

One of the earliest manifestations of Roosevelt's Wilsonian view of colonialism surfaced in August 1941, when the British were at war against Germany and Japan while the United States was still officially neutral. Roosevelt met with British prime minister Winston Churchill on a US naval ship near the coast of Newfoundland to discuss how the United States could be helpful to the UK war effort without actually entering the war. In addition to agreements regarding the loan of US war equipment, the two statesmen signed a document that came to be known as the Atlantic Charter, a statement of their joint view of postwar objectives.

Among the eight paragraphs in the document, the third was clearly Wilsonian: "They respect the right of all peoples to choose the form of government under which they will live, and they wish to see sovereign rights and self-government restored to those who have been forcibly deprived of them."[5]

Churchill and his Conservative cabinet could not have been pleased with this third paragraph. It essentially constituted an invitation to peoples living under colonial dependency, a large percentage of whom were subjects of the British Empire, to demand self-government after the end of the war and the defeat of the Axis powers, Germany and Japan. At the time of the Atlantic Charter, the UK was clearly not thinking about the sun eventually setting on the British Empire. But the effort to bring the United States into World War II was the highest priority at the time, and Churchill therefore must have accepted the third paragraph with his fingers crossed.

As further evidence of how seriously the United States considered the language of the Atlantic Charter, the State Department arranged for endorsement of the charter's language by the Inter-Allied Council in London on September 24, 1941. In addition to the United States and the United Kingdom, the council comprised the governments in exile of Belgium, Czechoslovakia, Greece, Luxembourg, the Netherlands, Norway, Poland, Yugoslavia, the Soviet Union, and the Free French forces based in London.

World War II ended in 1945, and the words of the third paragraph of the Atlantic Charter became a driving force in US policy toward colonialism, including colonialism in Africa. The fact that the United States never had colonies in Africa gave this vision of the postwar future even greater relevance to the early development of United States–Africa relations. In essence, the image of the United States in the minds of the embryonic African independence movements during the 1940s and 1950s was as the free world's champion of self-determination. This was in stark contrast to the absence of enthusiasm on the part of the European colonial powers for the idea of an early transition from colonialism to self-determination in the midst of their struggle to achieve reconstruction from the devastation of world war.

2

Franklin D. Roosevelt: 1941–1945

The first defeat in Africa for Axis powers Germany and Italy took place in the Italian colony of Eritrea on April 1, 1941. On that day, South African troops in the British army captured Asmara, the capital of Eritrea, where Italy had been the colonial power for the previous fifty years.[1] A week later, on April 8, the South Africans marched from Asmara to the Ethiopian capital of Addis Ababa, where they inflicted the final defeat of Italy in Africa. Ethiopia had been under Italian occupation for five years.

German military forces were present in four colonial African nations during World War II: Libya, Tunisia, Algeria, and Egypt. The Allied powers fought decisive battles in Egypt and Tunisia and defeated the German army in both sectors, leading to the Germans' total surrender and the Allies' taking of 267,000 German and Italian prisoners of war. The British army, made up heavily of colonial troops from India and Australia, was the principal force that defeated the German army in the western Egyptian town of El Alamein between July and November 1942.[2]

The American army was the principal force in Tunisia, beginning with their amphibious landing east of Algiers in January 1943 and ending with the final defeat of German forces in the capital city of Tunis in May 1943.[3]

The French Colonies in Africa: Divided Loyalties

The situation of France's African colonial dependencies during World War II was particularly ambiguous. Nazi Germany defeated France in July 1940 and occupied the northern half of the country. To replace the defeated republican government, the Germans installed a puppet regime called Vichy France, under the leadership of World War I hero Marshall Philippe Pétain. Thus, with the stroke of a pen, all French colonies came under the control of Vichy France and, by extension, Nazi Germany. When the Vichy French government was established, the United States was still officially neutral. For that reason, the United States and Vichy France established diplomatic relations.[4]

Regarding France's African colonies, Nazi Germany, except where it had military forces, was unable to exert control of the French colonial empire, nor was it interested in doing so after its total defeat in North Africa as of May 1943.

Morocco, for example, was a French protectorate ruled by a Sultan who was closely advised by French colonial officials. When US forces landed in Morocco in November 1942, the Vichy protectorate regime had no military forces there in a position to resist and surrendered within three days. This was the last straw for relations between the United States and Vichy France. Vichy prime minister Pierre Laval formally broke diplomatic relations with the United States on November 8, 1942, forcing Washington to close its embassy, thereby losing America's last window on occupied Europe. Shortly thereafter, on November 18, the German army occupied the city of Vichy and the southern half of France. This caused the US government to declare the Vichy regime extinct.

Two months later, in January 1943, US president Franklin Roosevelt and British prime minister Winston Churchill met in Casablanca, Morocco, to discuss strategy for the continuation of the war against Nazi Germany.[5] Free France leader General Charles de Gaulle was also present. The French leader-in-exile was happy to receive assurances from Roosevelt and Churchill that postwar France would remain intact and presumed those assurances included France's African colonies.[6]

In France's fifteen sub-Saharan dependencies, Vichy could exercise control only to the extent that the French administrations in each colony collaborated. Thus, each French governor had to decide: Would they agree to pledge allegiance to the Vichy regime, or would they heed the call of "Free France" from General de Gaulle operating in exile in London? The results were mixed. Some of the governors opted to remain loyal to the French government in Vichy. Others openly declared allegiance to General de Gaulle. Questioned after the war as to why they opted to remain loyal to Vichy France, several of the disgraced governors said that they had wanted to protect the pensions of French citizens in the colonial service.

The French high commissioner for all of Equatorial Africa, in Brazzaville in the Central African colony of the Congo, accepted a request from the United States to open a consulate. Lawrence W. Taylor was the first consul assigned there.[7] In the colony of Senegal, however, the French high commissioner for all of West Africa proclaimed loyalty to Vichy. This brought British naval warships to the port of Dakar on September 23, 1940, with a demand that the French high commissioner surrender and allow British military personnel to land and take charge. The high commissioner refused. After sending artillery shells into the center of the city, the British forces had to retreat. Their ships also failed to engage and destroy two French frigates loitering in the area, which managed to escape.[8]

French Africa was thus divided in two throughout the war. French West Africa, centered on Dakar, Senegal, remained loyal to Vichy. French Equatorial Africa, centered on Brazzaville, Congo, rallied to the Free French under General de Gaulle. With the appointment of a US consul in Brazzaville covering all of French Equatorial Africa, Under Secretary of State Sumner Wells told the Free French ambassador to Washington on April 13, 1942: "When Nazism is defeated, the people of France will be once more in full and sovereign control of their own destinies." Secretary Wells diplomatically avoided any mention of the importance of self-determination for dependent peoples, a theme US representatives were loudly championing in various Allied meetings during the war.[9]

The Free French representatives at meetings of the Allied governments during the war were careful not to emphasize their desire to restore the entire French empire after the defeat of Germany and Japan. This vast holding of dependent territories included French Indo-China (Vietnam, Laos, and Cambodia) as well as francophone Africa. In London, on September 24, 1941, for example, there was a meeting of the Inter-Allied Group to discuss postwar issues. In the final communiqué, the delegation representing General de Gaulle said: "The Free French take note of the Atlantic Charter, and make known their adherence to the common principles set forth in that declaration." When General de Gaulle came to power as the French prime minister in 1958, he began the process of transitioning France's African colonies to independence.[10]

One important US contribution to Free France's operations in Africa occurred in the eastern French territory of Djibouti, at the strategic entrance to the Red Sea and the Suez Canal. At the start of the war, Italian forces based in neighboring Italian Somaliland had captured Djibouti. In 1942, local French were able to recapture Djibouti when the Italians were defeated in Eritrea and Ethiopia. However, the restored French governor was reluctant to declare loyalty to de Gaulle because he felt a personal loyalty to General Pétain, though not to the Vichy regime, which he refused to recognize. But thirty-five miles across the Bab-el-Mandeb strait from Djibouti, the US consul in British Aden, Claire H. Timberlake, intervened. After long hours of discussion, Timberlake persuaded the governor to rally to de Gaulle.[11]

With the assistance of the pro–Free French governors, particularly the activist Franco-Martinique governor Félix Eboué in Chad, Free France was able to recruit and train both French and African troops in Central Africa for later service in the Allied invasion of southern France on August 15, 1944, in the amphibious landing called Operation Dragoon. The African troops involved in this operation pushed northeast through Alsace and into Germany, all the way to Munich, and constituted a major military contribution to the Allied success in the final victory over Nazi Germany.

Reconnecting the United States with Two Old African Friends: Ethiopia and Liberia

The only two African nations to escape colonialism were Ethiopia and Liberia. Both had been hosting US embassies since the mid–nineteenth century, and both attracted the attention of the US government in connection with the war.

Ethiopia

As war clouds grew over Europe in the mid-1930s, fascist Italy's invasion of Ethiopia from its neighboring colony of Eritrea on October 3, 1935, was the Fascist-Nazi alliance's first act of aggressive territorial conquest of World War II. The Ethiopian head of state, Emperor Haile Selassie, managed to escape to Europe, where he brought his case to the League of Nations. Countering aggression and preserving peace were the reasons for the creation of the League immediately after World

War I. The diminutive Ethiopian emperor made an excellent case for international intervention to reverse Italy's aggression. His plea stimulated worldwide sympathy.

The debate in the League was highly critical of Italy for its unprovoked aggression. Nevertheless, France and the United Kingdom were reluctant to punish Italy for its action. Italy had fought on the side of Britain and France against Germany during World War I, and London and Paris still hoped that Italy could be persuaded to join them in the coming war against Germany. So Emperor Haile Selassie, let down that his country would remain under Italian occupation until the end of the coming war, became a symbol as the war's first victim of aggression. The Ethiopian army had fought valiantly against the invaders but lost to the Italians' superior weaponry and technology.

After five years of Italian occupation, however, British troops from South Africa liberated Ethiopia in April 1941. Thus, having been the first victim of fascist conquest, Ethiopia became the first to be liberated by the Allied forces. In June 1943, President Roosevelt wrote to Emperor Haile Selassie offering to furnish assistance on a loan basis, under the mechanism known as Lend-Lease. In October 1943, the Americans began shipping equipment to Ethiopia for a 5,000-man army. They also sent missions to Ethiopia for the purpose of improving the country's agriculture, engineering, and mining capabilities. As a gesture of gratitude and goodwill, the emperor decided that the large compound the United States was renting for its embassy and staff residences would become official US property. This cemented a strong relationship between Ethiopia and the United States that lasted until a radical Marxist military rebellion overthrew the emperor in 1974.[12]

Liberia

Since its founding in 1822, the West African Republic of Liberia has essentially been America's African orphan child. The nation was created by freed American slaves who voluntarily agreed to return to the land of their ancestors in order to address the problem of "the incompatibility of races." This was the credo of the American Colonization Society, which raised private funds to finance the move to Africa of any former slave willing to go.

Between 1822 and 1860, approximately 12,000 former American slaves and freedmen accepted the opportunity to resettle in Liberia. Because of their superior knowledge and arms technology, the former slaves were able to dominate the indigenous people they found living in the territory, which they named Liberia. By any definition, the former slaves, constituting only 5 percent of the population of the new nation, had become colonizers of the various ethnic groups already living there.

The former slaves came to be known as Americo-Liberians, while the indigenous tribes were called country people. Until 1990, when a band of country people took power in a military coup, the Americo-Liberians governed much as the white people governed in the south of the United States before 1965, with racial segregation, curfews, and total minority rule.

All of the countries bordering Liberia were European colonies, both British and French: Sierra Leone, Guinea, Côte d'Ivoire, and Senegal. Needless to say, with no external protection, the Liberian regimes were constantly concerned about the French and British putting pressure on their borders.

President Roosevelt first took notice of Liberia on January 27, 1943, when he stopped in the Port of Monrovia while returning from the Casablanca summit conference. He toured the American-owned Firestone rubber plantation, Liberia's main source of income. He also held discussions with the long-serving president, Edwin Barclay. The visit would have been filed as "routine" except for the leader of Liberia's official political opposition, James F. Cooper.

Cooper made a public statement protesting the fact that Roosevelt's visit was too short, and that Roosevelt had refused to see him. Cooper wanted to call Roosevelt's attention to what he called "the continued exploitation of the aborigines by the Americo-Liberian oligarchy."[13]

Later, when Roosevelt was in his final year of life and World War II was almost over, the US president heard about Liberia once again. In January 1945, Roosevelt received a visit from two African American newspaper publishers. (In those days, African Americans were called Negroes.) They discussed how the government of the United States could assist the advancement of black people in postwar America. Toward the end of the conversation, one of the publishers asked Roosevelt about his postwar plans for Africa. Needless to say, Roosevelt was totally unprepared for the question. But in his own inimitable way, Roosevelt responded with a proposal that the two publishers visit Africa and return with some advice about what US postwar policy should be.

The publishers accepted Roosevelt's proposal and visited West Africa. When they returned, they debriefed to Acting Secretary of State Dean Acheson. Their thoughts were contained in a memorandum from Acheson to Roosevelt dated April 4, 1945. The publishers had visited three territories: Sierra Leone (a British colony), Côte d'Ivoire (a French colony), and the independent nation of Liberia.

Secretary Acheson began his memorandum to President Roosevelt with the following quote from the Negro publishers: "Liberia is a disgrace to the United States." Having visited Sierra Leone and Côte d'Ivoire, the publishers saw some of the advantages of European colonization, such as paved streets in the capital cities, power plants and reliable electricity service in the cities, retail stores, and some decent schools. By comparison, Liberia and its capital city of Monrovia were in a primitive state. Acheson summed it up as follows: "The inefficiency and lack of initiative of the ruling group, the corruption in government circles, the scandalous treatment of the native inhabitants, and the lack of democratic practices in this independent republic are of particular concern to us at a time when the problem of dependent peoples is under widespread discussion."[14]

Secretary Acheson advised the president, "Whether or not we admit it, Liberia is widely regarded as a responsibility of the United States." Acheson proposed that the United States extend some development assistance to Liberia and at the same time put pressure on the Liberian ruling class to institute reforms. Roosevelt wrote "OK" at the bottom of Acheson's memo, thereby releasing $12.5 million to construct a new harbor, complete an economic survey, conduct a health project, and provide agricultural advice.

In view of Liberia's weakness and vulnerable borders, Acheson also made the important decision to protect Liberia from territorial inroads on the part of the neighboring British and French colonies.[15]

Africa and Wartime Logistics

Until the Allied liberation of France in the second half of 1944, the Mediterranean Sea was too dangerous for the transit of military personnel and equipment between the United States and the Middle East and South Asia. In this respect, West African airports played a major role.

Before late 1943, all of the francophone West African airports were considered to be under the control of Vichy France and therefore not available for Allied air traffic. British colonies, however, were more than happy to cooperate. The US Army Air Forces arranged for US transport aircraft to use the airport facilities at Accra, Gold Coast (now Ghana), and Bathurst (now Banjul) in Gambia.

By the end of 1942, US transport air traffic through Accra had become sufficiently heavy for Lord Swinton, the British minister of state for West Africa, to request that the United States send a representative to Accra to "coordinate all aspects of the war effort." Back in Washington, the director of West African affairs, Perry N. Jester, recommended that the United States take advantage of this invitation in order to be positioned to protect US economic interests after the end of the war.[16]

The former French colony of Mauritania was located on the northern border of France's colony of Senegal. Because Mauritania was mostly desert, with no known resources at the time, it was administered from the northern Senegalese town of St. Louis. Although the governor of Senegal had opted for Vichy France, the Free French and US forces, operating out of Morocco, were able to take control of the northern half of Mauritania. The central Mauritanian town of Atar, about a hundred miles from the capital city of Nouakchott, has a plaque on the outer fence of its municipal airport that reports the construction of the field by the US Army Air Forces in 1943. They gave the field the name North Dakota. It served mainly as a refueling stop for aircraft flying to Cairo.

Belgian Congo Uranium and Development of the Manhattan Project

The Belgian Congo, now the Democratic Republic of the Congo (DRC), was one of the largest and wealthiest of the European colonies in Africa. In the extreme southeastern corner of the Congo, near the border with the former British colony of Northern Rhodesia, now Zambia, there are extensive rich mineral deposits in the province of Katanga. The main minerals exploited in the Congo today are copper and cobalt.

Until the independent Congolese government nationalized the Katanga mines in 1967, the mines were owned by the Belgian corporation Union Minière de Haut Katanga (UMHK). In 1915, UMHK geologists discovered a uranium deposit. At the time, the main uses for uranium were as a source for radium, one of the earliest means of treatment for cancer, and as a source of dyes for ceramics. The main sources of uranium were small mines in the United States and Canada. What was special about the Congolese uranium ore was its very high content of the metal, at over 80 percent uranium content. The uranium ore until then being mined had less than 10 percent uranium content.

A treatment plant in the Congo produced uranium oxide, which it then shipped to Belgium for international sales. Since the United States was the principal market for uranium in the late 1930s, the director of UMHK, Edgar Sengier, decided to place a stockpile of 1,200 tons of the metal in New York's Staten Island. In addition, he had 3,000 tons stocked at the mine in Katanga.

In 1940, after the Nazi army had overrun Western Europe, including Belgium, President Roosevelt gave the order to begin the Manhattan Project, which had as its mission the development of an atomic bomb. This required a large amount of uranium, and Colonel Ken Nichols was assigned to find it. He located the UMHK director and purchased both the 1,200 tons in Staten Island and the 3,000 tons at the mine site in Katanga. Subsequently, UMHK was shipping 400 tons of uranium oxide per month to the Manhattan Project.

Because of the high priority and sensitivity of the uranium supply, the United States provided security for the UMHK facility through the Office of Strategic Services (OSS). One OSS mission was to prevent smuggling of uranium oxide to Germany. When the UMHK mine developed flooding problems below the waterline level, the US Army Corps of Engineers came in to provide repairs.

After the war, the scientists involved in the Manhattan Project said that the rich uranium from the Congo had been crucial for the development of the separation plants and plutonium.

The Yalta Conference:
Roosevelt's Last Act of International Diplomacy

The three Allied wartime leaders, Franklin Roosevelt (United States), Winston Churchill (United Kingdom), and Joseph Stalin (Soviet Union), met for the last time in the beach resort of Yalta on the Black Sea from February 4 to 11, 1945. The main purpose was to coordinate strategies for the final military defeat of Nazi Germany and to prepare for the rehabilitation of the liberated countries in both Western and Eastern Europe. Africa was clearly not on the agenda, but decisions were taken that had an impact on Africa.

First, the "Big Three" agreed that in the new "international security organization" that would be established, to be called the United Nations, France would be one of the five permanent members of the Security Council with the power of veto. Thus, the two most important colonial powers in Europe would be in a strong position to resist pressure from powerful voices in the UN General Assembly to quickly grant independence to their colonies.[17]

Second, Roosevelt was determined to include the self-determination of peoples in the founding United Nations documents, along with a pledge that the United States would henceforth have to play a major role in the world in order to guarantee peace and security. The prewar policy of isolationism would no longer be acceptable. Reporting on the Yalta Conference in his final address to the US Congress on March 1, 1945, Roosevelt spoke of his hopes for postwar peace and security: "It will be a peace based on the sound and just principles of the Atlantic Charter. Responsibility for political conditions thousands of miles away can no longer be avoided by this great nation."[18]

3

Harry S. Truman: 1945–1953

The main preparatory work for the establishment of the United Nations was accomplished at the Dumbarton Oaks conference in Washington from August 21 to October 7, 1944. The official title for this conference was "Washington conversations on an international peace and security organization to succeed the League of Nations." It was at the Dumbarton Oaks estate of Mr. and Mrs. Robert Bliss that most of the language of the United Nations Charter was written.[1]

One of the subjects not discussed at Dumbarton Oaks was the status of non-self-governing nations. Within this group were the former German colonies mandated by the League of Nations after the end of World War I to the control of the victorious countries: Great Britain, France, Japan, Italy, and South Africa. Within Africa, these territories included Tanganyika (now Tanzania) and English-speaking Cameroon, which were administered by Britain; Togo and French-speaking Cameroon, administered by France; Rwanda-Urundi (now Rwanda and Burundi), administered by Belgium; Somalia, administered by Italy; and Southwest Africa (now Namibia), administered by South Africa.

The San Francisco Conference

The official conference for the establishment of the United Nations began in San Francisco on April 25, 1945. President Truman decided that the US delegation would be bipartisan. The chairman of the US delegation was Secretary of State Edward R. Stettinius, representing the Democratic administration. The two most prestigious Republicans in the delegation were Senator Arthur Vandenberg of Michigan and former governor Harold Stassen of Minnesota. Prior to World War II, Senator Vandenberg had been one of the strongest advocates for the United States remaining isolationist and aloof from international crises. The experience of the war caused him to change his view. In early 1945, he made an important speech in the Senate that proclaimed his adherence to a vigorous US involvement in international affairs. He also coined the phrase "Political partisanship stops at the water's edge."[2]

During the committee work at the San Francisco conference, the issue of non-self-governing territories arose in the form of unfinished business from the League of Nations. What was to be done about the territories mandated under League auspices to European nations and South Africa? In response, the conference established the Trusteeship Council as one of six organs of the United Nations, to take over the supervision of the League-mandated territories that were to be transferred to it. The conference anticipated that in addition to the transfer of the League's mandated territories, the Trusteeship Council would also take jurisdiction over new territories seized from the defeated countries in World War II. Further, the conferees stated that the Trusteeship Council would be open to taking jurisdiction over non-self-governing territories voluntarily handed over by the colonial powers.

Germany had already relinquished all of its colonies after its defeat in World War I. After Japan's defeat in World War II, it lost several territories in the Pacific Ocean to US armed forces, including the Marshall Islands, the northern Marianas, and Palau. In Africa, Italy lost its Eritrea colony that British troops had seized early in the war, but it was still in control of Italian Somaliland at war's end.

The "International Trusteeship System" was written into the UN Charter as Chapters XII and XIII. Article 73, regarding non-self-governing territories, stated that the "interests of the inhabitants of these territories are paramount." Members assuming trusteeship responsibility for these territories, designated under Article 81 as the administering authorities,[3] accepted as a sacred trust the obligation to promote the well-being of the inhabitants, promote self-government, and submit relevant information to the UN Secretary-General. The term "to promote" self-government was much softer language than the US delegation would have preferred. The Chinese and Soviets were in favor of designating "independence" as the desirable goal for non-self-governing territories under UN Trusteeship administration. The UK and France were adamantly opposed. The United States, therefore, accepted "the promotion of self-government" as a compromise.[4]

Within the UN system, the General Assembly, in which each member has one vote, is the overall authority, with the exception of the Security Council, which works independently in support of peace and security. To provide supervision and direction over the Trusteeship Council, the General Assembly established the Fourth Committee, bearing the name Special Political and Decolonization Committee. It is within this committee that the main debates over non-self-governing territories have taken place over the seven decades of the UN's existence.

Unlike the UN Security Council, the five major powers did not have a veto in the Trusteeship Council, where all UN members had a right to vote. However, in order to protect the interests of the trust-administering powers, a two-thirds vote is necessary for decisions of the Trusteeship Council to be enacted.[5] The two-thirds requirement was particularly important to the US military, which did not want to be forced to relinquish control over the Japanese Pacific islands captured during the war. The US military considered control over these islands to be crucial to the US strategy of maintaining its dominance over the western Pacific.[6] For this reason, the US delegation had to resist any tendency on the part of members to introduce the concept that all non-self-governing territories, regardless of colonial origin, be placed under the jurisdiction of the Trusteeship Council. The United Kingdom and France were in total agreement with the United States on this point.

After the required number of Charter ratifications, the United Nations came into formal existence on October 24, 1945. At that point, all member nations administering territories under League of Nations mandates were requested to transfer their territories to UN trusteeship status. All of the mandate-holding governments complied, except one. South Africa had control of former German Southwest Africa under a League mandate and indicated forcefully that it considered the League mandate still valid. It had no intention of transferring that mandate to UN trusteeship status. This situation would later become a major political issue for the UN General Assembly, which grew increasingly impatient with South Africa's refusal to adhere to the international consensus that all territories held in trust must eventually be prepared for self-government. Above all, Southwest Africa would become a major policy issue for the United States.

Organizing the UN Trusteeship Council

The first meeting of the United Nations General Assembly took place in London in January 1946. One of the main orders of business was to organize the machinery of the Trusteeship Council, as laid out in Articles XII and XIII of the Charter.

The least controversial aspect of the Trusteeship Council was the proposed transfer to the Council's jurisdiction of the League of Nations–mandated territories dating from the end of World War I. The General Assembly formally requested all governments administering League mandates to make the transfer.

The US delegation had taken the lead in persuading the General Assembly to request the transfer of the League mandates to the Trusteeship Council. The US draft resolution referred to Chapter XI of the Charter, in which the administering authorities agree to give highest priority to the welfare of the peoples in the non-self-governing territories, "including the obligation to develop self-government, and to assist the inhabitants in the progressive development of their free political institutions."[7]

On January 16, 1946, the United Kingdom announced that it would place its African mandates under the UN Trusteeship system. These included Tanganyika (Tanzania), Cameroon, and Togoland (Togo). The Belgians quickly followed with Rwanda and Burundi, and the French with their regions of Cameroon and Togoland.[8]

The US delegation was so focused on the desirability of bringing the non-self-governing peoples to eventual independence that they proposed rules and agreements within the Trusteeship system that would ensure such an outcome in every case. The United States proposed, for example, that "all rights and titles in the trust territory shall be vested in the UN. The UN shall exercise these rights as trustee for the inhabitants of the trust territory." In other words, the governments who will be administering these trust territories will be agents working on behalf of the UN, and not colonial powers in the traditional sense. The United States insisted that each of the nations placed under trusteeship be the subject of a separate agreement between the administering government and the UN and that each agreement include a commitment to "promote their progressive development toward self-government or independence."[9]

When the French announced their intention to transfer their mandated African territories to the UN Trusteeship system, they declared their hope that these nations would eventually choose to remain in the French Union.[10]

The British and French expressions of intent to place their League of Nations mandates under the jurisdiction of the United Nations enabled the second meeting of the General Assembly in October 1946 to officially announce the existence of the Trusteeship Council. Despite its enthusiasm for this process on the part of Britain and France, the United States hesitated when it came to the Pacific islands seized from Japan during World War II. The US military wanted to annex these territories outright as vital elements of US security in the Pacific.[11]

The annexation issue came to a head at the October 1946 General Assembly meeting. The South African government announced that it had no intention of transferring its League-mandated territory of Southwest Africa to the UN Trusteeship system and, indeed, expressed its intention to annex Southwest Africa. In view of the vast size of Southwest Africa and its strategic location just north of South Africa, the possibility that the territory might be annexed by the administering power was unacceptable to the other UN members. With its own problem of the Pacific islands as background, the US delegation proposed the establishment of a UN commission to investigate the Southwest Africa issue. The South Africans responded that they would engage in consultations with the inhabitants of Southwest Africa and issue a report to the General Assembly at an appropriate time.

Although still early, the prospect of South Africa's white minority rule being extended to Southwest Africa was becoming a significant issue. For its part, the United States did not want to do anything that would help to justify such an outcome. Hence, in December 1946, the United States agreed to place under trusteeship those Pacific islands that had originally been mandated to Japan. In bilateral discussions, the South Africans indicated that they had no basic objection to placing Southwest Africa under trusteeship, but they feared the requirement to sign a separate agreement with the UN would mandate progress toward "self-determination or independence."[12]

Over the years after that October 1946 General Assembly meeting, the South African government continued to refuse to change the status of Southwest Africa and maintained that it continued to control Southwest Africa under the original League of Nations mandate. The issue of Southwest Africa issue achieved critical importance for US policy starting with the administration of Ronald Reagan (1981–1989).

UN Debate on the Colonial System

The number of non-self-governing territories entering the UN Trustee-ship system was tiny compared to the overall number of colonial pos-sessions. Inevitably, the question arose of including these territories in the Trusteeship system.

Chapter XI, Article 73, of the UN Charter concerns non-self-governing territories regardless of origin. All colonial powers that belonged to the UN thus accepted the obligation to develop self-government and free political institutions among their dependent peoples. In view of Article 73, some sentiment existed that all colonial dependencies should be placed under the UN Trusteeship system.

Within the US delegation to the first General Assembly in London in January 1946, the leading Republican on the team was John Foster Dulles, a senior partner of the New York law firm Sullivan and Cromwell. In his overall politics, Dulles was a strong conservative, but when it came to colonialism, he was a strong abolitionist. In his address to the US delegation at the first General Assembly, Dulles said: "We should consider asking the [General Assembly] to declare all states with colonies to submit to trusteeship, not just the mandatory powers. The real problem in this whole field of dependent areas was that people of one color were ruling those of another."[13]

The debate within the UN about colonial possessions, and whether or not they should be submitted to Trusteeship Council jurisdiction, became quite lively. The leaders of the pro-trusteeship argument were China, Soviet Union, and India. The colonial powers, Britain and France, were adamantly opposed, and made it clear in their discussions with US diplomats that they were not prepared to give up sovereignty. The so-called anticolonial powers, China, the Soviet Union, and India, clearly took their stand for the purpose of acquiring prestige through championing the cause of dependent peoples.[14]

The US position on the colonial issue fell between the European colonial powers and the anticolonial bloc in the General Assembly. Arti-cle 73 of the Charter called for colonial administrators to submit infor-mation to the UN Secretary-General about the progress they were making toward self-determination or independence. The United States decided to comply with this requirement in order to demonstrate to dependent peo-ples that the United States was on their side. In July 1947, the United States submitted information to the Secretary-General on Alaska, Ameri-can Samoa, Guam, Hawaii, Panama Canal, Puerto Rico, and the Virgin

Islands. In essence, the United States was informing the world that its dependent territories would eventually gain self-determination.[15]

The General Assembly created the Fourth Committee in order to debate the administration of Trustee territories. Because the General Assembly would also be debating non-Trust territories, the Fourth Committee was divided into two subcommittees, one for trusteeships and one for general colonialism. In this entire process, US policy was to "thwart the extreme tactics of the anticolonial block, and at the same time avoid identification with the colonial powers."[16]

While debate on colonialism was lively within the UN system, African nationalists were becoming active in their territories, thanks in part to US anticolonialist rhetoric. In one of his many reports on the status of colonialism in the French protectorate of Morocco, Edward A. Plitt, US diplomatic agent in Tangier, wrote in a telegram to the State Department dated October 29, 1947: "The Atlantic Charter and contacts with western armed forces fostered aspirations for independence." He went on to complain that infrastructure development in Morocco brought wealth to the French settlers there but did little for the indigenous population. "Very little effort was made to instruct the native population with a view to bettering their living conditions and preparing them for active participation in governing the country."[17]

Similar nationalist stirrings were taking place in French-ruled Tunisia, where Habib Bourguiba, leader of the Tunisian Nationalist Party, was agitating for independence. One US diplomatic report said that Bourguiba was complaining about Tunisia's bad luck in not having been owned by an enemy regime such as that for Syria and Lebanon after World War I. In those mandated territories, France was obligated to bring the people to self-government by League of Nations rules. But in Tunisia, those rules did not apply, and thereby France felt free to take its time.[18]

In general, the United States was torn by two imperatives with respect to European colonialism in Africa during the years immediately after World War II. On the one hand, Washington wanted to do everything possible to hasten Western European recovery from the ravages of war. This aim gave rise to the Marshall Plan and, later, to the North Atlantic Treaty Organization (NATO). Thus, Washington did not want to put pressure on Europeans to give independence to their colonies too rapidly, because these territories were sources of raw materials and preferential trade.

On the other hand, the Truman administration was facing the rise of world communism as a threat to Western security. The Soviet and Chinese communist regimes were telling the colonial peoples that the Europeans, with the help of the American imperialists, were exploiting them and would never grant independence. For this reason, US diplomats on the ground in Western Europe were warning about the danger of communism co-opting the anticolonial message.

As US diplomat Paul Alling in Morocco told the State Department on January 30, 1947, "In general, my impressions are that the best means of preventing communism in North Africa are for the French to accelerate the tempo by which they are liberalizing various regimes in this area."[19]

In May 1947, the US embassy in Paris informed the State Department that the French had decided to "begin democratic reforms in Morocco leading to slowly expanding self-government."[20] In response, Washington informed Paris that "the United States will block consideration of North Africa in the General Assembly by nationalists, but in return, France must come up with a plan to bring North Africans toward self-determination."[21]

Exceptions to the Colonialist Self-Determination Commitments

By mid-1947, it was clear that Britain and France had made a firm commitment to bring their African colonies to independence. The only ambiguous aspect involved the pace of transition. However, there were four exceptional cases in Africa involving reticence on the part of the colonial powers. These were destined to cause significant violent instability in future years, as well as headaches for US policy.

France's Algerian Dilemma

France smoothly brought its North African colonies of Morocco and Tunisia to independence in November 1955 and March 1956. But its Algerian dependency, situated between Morocco and Tunisia, was in a different category. With a large French settler population of 1.5 million, Algeria was considered part of metropolitan France. Therefore, the idea of independence for Algeria was not on the table.

The "colonial-racial" problem was inaugurated in October 1870, when the French government granted French citizenship to 37,000 Jews who had been living in Algeria since the fifteenth century. At the same time, the French government decreed that French citizenship was not to be granted, with few exceptions, to Algeria's Muslim populations of 2.5 million Arabs and Berbers. Over the years, this act of discrimination caused considerable animosity between Algerian Muslims and Jews, and between Algerian Muslims and the French.

In May 1945 anti-French demonstrations began in Algeria, to which the French authorities responded with violent repression. Guerrilla war against the French began in August 1955 and ended with Algerian independence in July 1962. The Truman administration did not talk much about the Algerian insurgency during its time in office, but later the Kennedy administration was quite vocal in support of Algerian self-determination.

South Africa and Southwest Africa (Namibia)

Despite continuing pressure from the UN Trusteeship Council, the UN General Assembly, and the United States during the early years of the Truman administration, South Africa dragged its feet with respect to bringing its League-mandated territory of Southwest Africa under the jurisdiction of the UN trusteeship system. South Africa refused to transfer its League mandate to the UN despite a decision by the International Court of Justice on June 11, 1950, that the United Nations had legally assumed all League responsibilities. The court's decision with respect to Southwest Africa was nevertheless ambiguous. The Court said that Chapter XII of the UN Charter provided a mechanism for the transfer of League mandates to UN Trusteeship jurisdiction but that South Africa was under no legal obligation to do so. However, the Union of South Africa could not modify the status of Southwest Africa without UN consent. Thus the Court allowed South Africa to administer Southwest Africa indefinitely but would not authorize it to make such major changes in the relationship as annexation.[22]

During World War I, the South African army had conquered the German colony of Southwest Africa and administered it ever since as an extension of South Africa. It was not surprising, therefore, that the South African regime was reluctant to give up jurisdiction. As in South Africa, Southwest Africa was governed by the apartheid system, under which the black African majority had no political voice.

While continuing to advocate the transfer of Southwest Africa to the UN Trusteeship system, after 1947 the Truman administration became totally preoccupied with national security in the context of the threat of potential Soviet aggression. The US view of South Africa thus shifted from a colonial irritant to one of strategic partnership in the defense against communism. Southwest Africa as a colonial problem disappeared from the Washington agenda and would not surface again until the Nixon and Ford administrations (1969–1977). In 1974, an anti–South African insurgency broke out in Southwest Africa, with the guerrillas receiving assistance from Cuban troops based in neighboring Angola. Needless to say, this became a major crisis for US policy.

All subsequent administrations continued to refer to the decision of the International Court of Justice as the baseline for all policies toward the Southwest Africa issue, thereby preventing South Africa from annexing the territory.

Eritrea: Torn Between the UK, Ethiopia, and the United Nations

When World War II broke out, Eritrea had been an Italian colony for half a century. In 1935, fascist Italy used Eritrea as the base from which it conquered neighboring Ethiopia. This was the act of aggression that brought Ethiopian emperor Haile Selassie to request assistance from the League of Nations, which shamefully failed to act.

In 1941, British army units from South Africa recaptured Eritrea and liberated Ethiopia from Italian occupation. When World War II ended, the UK had a problem with respect to Eritrea. Normally, Eritrea should have been placed under UN Trusteeship jurisdiction, with the UK as the administering power. But Ethiopia objected, claiming that Eritrea had been part of greater Ethiopia prior to the Italian colonization. The UK decided to do nothing until the international community could decide Eritrea's status.

US policy toward the Eritrean issue reflected the Truman administration's sympathy for Emperor Haile Selassie, whose plea for help in 1935 against Italian aggression had been ignored. Perhaps even more important, after the start of the Korean War in 1950, when the United States was in charge of the UN "police action" against North Korea, Ethiopia sent a battalion of 1,200 troops to fight with the UN forces. Known as the Kagnew Battalion, the Ethiopian troops came from the emperor's personal guard and fought valiantly alongside the US Seventh Infantry Division, suffering significant casualties. In view of this enormous gesture on the emperor's part, the Truman administration remained neutral on the subject of Eritrea's fate.

In 1952, the British asked the UN to determine the will of the Eritrean people. As a result of the UN's survey, Eritrea entered into a loose confederation with Ethiopia, with its own parliament and security force. Ethiopia remained responsible for the currency, trade, and foreign and defense policies. The Truman administration supported this arrangement enthusiastically. Unfortunately, Ethiopia annexed Eritrea by force ten years later, in 1962, thereby starting a guerrilla war that would perturb US policy for another twenty-nine years.

Portugal

Portugal and its African colonies constituted a single family that could not be torn asunder. Portugal began to establish coastal supply stations in sub-Saharan Africa as early as the sixteenth century. By 1885, when the Berlin Conference drew the final colonial boundaries in Africa, Portugal had enormous properties in Angola, Mozambique, Guinea-Bissau, Cape Verde, and São Tomé. Until the end of World War II, the Portuguese colonies in Africa were essentially producers of tropical agricultural products for export to Portugal and the rest of Europe. After the war, Angola and Mozambique began receiving large numbers of Portuguese emigrants, who were escaping dire economic conditions under corporatist fascist rule in Lisbon. Because Portuguese Africa was such an important outlet for unemployed Portuguese, the idea of bringing these territories to independence under African rule was anathema to the Portuguese authorities. For this reason, Portugal was absent from the international debate about trusteeship and self-determination for the non-self-governing territories.

The Truman administration was relatively silent about Portugal's refusal to even consider self-government for its African territories because of the growing perception of threat from Soviet aggression. Portugal was a founding member of the North Atlantic Treaty Organization, officially established on April 4, 1949, to provide collective defense against the Soviet threat. Portugal agreed to allow the United States to have an airbase in the Azores Islands in the Atlantic Ocean as part of the NATO system.

Its Western allies did not bother Portugal about its African territories. But it all came to an end in 1974, when young army officers overthrew the Portuguese fascist regime and quickly granted independence to Portugal's African colonies. Two of them, Angola and Mozambique, rapidly descended into civil war. The US government was later forced to pick up the pieces, starting with the Reagan administration in 1981.[23]

The Soviet Threat Changes the Truman Administration's View of Colonial Africa

Not long after the Japanese surrender in 1945, the Truman administration had to begin thinking of the possibility of a new world conflict. When the Allied forces liberated the nations of Western Europe from Nazi occupation in 1944–1945, the prewar democratic systems were restored immediately. The biggest concern became postwar reconstruction.

When Soviet forces liberated nations in Eastern Europe from Nazi occupation in 1944–1945, they imposed new communist governments by force, backed up by the extended presence of Russian troops. This was in direct violation of promises Soviet dictator Joseph Stalin made to President Roosevelt at the Yalta Conference in the Crimea resort from February 4 to 11, 1945. Stalin had promised that the liberated nations would choose their governments through democratic elections. Matters were made worse for US policy when the Maoist communists took over mainland China in 1948, and communist North Korea invaded South Korea in 1950.

In addition, Soviet propaganda was threatening to bring communism to the Western world. In France and Italy, the communist parties were able to win about 20 percent of the votes in the earliest elections, continuing to the 1980s. Both of these communist parties were totally loyal to the Soviet Union and in some instances desired it to liberate them from capitalism.

The net result of the Soviet threat in its various facets was to cause the Truman administration to make foreign and national security policy concentrate on defense against the Soviet menace. The jewel in the crown in the common defense was the creation of the North Atlantic Treaty Organization in 1949. All the NATO member countries that had colonies in Africa effectively made those colonies part of the common defense system. It is no surprise, then, that US policy toward Africa during the second half of the Truman administration was fully focused on how Europe's African colonies would fit into planning for the common defense.

US military planners were particularly interested in Africa for several reasons:

- To protect the sea routes around South Africa.
- To maintain access to strategic minerals available in Africa. The military's list included uranium, cobalt, and crushing diamonds from the Belgian Congo; uranium from South Africa; chromium from Southern Rhodesia (now Zimbabwe), and manganese from Gabon. With the Soviet Union and the Belgian Congo as the only two suppliers of the world's cobalt, it was absolutely imperative to maintain control over the Congo.
- To plan for the takeover of Europe's African territories in the event Soviet forces overran Western Europe.
- To build a NATO-capable airbase near the mining town of Kamina in the southeast Belgian Congo.
- To develop a strategic relationship with nationalist, white racist South Africa in order to prevent it from annexing both Southwest Africa and the British High Commission territory of Bechuanaland (now Botswana), and to encourage their anticommunism.[24]

Africa as a Target of the Communist Ideological Threat

In 1950, five years after the end of World War II, the Soviets continued to maintain several hundred thousand troops in Eastern Europe in support of their satellite communist regimes. At the same time, Soviet propaganda was telling the European colonies in Africa that they were being exploited by their colonial masters and should rise up against them. This gave rise to a debate within the State Department as to the proper response to this challenge.

The Truman administration, through the Marshall Plan, officially named the European Recovery Program, had the objective of assisting the liberated nations of Europe to rebuild their economies and even offered participation to the Soviet Union, which refused. Subsequently, the idea of providing economic development assistance to poor, less developed nations came to the fore as the primary means of fighting communist ideology. This idea was not universally accepted at first.

Ambassador George Kennan, the iconic diplomatic expert on the Soviet Union, was Secretary of State Dean Acheson's chief of policy planning. In a memorandum to Acheson dated February 17, 1950, titled "Fighting the Threat of Communism Worldwide," Kennan discussed the challenge of communism in the developing world. He took issue with the idea that providing financial assistance was the best way to fight communism in those territories: "I think we should fight the assumption that these relations cannot be normal and satisfactory ones unless we are extending some sort of unrequited assistance to the respective peoples. In particular, we should beware of the favored stereotype to the effect that low standards of living produce communism, and high standards of living do not. This is an unproven thesis, and probably unsound."[25]

In earlier policy recommendations, Kennan was all in favor of economic recovery assistance for the reconstruction of Europe. By 1950, he was ready to state that the military threat to Western Europe was receding, with NATO forces in place, and that the European economies were recovering steadily.

Kennan's view was challenged a month later by George McGhee, assistant secretary of state for the Near East, South Asia, and Africa. In a memorandum dated March 7, 1950, McGhee said that with China under the control of Maoist communists, thereby threatening US interests in East Asia, the Western world must look to Africa as the most reliable source of vital natural resources. So far, McGhee said, communism had not penetrated Africa as an ideology. Therefore, the United States should assist Africa economically, working through the European colonial powers.

As in the normal course of things, the disagreement over Africa policy in the State Department in early 1950 led to an official policy debate, with the resulting production of an official policy statement, issued on April 18, 1950, titled: "The Future of Africa."[26] The paper pointed out the growing interest in Africa within different American communities, including humanitarian groups, religious denominations, and business establishments. All saw an interest in Africa's economic advance.

The paper emphasized the importance of African growth and development to the growing economic and political strength of the European colonial powers, who were US allies in the defense against the spread of communism in Western Europe. In addition, the paper predicted that the importance of Africa in world affairs could only grow in view of the continent's enormous wealth in natural resources, and it noted that the new generation of African nationalists seeking independence from colonialism was actually quite suspicious of the motives of the Soviet Union and their European communist friends. Finally, the paper emphasized America's reputation in Africa for promoting self-government and transitions to independence. It said that the United States should continue to advance that view in its rhetoric toward the African people.

The net result of the Africa policy paper was the decision to include Africa in US foreign development assistance programs, working through the colonial powers so as not to offend them and cause them to suspect that the United States was seeking to displace them. This policy was implemented by allocating certain funds in the European Recovery Program to projects in Africa.

Within the State Department, Africa was elevated in status by the creation, on August 10, 1950, of a separate Office of African Affairs within the Bureau of Near East, South Asia, and African Affairs. The first Foreign Service officer to head the office was E. H. Bourgère.

Growing Anxiety About South Africa Takes a Back Seat to the Soviet Threat

The Truman administration never abandoned its objective of persuading South Africa to relinquish its control over Southwest Africa, but the issue was played out exclusively at the annual meeting of the UN General Assembly. Because of the emphasis on countering the Soviet threat, dealing with South Africa's deepening racial problem would have to wait for later administrations. Indeed, even in the UN, the US policy toward Southwest Africa changed from "South Africa has a legal obligation to transfer the territory to international trusteeship jurisdiction" to "South Africa has a moral obligation to do so." In short, during this nervous initial period of the Cold War, the United States could do no more than maintain the status quo in southern Africa.[27]

First Gesture of Support to Self-Government in Sub-Saharan Africa

In 1951, the African colony that had made the most progress toward self-government was the Gold Coast (now Ghana). Under the new Gold Coast constitution dated January 23, 1951, eight of the eleven ministers in the territory's Executive Council were Africans. Kwame Nkrumah, leader of government business in the Gold Coast Legislative Assembly, was the effective prime minister. In this capacity, Nkrumah was invited to make an informal visit to the United States as a guest of Assistant Secretary of State George McGhee on June 7 and 8, 1951. During a lunch in Nkrumah's honor, McGhee said that Britain's action to bring its African colonies to independence contrasted sharply with the Soviet Union's imposition of communist dictatorships throughout Eastern Europe.

Nkrumah had graduated from Lincoln University in Pennsylvania. His Convention People's Party won the nation's first-ever legislative elections. Upon his return to Accra, the capital city, Nkrumah sent a warm note of appreciation to McGhee. In recognition of the Gold Coast's progress, the US consulate in Accra was elevated to consulate-general status, and the US Economic Cooperation Administration centralized its West African operations there.[28]

Truman's Legacy on Africa

Truman bequeathed to the successor Eisenhower administration the policy that Africa had become a full partner in the Cold War against the Soviet Union. As African colonial territories started their advance toward independence during the 1950s, and as the danger of Soviet military intervention in Western Europe began to recede, Eisenhower analyzed United States–Africa relations with greater perspective and nuance.

4

Dwight D. Eisenhower:
1953–1961

Coming to power in January 1953, the Eisenhower administration was significantly less nervous about the worldwide challenges to
US security than was the Truman administration. Within months of taking office, President Eisenhower was able to bring the Korean War to a
ceasefire and bring home thousands of US troops. In Western Europe,
the full military force of the North Atlantic Treaty Organization had
been deployed in West Germany, facing the Soviet armies in East Germany. In France and Italy, the respective communist parties were talking more about coming to power through elections than about being liberated by the Red Army.

Eisenhower's secretary of state was John Foster Dulles, the New York
lawyer who had represented the Republican Party in the bipartisan US delegations to the annual UN General Assembly during the Truman years.

Dulles had three major characteristics when it came to public policy:

- He was a strong conservative with respect to US domestic politics.
- He was a staunch advocate of self-determination for people living
  under colonial rule.
- He was a fierce "cold warrior," expressing hatred for the Soviet
  Union and its satellite communist regimes in Eastern Europe at
  every opportunity.

31

The complexity of Dulles's political views came into play in the administration's debate over US policy toward the newly independent African nations. A good example of Dulles's approach at the time is available in the record of his conversation with the British foreign secretary Selwyn Lloyd on March 23, 1957, on the subject of Africa. Dulles expressed satisfaction that the concept of independence for non-self-governing peoples had finally been widely accepted. However, he was worried about the ability of future independent African nations to maintain their independence. He said: "We are facing a major problem. How do we keep these newly independent nations from being taken over by communism? We will be in serious trouble if Africa were lost to the free world."[1]

What was Secretary Dulles's first sign that the communists were starting to make inroads in Africa? The newly independent government of Ghana had announced that it intended to establish diplomatic relations with the Soviet Union. Hence the door was open to the Soviets to bring their brand of subversion into West Africa. Dulles was clearly worried.[2]

Unperturbed, Foreign Secretary Lloyd bragged that the gigantic colony of Nigeria would soon follow Ghana into independent statehood. That really made Dulles paranoid: "The UK should not feel we are putting pressure on the UK to grant premature independence. Attainment of independence should depend on the ability of people to sustain the responsibility, otherwise independence could be followed by communist takeover."[3]

Clearly, after having championed the concept of self-determination for non-self-governing peoples as a member of US delegations to several sessions of the UN General Assembly, Dulles was having some buyer's remorse.

The Eisenhower Team Develops Options for US Africa Policy

While the secretary of state was worrying about the possibility of independent African states being "taken over by communism," his colleagues in the State Department, the National Security Council staff, and the intelligence community were working diligently to develop the knowledge base necessary for the elaboration of sophisticated policy toward these new nations.

Arrival of the Diplomats

The most efficient method for the development of a knowledge base about the newly emerging nations of Africa was to put skilled observers on the ground in those territories. For this reason, by the end of 1956 the State Department had opened US consulates in every colonial African capital city, staffed by Foreign Service officers with the titles of consul and vice consul. In earlier years, the United States had already been operating consular offices in the major trading cities of Africa, including Dakar, Senegal; Nairobi, Kenya; Léopoldville, Belgian Congo; Lagos, Nigeria; and Durban, South Africa.

Senior Washington Officials Travel to Africa

Several of Washington's senior officials decided that they wanted to travel to Africa to see for themselves. When they came back, they wrote and distributed memorandums providing their observations, predictions, and recommendations for policy.

One of the earliest travelers was Mason Sears, US representative on the UN Trusteeship Council. In February 1956 he visited Ethiopia, Kenya, Uganda, Tanganyika, Southern Rhodesia, South Africa, Ghana, British Togo, and Nigeria. The absence of francophone territories on his itinerary was conspicuous. After that tour, he felt expert enough to comment on significant issues:

- The repressed black African majority in racist, white minority–ruled South Africa will run out of food in twenty years because they are relegated to rural reserves with the least-productive land.
- After defeating the Mau Mau insurgency, Kenya is heading toward a successful transition to independence.
- Nigeria and the Gold Coast are moving nicely toward independence.
- Yes, there will be a danger of communist subversion in the independent African nations. Communism will penetrate through the labor unions, which were quite healthy in the colonies before independence.
- Without having visited Algeria, he predicted that the French would lose to the fighting nationalist insurgents there in the same way they lost to nationalists in Vietnam in 1954.

Mason Sears made one principal recommendation with respect to the segregated white minority apartheid regime in South Africa, as well as the white minority–ruled UK colony of Southern Rhodesia: "Instruct United States diplomats in those two countries to open their July 4th receptions to non-whites, thereby mixing the races at these prestigious annual social events." This recommendation went all the way up to Secretary of State John Foster Dulles for decision. The secretary decided against the recommendation. He said that US diplomats should give priority to the cultivation of moderation among the white leaders and not irritate the white governments through the mixing of races at official receptions. Sears was quite accurate in his indirect prediction that the race issue in southern Africa would become a major headache in US policy toward Africa in future years.[4]

A short two months after Sears's Africa trip, he voted in the UN Trusteeship Council to ask Britain and Belgium to establish "intermediate target dates" toward political, economic, social, and educational goals in Tanganyika (now Tanzania) and Ruanda-Urundi (now Rwanda and Burundi). The British and Belgians, our NATO allies, showed displeasure at being pushed in this way.[5]

Vice President Nixon Joins the Travelers to Africa

The British colony of Gold Coast became the independent nation of Ghana on March 6, 1957. It was the first colonial territory south of the Sahara to cross this threshold. The country's first head of state was Kwame Nkrumah, who had visited Washington earlier when he was the leader of government business in the colonial parliament. Vice President Nixon represented the United States at the independence ceremony. He took advantage of this event to visit several countries in Africa during the period February 28–March 21, 1957.

What was significant about Nixon's tour was the way he approached each territory or nation. He was not visiting just to shake hands and express the goodwill of the United States. He was on an educational visit to analyze the situation in each country and make relevant recommendations to the policymakers and practitioners in various agencies. Among his recommendations were that the United States should try to improve relations with Morocco and Tunisia without seeking to supplant the French. Above all, the United States should avoid identification with the "repressive" French policy in Algeria. The United States should also assist the Arab governments of North Africa to resist the extremist, anti-West, pan-Arab rhetoric of President Nasser of Egypt.

Following are some other Nixon observations and recommendations:

- Ghana is suffering growing pains over an internal dispute on the issue of decentralization. It wants to end its heavy dependence on cocoa and would like to harness the energy of the Volta River to build a dam and aluminum smelter. Nixon recommended that an experienced career Foreign Service officer be assigned as the first US ambassador and that the United States should follow Ghana closely because that country will influence all of Africa.
- Nixon was deeply concerned about Liberia, because it was far less developed politically, economically, and socially than Ghana. He compared Liberia to a South American dictatorship. He recommended that the United States start being tough with Liberia about broadening the base of political power. "Tell them what they do not want to hear."
- In independent Ethiopia, Nixon quite accurately described the dominant Amhara ethnic group as uninterested in democracy. What they wanted was to continue to monopolize power with the assistance of US military material and training. Nixon's recommendation was to provide the military assistance in return for US military base rights overlooking the Red Sea.
- Nixon described the Sudan as being "torn between Africa and the Middle East." He recommended support for the prime minister, whom he described as "anti-communist." He also recommended that the United States provide economic and technical assistance and that the Africa office of the State Department rather than the Middle East office cover Sudan.
- Nixon described Libya as important because of its location on the flank of NATO. With the large US investment in the Wheelus Field Airbase near Tripoli, he said, the United States should try to replace the departing British military and help to build a Libyan army.

After his specific country recommendations, Nixon had general recommendations for overall US policy toward Africa. The Defense Department and the International Cooperation Administration (now the US Agency for International Development [USAID]) should pay more attention to Africa. In addition, the United States should:

- Increase the State Department presence in Africa.
- Prepare to give assistance to the new states as they become independent.
- Review how aid is delivered to avoid frustrating bottlenecks.
- Review US information output to Africa.

Nixon's trip gave him significant leverage in the subsequent making of overall policy toward Africa as the wave of newly independent nations accelerated.[6]

Overall, the period 1953–1958 was one of bureaucratic excitement throughout the national security agencies about the newly emerging African nations. Everyone was writing memorandums with recommendations to everyone else in an effort to influence the final policy framework that was working its way through the National Security Council system.

Intelligence Analysis of Decolonization in Africa

Ever since President Truman created the National Security Council (NSC) in 1947, the various intelligence agencies and offices have worked together to produce a flagship product called national intelligence estimates (NIEs). Reserved for national security issues of high priority to the president and other members of the NSC, the NIEs represent a consensus view reached by the several analytic branches. Needless to say, a number of NIEs contained minority dissenting views. The prospect of a large number of new nations in Africa entering the international scene stimulated a significant amount of analysis and discussion within the community.

Early in the Eisenhower administration, the community produced NIE-83, dated December 22, 1953. The title was "Conditions and Trends in Tropical Africa."[7] As a rule, senior intelligence analysts think first about priority US national interests. Therefore, they ask the first question: What are the strategic interests of the United States in Africa? Their response in NIE-83 was that US strategic interests arose chiefly from the supply of important minerals, especially uranium, columbium, cobalt, and diamonds.

Second, Africa was important because of its sea and air lanes in the Indian Ocean, the South Atlantic, and the Red Sea. For commerce and military purposes, the United States required unimpeded access to these lanes.

The rise of African nationalism would weaken European control of Africa's resources. Independent African nations were likely to be unstable, thereby threatening US access to the strategic minerals and to the sea and air lanes. Instability would increase in Africa in direct proportion to the increase in self-government. As instability increased, African exports of strategic commodities would be impaired.

What about the potential influence of international communism in Africa that was worrying some high-level policymakers, especially Secretary of State Dulles? The analysts agreed that under colonial rule, "communism was weak, but the influence of communism [would] grow among young African intellectuals."[8]

National intelligence estimates do not recommend policy. They provide the basic analysis that assists policymakers. NIE-83 was the earliest intelligence product to address prospects for US policy in Africa. The basic policy thrust of NIE-83 was to warn policymakers not to push the colonial powers too hard on transitioning their territories in Africa toward independence. It was issuing a warning. Africa, with fifty independent nations, could be a very unstable continent.

Three years later, the intelligence community updated its view of emerging Africa in NIE-72, dated August 14, 1956, and titled "Conditions and Trends in Tropical Africa."[9] Looking forward to imminent mass transitions to independence in Africa, NIE-72 predicted "formidable political and economic problems." The estimate foresaw communist countries, as well as some in the Middle East and Asia, competing with the West for power and influence. The analysts expected that Egypt would try to become the leader in external influence through its support of "native nationalism and the spread of Islam."

Addressing the uppermost concern in the minds of most US policymakers, the estimate considered the influence of communism in Africa to be weak under colonialism. However, they expected the Soviet Union to come in with offers of assistance, especially military, thereby increasing the prospects for the penetration of communist ideology. Nevertheless, NIE-72 was prescient in forecasting an overwhelming desire on the part of the newly independent African governments to stay aloof from the ongoing East-West great power struggles: "It is unlikely that most Africans will identify themselves closely with either side in the East-West struggle. Very few of the new African states are likely to be prepared to ally themselves formally with the West; in general, new states will seek to avoid any type of agreement that appears to involve any commitment to either side."

The message of NIE-72 was that the United States must be prepared for new challenges in Africa with the arrival of as many as fifty new independent governments. With the right approach, one that accepts

African neutrality and provides assistance to the new regimes in their struggles for economic development, the United States should be able to maintain access to Africa's strategic minerals and vital sea and air lanes.

Basic US Policies Toward the Newly Independent African States

After Ghana's independence in March 1957, it was clear to President Eisenhower and his senior policy advisers that the march toward independence for the British and French colonies had become irreversible. It was time, therefore, to pivot away from the policy of encouraging self-determination for the African colonies and to concentrate instead on the formulation of policies to guide US relations with the newly independent African nations.

It was not surprising that President Eisenhower, as a former top military commander in World War II, established a methodical procedure for development of policy toward Africa. First came the series of national intelligence estimates summarized earlier. Second was National Security Council Report 5719 of August 23, 1957, prepared on the basis of discussions among the agencies having official status in the National Security Council, led by the Departments of State and Defense. For this particular discussion, the Treasury Department and the Bureau of the Budget were included. After the president approved it, NSC 5719 became the first official document defining US policy toward Africa.[10]

NSC 5719 echoed earlier statements of US national interests in sub-Saharan Africa: The United States needs access to certain strategic minerals. The United States needs access to Africa's sea and air lanes at all times, and especially in the event that Soviet forces might block access to the Mediterranean corridor. The United States has an interest in preventing the growth of communist influence among the new African elites slated to come to power.

Appearing for the first time was a new theme—a realistic understanding that some of the new nations were likely to suffer instability accompanied by violence. There was also the prospect of questionable governance in some countries. Against this background, NSC 5719 made it clear that the United States was definitely not preparing to take responsibility for solving sub-Saharan African national problems. The primary aim of this US policy was to encourage a continuing close relationship between the European powers and their former colonies. The

United States was prepared to provide economic assistance to the African countries within the context of the administration's support of European recovery. Under no circumstances, however, would the United States use foreign aid to undermine Europe's primary role in support of Africa's transition to independence. Rather, it desired that Europe continue to play a primary role in Africa post-independence.

Decisions About Bilateral Relations
Between the United States and Africa

The final element of policy formulation was the conduct of bilateral relations with African countries on a day-to-day basis. This aspect gave rise to the most important debate about Africa that took place under President Eisenhower's leadership. A number of decisions had to be made with respect to the conduct of bilateral relations with each newly independent African nation.

The first issue concerned the number of US embassies to establish in Africa. Should there be a US ambassador in each hub city, with multiple accreditations to the governments in neighboring countries? Or should there be a US ambassador in every independent country? Eisenhower and his senior national security advisers embraced the concept of treating every newly independent African nation with dignity and with respect for their sovereignty, regardless of the size of their respective populations. In short, the United States would treat every independent African government as an equal. Against this background, Eisenhower decided to establish an embassy headed by a US ambassador in every independent African country. Implementing this decision was facilitated by the earlier opening of consulates in the most important African cities between 1953 and 1955. During the period 1958–1960, there was much activity in the State Department devoted to the planned opening of new embassies, as each new nation reached independence.

The most important substantive debate that took place at NSC meetings devoted to Africa policy was one between Vice President Richard Nixon and Secretary of State John Foster Dulles. It occurred during the 375th meeting of the National Security Council on August 7, 1958. The secretary sincerely believed that the defining issue in the postwar era was the menace of Soviet communism. He saw it as a threat both to Western civilization and to the survival of capitalism. So when it came to the conduct of US diplomacy with the newly independent

African governments, Dulles proposed that the issue of Soviet communism be placed at the top of the agenda.

Taking Sides in the Ideological Struggle

Secretary Dulles came to the debate under the influence of his special
assistant, Julius Holmes, who had spent ten weeks touring Africa during
October–December 1957. Holmes was a career Foreign Service officer
who later became ambassador to Iran. In his memorandum to Dulles
dated February 6, 1958, Holmes depicted a very unstable beginning for
the newly independent African nations: "I foresee a very difficult and
probably long period of uncertainty, bad management, retrogression and
conflict, with a strong chance of violence in some areas. There will be
plenty of troubled waters for communist fishing."[11]

Dulles's proposed approach for US bilateral relations with individual sovereign African governments was quite simple. "Please join us in
this holy war against communism. We believe that Americans and
Africans share the same values. We hope that you will be on our side
in this Cold War." Dulles told his NSC colleagues that any African government that decides not to join the West in this mighty ideological
struggle must be considered to belong to the other side. In other words,
you are with the United States or you are against the United States.

With his extensive travels in Africa as background, Vice President
Nixon took issue with Secretary Dulles's thesis. Nixon said that the
African nationalist leaders had struggled hard to achieve independence
for their peoples. The last thing they wanted was to be forced to join one
of the two superpower blocs. They had struggled for independence, and
they wanted to remain independent. Nixon said: "We should encourage
neutrality, which the national independence movements favor, instead of
assuming that a neutral is on the Soviet side."

After listening to both arguments, President Eisenhower opted for
the Nixon thesis. Eisenhower said that what the new African nations
needed was education and economic development. He said: "We should
first work through education and cultural relations. We must first win
the people." Thus, the US acceptance of African nonalignment became
embedded in US policy. Between 1960, when the majority of African
colonies gained their independence, and 1990, when the Soviet Union
collapsed, US respect for African nonalignment was seriously challenged on more than one occasion, but never faltered.[12]

Almost as a symbol of Eisenhower's decision of August 7, 1958, the State Department established a separate and independent Bureau of African Affairs on August 20, 1958. The first assistant secretary of state for African affairs was Ambassador Joseph Satterthwaite, a career Foreign Service officer.[13]

The Potential for Serious Instability in African Subregions

The final aspect of policy toward US-African bilateral relations was the issue of preparing for the likelihood of serious instability in several of the fifty new nations that were on the verge of coming into existence. In the national intelligence estimates, summarized earlier, all predicted instability was caused by ethnic conflict. Vice President Nixon emphasized that possibility in his travel reports, and in his post-travel statements.

President Eisenhower's view was that it would not make sense to send military forces to Africa from NATO nations to deal with serious violent instability. Seeing European and US military units back in their countries, Africans would believe that colonialism had returned. Eisenhower reached the conclusion that if stability operations would be needed in Africa, the military units should be wearing the blue helmets of the United Nations. The so-called police action that took place in Korea between 1950 and 1953 was authorized by the UN Security Council, though implemented by the US military with the assistance of friendly countries, including Ethiopia. What Eisenhower was contemplating were future stability operations taking place in Africa under the direct command of the United Nations in New York, with military units being contributed by all UN member nations. The entire NSC fully supported Eisenhower's view.[14]

Eisenhower's First Challenge in Africa: Collapse of the Belgian Congo

President Eisenhower's theory of UN intervention to stabilize violent situations in Africa was soon tested in June 1960, when the Belgian Congo collapsed into chaos within days of its independence.

Belgium decided to bring the Congo to independence only at the last minute, and with minimum preparation. Unlike Britain and France,

Belgium did not begin preparations to bring its Congo colony to independence during the early 1950s. The Belgian government's outlook was more long-term. This was not surprising in view of Belgium's interest in the Congo's vast mineral wealth. In 1955, the Belgian Congo was one of the world's major producers of copper and uranium and, along with the Soviet Union, only one of two producers of cobalt. For the sake of its own economy, and for the sake of thousands of its expatriates employed in the Congo, Belgium was in no hurry to bring the Congo to independence.

During the second half of the 1950s, Belgian internal politics shifted in favor of the left-wing parties that believed Belgium should not remain a colonial power while other Europeans were freeing their colonies. In 1958, Belgium decided to schedule the Congo for independence in 1960. Preparations were made rapidly to hold elections in the Congo in 1959. Unfortunately, nothing had been done to train Congolese administrators, civil servants, and business managers. During the colonial period, the Belgians refused to allow Congolese high school graduates to attend universities in Belgium. The Belgians did an excellent job of providing vocational training to electricians, carpenters, and plumbers. But when independence took place on June 30, 1960, the Congo had only eighteen university graduates, who had managed to obtain their higher education clandestinely, in either Europe or the United States.

The thinking of the Belgian government was that the Congolese were so far away from being able to govern themselves that they would readily accept a continuation of Belgian management for a significant period after political independence. General Emile Janssens, the Belgian commander of the Congolese security force known as the Force Publique, said on the eve of independence: "Before independence and after independence are the same. There will be no change."[15]

Elections for president, prime minister, provincial governors, and the national and provincial assemblies were held in April and May 1960. As a result, elected officials were in place for Congolese independence on June 30, 1960. Unfortunately, the newly independent Democratic Republic of the Congo became a very unstable and violent country very shortly after independence. The Congolese army mutinied against the Belgian officers, becoming an undisciplined band of looters and rapists.

The newly elected president, Joseph Kasavubu, and the newly elected prime minister, Patrice Lumumba, were totally incompatible. President Kasavubu was pro-Belgian and willing to continue Belgian management of the government and the economy. Patrice Lumumba was an ardent nationalist who demanded a rapid exit of the Belgian administration. Lumumba was popular with the Congolese population. The president and prime minister argued bitterly in public and at one point engaged in dismissing each other. Belgian and other expatriates began leaving the Congo to escape the rampaging military, thereby reducing government services.

To make matters worse, the governor of the mineral-rich Katanga province, Moïse Tshombe, declared secession from the Congo. The Belgian business community, which had financed a special military force under Tshombe's command, supported him. Violence developed between Katanga and the central government. The secession of Kasai and Orientale provinces followed that of Katanga. It had become a situation of extreme national disintegration.

What caught President Eisenhower's attention during July and August 1960 was the arrival of Soviet diplomats, who flocked to the support of the anti-Belgian, anti-Western prime minister, Patrice Lumumba. Eisenhower envisaged the Soviets taking advantage of the chaos to assume control of the entire Congo, a massive territory equal to the size of the United States east of the Mississippi River.

Eisenhower panicked and sent an order to the US commanding general of the North Atlantic Treaty Organization in Belgium to prepare forces to intervene in the Congo to restore order. Before this directive could be implemented, however, Vice President Nixon reminded Eisenhower of his earlier policy decision to look to the United Nations to engage in stability operations in Africa if needed. Eisenhower changed his mind about a possible NATO intervention and, instead, ordered that the United States propose a UN peacekeeping operation for consideration by the UN Security Council.

As part of his initial panic reaction, Eisenhower ordered the Central Intelligence Agency (CIA) to instruct their station in Léopoldville to "arrange" the assassination of Prime Minister Patrice Lumumba. The CIA station chief in Léopoldville, Larry Devlin, did not feel comfortable with this directive and managed to avoid implementing it through deliberate delay.[16]

As it turned out, other people had the same idea about Lumumba. Toward the end of 1960, Lumumba was taken into custody by members of the Congolese military and transported to Katanga province, where security people working for secessionist governor Moïse Tshombe executed him on January 17, 1961. Historians differ on the exact circumstances of Lumumba's assassination, but there is a consensus that foreign governments were involved, possibly Britain, Belgium, and even the United States.[17]

Lumumba's death removed the central person around whom Soviet diplomacy had tried to create a communist path of influence in the Democratic Republic of the Congo, and thereby weakened the Soviet effort. Lumumba's political disciple, Antoine Gizenga, continued Lumumba's nationalistic, anti-Belgian rhetoric and maintained control over the provincial capital of Kisangani. But he did not have the position of prime minister, and thus had much less influence on politics. While this was good news for the Eisenhower administration, the disintegration of the Congo remained a major concern.

Meanwhile, it was important that the United Nations intervene urgently to stabilize the Congo and prevent disorder from spreading throughout Central Africa. Meeting on July 14, 1960, in New York, the UN Security Council adopted Resolution 143. Quite brief, the resolution contained two decisions: Belgium must withdraw its forces from the Congo, and the UN Secretary-General is authorized to provide the government of the Democratic Republic of the Congo with such military assistance as may be necessary.[18] It is noteworthy that the UN decision to engage in stabilization action in the Congo took place before the January 1961 assassination of Patrice Lumumba, an event that exacerbated the disorder in the Security Council.

Over the next few months, the two-paragraph Resolution 143 resulted in the deployment of 20,000 UN military personnel to the Congo, coming from several nations, including Ethiopia. Pursuant to Eisenhower's policy decision, no European or US personnel were among the military units deployed to the Congo. Nevertheless, there was one important US contribution to the UN military operation. Only the United States had the military airlift capability to move military units and their equipment to and from the Congo, as well as within the Congo; thus, the US Air Transport Command was kept quite busy transporting blue-helmet military units during the four years of the UN operation.

In addition to the military deployment, UN civil servants and other contractors were brought in to replace the departing Belgian managers and train the Congolese to take their place. The UN operation in the Congo lasted from 1960 to 1964. It was credited with keeping the country territorially intact and with providing the former Belgian colony with a decent start toward real self-government.[19]

Eisenhower's Farewell Address to the UN:
Much About Africa

In his final annual address to the UN General Assembly, on September 22, 1960, President Eisenhower devoted many of his remarks to Africa, saying:

- There should be noninterference in Africa's internal affairs.
- The international community should assist African nations in ensuring their security without "wasteful and dangerous competition in armaments."
- The international community should maintain emergency assistance to the Congo.
- The United Nations should provide assistance for Africa's educational and economic development.[20]

Eisenhower's final UN speech was fully consistent with his policy decisions about Africa during his eight-year presidency. His key points: keep the Cold War out of Africa; concentrate on economic and cultural development; and safeguard the independence of African nations. Those decisions formed the basic policy document with regard to Africa for all subsequent administrations. Though severely challenged during future administrations, those decisions always managed to survive.

5

John F. Kennedy:
1961–1963

The good news about Africa, as the Kennedy administration took over on January 20, 1961, was the presence of UN peacekeepers on the ground in the Congo. The Kennedy policy team was pleased that Eisenhower had decided to call on the United Nations to restore order instead of deploying the US military as part of a NATO operation. The UN force had effectively stabilized the military situation in most of the Congo, but the overall situation was still one of political chaos. The administration was faced with several challenges to its early diplomacy.

In the mineral-rich Katanga province, Governor Moïse Tshombe was continuing to demand the right of "secession through self-determination." He had a force of Katangan troops trained and supplied by Belgian mercenaries and white citizens of the two British Rhodesian colonies across the Congo's southeast border. The UN force did not want to engage in warfare if it could help it, so the emphasis in early 1961 remained with diplomacy.

Patrice Lumumba, the newly independent Congo's first elected prime minister, was assassinated only three days prior to Kennedy's inauguration on January 20, 1961. That event significantly reduced the threat of a "communist" takeover of the Congo, but Lumumba's followers were still effectively in control of the provincial capital of Kisangani. The new leader of the Lumumbist political grouping, Antoine Gizenga, continued his late mentor's demand that the Belgians depart and that the Congo become a "Pan-Africanist" anti-Western state. He had a homegrown militia that was supplied by Soviet military flights. In January 1961, the United States complained to the UN Secretary-General, Dag Hammarskjöld, that the UN peacekeepers were not doing enough to prevent Gizenga's fighters from advancing toward the eastern province of Kivu.[1]

The Katanga problem had become a major internal political issue for NATO ally Belgium. Brussels saw the idea that the Belgian military should depart the Congo as a threat to the thousands of Belgian citizens employed there and their families. In addition, there was a perceived threat to the giant Belgian mining conglomerate UMHK, which was the main employer of Belgian citizens in the Congo as well as a major earner of revenue for the Belgian government.

At the beginning of 1961, Belgium's interests would have probably been best served if Katanga province could have been allowed to become an independent country. But considering the views of the other independent African governments, as well as those of other leading "nonaligned" nations such as India, the United States could not possibly espouse the breaking up of an African country. Belgium, however, had an internal political imperative to do just that.

In the Congolese capital city of Léopoldville, President Kasavubu needed to find a new prime minister more compatible with his own moderate view of the Belgians and the West in general. Under the command of Colonel Joseph Mobutu, the Congolese army protected Léopoldville, and Kasavubu's government. Mobutu had started out as a journalist-turned-sergeant when the Belgians were still in charge two years earlier. After returning from journalism studies in Belgium in 1959, Mobutu joined the army and also adhered to Patrice Lumumba's party. His command of the Congolese army in the capital city at independence was cause for concern on the part of the United States.

Quickly Making US Policy Toward the Congo Crisis

President Kennedy and Secretary of State Dean Rusk made some initial decisions about the US approach to the Congo crisis, contained in a memorandum from Secretary of State Rusk to the president dated February 1, 1961:

- The United States should obtain a new UN mandate to control and neutralize all Congolese armed elements to keep them out of politics, by force if necessary.
- The UN needs to prevent all outside military assistance.
- President Kasavubu should establish a middle-of-the-road cabinet.
- The UN needs to have a greater administrative role in the governance of the Congo.[2]

Support for the United Nations

The highest US priority was to make sure that the UN operation had what it needed to maintain stability in provincial subregions, especially Katanga. It was particularly important that the UN prevent Katangan governor Tshombe from achieving secession by force of arms. For this purpose, the administration allocated $40 million to the UN operation as its share of the peacekeeping burden. In addition, the US mission to the UN in New York, including the US military and intelligence components, kept in close touch with Secretary-General Dag Hammarskjöld on the day-to-day problems of managing the operation in the Congo. Ending the Katanga secession rapidly was also important in order to shift the payment of copper revenues from the Katanga regime to the Congolese central government. It was also important for the UN to make sure that the copper and cobalt mining operations continued unimpeded so that the revenues could continue to flow.

US Consulate in Elizabethville Keeps in Touch with the Secessionists

In Katanga's capital city, Elizabethville, the Eisenhower administration had wisely established a US consulate before the Congo's independence. Secretary Rusk instructed Consul William Canup to keep close contact with Governor Tshombe and continue trying to persuade him that the secession of Katanga from the rest of the Congo was unacceptable.

On April 3, 1961, Consul Canup, accompanied by Robert Eisenberg, the visiting deputy director of Central African affairs in the State Department, met with Tshombe to talk about the need to preserve the unity of the Congo. They talked about divided Germany and how the United States was working hard with its allies France and the UK to bring about German unification in order to prevent that country's total disintegration. They explained to Tshombe that all of Africa opposed breaking up newly independent countries. This conversation did not persuade Tshombe. There was so much general hostility toward Consul Canup in Elizabethville that Nepalese Gurkhas in the UN force were assigned to protect him.[3]

Influence of the African Asian Group

With respect to US policy, various elements within the United Nations were voting on the Congo operation. The so-called African Asian Group tended to favor Lumumba and Gizenga, because they were seen as the true anticolonialist nationalists. The African governments were divided into pro-Kasavubu and pro-Lumumba/Gizenga factions. Ghana and Guinea led the latter group. The US approach was to instruct US embassies in Africa to argue that the only way to prevent the Cold War from becoming a major factor in Africa, and to ensure neutrality in the East-West struggle, was to support the United Nations in the Congo.

The US diplomatic approach to the Africans generally succeeded. On March 8, 1961, President Kennedy had a conversation with President Kwame Nkrumah of Ghana, considered the leader of the nonaligned, anticolonial, anti-Western faction in Africa. Nkrumah expressed the view that the priorities in the Congo were to restore law and order, remove the Belgians, and insulate the Congo from all outside influence except that of the United Nations. In other words, in the face of a chaos that could become contagious in Africa, this left-wing radical head of state abandoned ideology and opted for both law and order, and the UN.[4]

Keeping the Congolese Army Out of Politics

Finally, the CIA station at the US embassy managed the problem of having Lumumbist sympathizer Colonel Joseph Mobutu as commander of the Congolese army in Léopoldville. Mobutu was co-opted into the Kasavubu moderate, pro-Western camp and remained there after he became president of the Congo in 1965 through a military coup.[5]

In July 1961, one year after the Congo's official independence, it was clear that the United States had become the key foreign actor in the management of the ongoing Congolese crisis. The US embassy in Léopoldville, the US consulate in Elizabethville, the US embassy in

Brussels, and the US mission to the United Nations were the main agents responsible for implementing Washington's policy.

US policy had three main challenges during the second half of 1962:

- To help President Kasavubu organize a broad-based government that could attract support from all factions and ethnic groups.
- To prevent Katanga governor Moïse Tshombe from making that final jump into secession, with the support of Belgian and UK business interests, and of white settler extremists in Northern and Southern Rhodesia.
- To keep stroking the Belgians to remain confident that a unified central government in the Congo would not necessarily jeopardize their substantial economic interests there.

Adoula Becomes Prime Minister

In June 1962, President Kasavubu called for a meeting of parliament to select a new prime minister. Delegates came from every province, including secessionist Katanga. After much debate, the delegates elected Cyrille Adoula as the new prime minister. US ambassador Claire Timberlake worked closely with Kasavubu in the identification of Adoula as the best choice.

Adoula was known as a "moderate socialist." He had come up through the ranks of the labor unions authorized under Belgian rule. At independence, he joined Patrice Lumumba's party. After Lumumba's assassination, he left the party because of disagreements with the extremism of Lumumba's replacement leaders. His election as prime minister was seen as a defeat for the Soviet diplomats grouped around Antoine Gizenga in Stanleyville.[6]

Adoula formed a broad-based regime representing all of the provinces and the major ethnic groups. The United States refused to become involved with revisions to the constitution and with such questions as whether the Congo should be a unified or confederal state, indicating that these were purely "internal affairs."[7]

To demonstrate high-level US support for the new government, President Kennedy invited Adoula to pay an official visit to Washington. Their meeting at the White House took place on February 5, 1962.[8] During their first meeting in the cabinet room, with associates and advisers on both sides, Prime Minister Adoula looked around and asked,

"Where is Carlucci?" President Kennedy responded, "Who is Carlucci?" Kennedy quickly learned that Adoula was looking for Frank Carlucci, a Foreign Service political officer who had recently served at the US embassy in Léopoldville. Kennedy arranged for Carlucci, who was then working at the State Department, to be available at subsequent meetings. This anecdote illustrates how the US embassy in Léopoldville kept close and friendly ties with all of the Congolese political leaders and were therefore in a position to exert considerable influence.[9]

US Diplomacy Intensifies over the Congo Crisis

In Léopoldville, the US message to Prime Minister Adoula was to prevent civil war. Do not send the Congolese army to fight the rebels in Katanga. Emphasize negotiations. Let the UN force maintain order in Katanga. Adoula's response was that he was prepared to negotiate with Tshombe.

In Elizabethville, Lewis Hoffacker replaced Bill Canup as consul in September 1961. Hoffacker's message to Tshombe was that an independent Katanga could not succeed. Negotiations with Adoula were the only way to achieve peace and stability. He emphasized that President Kennedy approved this policy. Hoffacker also reported to the embassy and the State Department that he found Tshombe more moderate than his hard-line associates such as Godefroid Munongo, his chief of security. Tshombe had been educated by American Methodist missionaries and was better able to dialogue with American diplomats and visitors.

In Brussels, Foreign Minister Paul-Henri Spaak was crying on Ambassador Douglas MacArthur's shoulder. He said that the Belgian-owned mines represented a major economic asset. The Belgians hated the UN for refusing to permit Katanga to secede, and they were losing confidence in the United States because Washington was giving full support to the UN operation. Spaak said that the entire Congo experience could possibly cause the fall of the Belgian government.[10]

In the United Nations, the US mission had instructions to resist resolutions calling for the imposition of UN economic sanctions against Tshombe and the Katangan secessionists. In a memorandum to President Kennedy dated November 11, 1961, Secretary of State Rusk recommended against the proposed sanctions. His position reflected some long-range State Department thinking. Rusk said: "It would be undesirable to have the UN adopt such a policy (economic sanctions) at this time, since it could create an instrument for possible use against South Africa or Portugal in situations in which the United States would not want to support such action." Rusk also informed Kennedy that the Congo crisis was the most important subject of discussion at the annual meeting of the North Atlantic Council (of NATO) in Brussels in December 1961.[11]

To make matters worse, Dag Hammarskjöld, the UN Secretary-General, was killed when his UN aircraft crashed while attempting to land at Ndola Airport in Northern Rhodesia on September 17, 1961, in the dark of night when there were no witnesses. The crash took place under mysterious circumstances, with suspicions pointing to the white Rhodesians and their wanting the UN mission to fail and Moïse Tshombe to succeed in his efforts to bring about Katanga secession.

The UN Finally Persuades the Katangans That Secession Cannot Happen

The overall situation in the Congo began to turn in late 1961 when the UN carried out a targeted military operation against the non-Congolese mercenaries assisting the Katanga secessionist forces. To bolster this operation, President Kennedy authorized the US Air Force to transport an Ethiopian UN battalion from Kisangani to Elizabethville, enabling the UN to defeat the non-Congolese fighters.

After the success of the UN military operation, Prime Minister Adoula was able to persuade Governor Tshombe to meet him on neutral ground to negotiate the future of the Congo. Edmund Gullion, now the US ambassador, had Tshombe transported to the Kitona airbase, where he met Adoula for talks. This began eleven months of tough negotiations between Adoula and Tshombe. Because of its earlier role, mediation of the negotiations became the responsibility of the United States. Between January and November 1962, there were many high-level interagency meetings in Washington to help guide these negotiations. President Kennedy presided over several such meetings.

Tshombe was finally forced to accept full integration into the greater Congo in November 1962, when US diplomacy persuaded the Belgians that their mining investment would be safe with Katanga remaining inside the Congo. At that point, the mining company UMHK began to pay royalties to the central government rather than to Katanga. Tshombe was able to claim partial victory with Adoula's promise to revise the constitution to give the provinces greater decentralized power.[12]

From mid-1962, the United Nations was able to concentrate on restoring the Congo's infrastructure and establishing workable governance. UN civilians replaced UN military little by little. By the time of the UN's departure in 1964, the Congolese government was able to take ownership of power with a modicum of capability.

The US management of the Congo crisis was a clear diplomatic victory for the Eisenhower and Kennedy administrations. Particularly impressive was the well-coordinated action among the State Department and four separate US diplomatic missions—in Léopoldville, Brussels, and Elizabethville, and at the United Nations.

New Policy Toward Other Newly Independent African Countries

While the Congo crisis was the highest African priority for the Kennedy administration, relations with the other newly independent African countries also needed to be addressed. In managing those relations, the administration created some interesting new policy, especially in the sector of development assistance.

Very early in his administration, President Kennedy made a symbolic gesture of friendship toward the newly independent nations of Africa. As his very first political appointment to a senior-level position, Kennedy nominated an assistant secretary of state for African affairs, G. Mennen Williams, the outgoing Democratic governor of Michigan. Williams had significant US political experience but little experience with foreign affairs. However, he turned out to be a fast learner and very astute at identifying key issues for US policy.

In general policy terms, Kennedy accepted the overall formulations of his predecessor, President Eisenhower, with some nuances. Above all, Kennedy endorsed the fundamental policy of preventing the Cold War from becoming significant in Africa. Secretary of State Dean Rusk, in many of his conversations with European counterparts, emphasized this point when discussing policy toward Africa.

Special Relations Between Africa and the Former Colonial Powers

At one of the earliest meetings of the National Security Council, on February 9, 1961, the president decided that the secretary of state should have the flexibility to supplement Western European support to newly independent areas with US aid whenever such action would be in the US interest. In a memorandum to the president dated February 15,

1961, Secretary Rusk recommended: "We need to be less rigid in our approach to aid for Africa. In other words, we can give aid without worrying about whether other donors are giving aid."[13]

United States–Africa Military Relations

The most sensitive aspect of foreign aid to Africa was military assistance. If the former colonial powers were worried about inroads on their influence, it was clearly in the area of military cooperation. The US Defense Department did not believe that United States–Africa relations should fail to include military relations. In one internal memorandum, in February 1961, Haydn Williams, deputy assistant secretary of defense for international security affairs, pointed out that African countries did not want to be totally dependent on the former colonial powers for military support. The Africans were asking for US military assistance. He said, "If we want to stop relying only on former colonial governments for military aid to Africa, we should make a new policy, with a separate policy for South Africa."[14]

Access to the African Continent
to Carry Out Contingency Operations

With a large majority of African territories slated to achieve independence by 1964, the US military was concerned about having access to the continent in the event of needed contingency operations. They had had total access for transit through Africa to the Middle East and South Asia during World War II. During the postwar colonial period, which was about to end, the US military was granted unlimited access by the colonial powers, who were also NATO allies. But with the massive influx of independent African nations, the access issue had become a big question mark.

The Defense Department's first approach to the access problem was to ask the State Department to request permanent access and overflight rights from a selected group of African countries with the largest and best-maintained airports. The State Department responded that such a request was politically impossible, because it would create concerns about our intentions among the African governments. Also, the State Department did not want to jeopardize existing US access and base rights in Morocco, Libya, and Liberia.[15] Refusing to concede defeat on Africa, the Defense Department finally persuaded State to negotiate base and overflight rights in the UK-controlled South Atlantic Ascension Islands, rights that were granted and continue to exist today.[16]

Kennedy's Ideas About Development Aid

Immediately after the end of World War II, the Truman administration adopted as a policy concept the idea that providing economic and technical assistance to poor countries in the so-called third world serves to inhibit the rise of radical ideologies. Truman's initial attention focused on the liberated nations of Western Europe that badly needed help for reconstruction, giving rise to the European Recovery Program, also known as the Marshall Plan. Under Truman, other programs developed, including "Point Four" technical assistance and use of surplus US agricultural commodities to assist in alleviating hunger and developing foreign agricultural capacity.

Based on his experience as a senator from Massachusetts, President Kennedy came into office with well-defined ideas about aid to the developing world. Within weeks of taking office, on March 1, 1961, he issued an executive order creating the Peace Corps, designed to send American citizen volunteers to developing countries to transmit expertise. The first volunteers to go overseas under the Peace Corps program went to two African countries, Ghana and Tanzania. Kennedy firmly believed in the value of foreign economic assistance to the developing world. While he acknowledged that there was a real threat that communist nations would subvert these countries, exploiting poverty and misery, he insisted on the democracy-building value of foreign aid programs. In a special message to Congress on foreign aid dated March 22, 1961, Kennedy said: "There exists, in the 1960s, an historic opportunity for a major economic assistance effort by the free industrialized nations to move more than half the people of the less-developed nations into self-sustained economic growth, while the rest move substantially closer to the day when they, too, will no longer have to depend on outside assistance."[17]

Kennedy had two objectives in this special message. First, he wanted to persuade Congress that foreign aid to the developing world constituted a necessary component of US national security. Second, he wanted Congress to enact legislation that would place foreign aid on a firm legal footing, with a consolidated administrative base, a long-term funding outlook, and a dedicated cadre of talented professionals. Kennedy succeeded in his effort on a bipartisan basis. He created the US Agency for International Development as the coordinating government department for all foreign aid programs, with personnel serving abroad as career Foreign Service officers. He also decided that the US ambassador in each country would coordinate all foreign aid programs.

Needless to say, from the outset, US foreign aid became a major element in United States–Africa relations and has remained so ever since. A year after Kennedy's special message to Congress, he received a memorandum from the National Security Council staff, dated March 6, 1963, providing a breakdown on US assistance to Africa. For fiscal year 1963, Africa was allocated $262 million, with 75 percent of the total going to eight countries: Sudan, Tanzania, Libya, Ethiopia, Liberia, Morocco, Tunisia, and Nigeria.[18]

Acknowledging that the United States cannot, and should not, be working alone in the cause of economic development, Kennedy said that foreign aid should be coordinated among the Western donor governments through the Organisation for Economic Co-operation and Development (OECD), established by Eisenhower.

Assistant Secretary of State for African Affairs G. Mennen Williams also made a valuable contribution to the foreign aid debate. After his first trip to Africa in March 1961, Williams expressed the view that one objective of foreign aid to Africa should be to promote the education of girls. Educated girls have fewer children and healthier children. With this excellent recommendation, Secretary Williams was years ahead of his time.[19]

The Persistence of White Minority Rule

With each successive administration after World War II, the problem of white minority rule in South Africa, Southwest Africa, and the Portuguese colonies continued to be viewed as a tragedy in the making. The Kennedy administration was no exception.

While the decolonization process for the French and British African territories was proceeding smoothly, the problem of Portugal's refusal to even consider moving its colonies of Angola, Mozambique, Guinea-Bissau, and São Tomé toward independence was becoming more and more of a headache for the Kennedy administration. In addition, South Africa's refusal to transfer the territory of Southwest Africa to UN Trusteeship jurisdiction and South Africa's own deepening racial oppression were a growing source of friction between the United States and the community of newly independent African nations. Although Southern Rhodesia was still legally a British colony, the small white settler minority exercised self-government and ruled over the vast majority of African citizens, with total segregation and racial discrimination.

In a national intelligence estimate dated April 11, 1961, the intelligence community predicted, "As Portugal refuses self-government and independence, there will be violence, and we expect that Portugal will not be able to bear the long and bloody struggle to come."[20] As the Portuguese colonies became surrounded by newly independent African states, it was inevitable that these states would sponsor and encourage insurgencies against Portuguese rule.

When Assistant Secretary Williams returned from his second trip to Africa in February 1963, he said: "Southern Rhodesia is a new African time bomb. A major anti-white flare-up is to be expected."[21] Earlier, in an analytic paper dated June 28, 1962, the State Department Policy Planning Staff had issued a gloom-and-doom prediction about southern Africa: "The seeds of another Algeria have been sown in Southern Africa. Blacks face Whites across a sea of developing hate. With this confrontation, and the increasing polarization of racial tensions, the White supremacists are seeking to strengthen their established positions."[22]

As each African territory celebrated independence, their first action was to join the United Nations. As their number grew, their collective outcry against the Portuguese, white South Africans, and Southern Rhodesians became louder and louder. They were demanding international action to bring freedom to their oppressed brothers. During his annual speech to the UN General Assembly, President Kennedy, unfortunately, had to oppose sanctions because of the objections of Britain and Portugal.

Adlai Stevenson, former governor of Illinois and presidential candidate, was Kennedy's permanent representative to the United Nations. Preparing for the annual UN General Assembly debate in September 1962, Stevenson sent a message to President Kennedy predicting that the United States could expect to be criticized for refusing to condemn or sanction South Africa and Portugal. Stevenson recommended that the US response should be to stress in private conversations US efforts to limit arms sales to Portugal and South Africa, and to reiterate the US commitment to the liquidation of colonialism and racism.[23]

Kennedy was in a bind. Portugal was a US ally through NATO and was providing the United States with a naval and air facility in the Azores Islands that gave US military assets direct access to all of Western Europe. As for South Africa and Southern Rhodesia, there was absolutely no interest on the part of the United Kingdom to get tough with them, and there was virtually no domestic interest in the United States. At that point, the United States had to grin and bear criticism in the UN from African and other third world groups, as well as taunting from the Soviet bloc that behind its anticolonialist rhetoric the United States was really engaging in neoimperialism.

Arrival on the Diplomatic Scene
of the Organization of African Unity

As the number of newly independent states grew to a critical mass, it was normal that they should band together and form their own multilateral organization. During the period May 22–25, 1963, thirty African heads of state and government met in the Ethiopian capital city, Addis Ababa, to sign the founding charter of the Organization of African Unity (OAU). In their summit statement, the heads of state:

- Condemned racism everywhere.
- Urged the great powers to stop aiding Portuguese and South African racist regimes.
- Declared disarmament and a nuclear-free zone, and demanded an end to military bases and nuclear testing in Africa.
- Set up a special committee to animate a movement to oppose the apartheid regime in South Africa.
- Agreed to engage in general support for nonalignment.[24]

The State Department must have breathed a sigh of relief that the United States was not specifically singled out for aiding Portugal and South Africa. It was clear that in the final months before President Kennedy's tragic assassination, the OAU was destined to become a major diplomatic player in the evolution of US policy toward Africa.

Africa and the Cuban Missile Crisis

Somewhat surprisingly, Africa played a role in Kennedy's management of the Cuban missile crisis during the month of October 1962. Just prior to the crisis, President Milton Obote of Uganda was invited to Washington to meet and have lunch with President Kennedy. When the crisis started, both Obote and the US embassy in Uganda's capital city, Kampala, assumed that the visit would have to be postponed. But word came in from the State Department to inform President Obote that he should come ahead to Washington as planned. Obote did so and had lunch with President Kennedy in a relaxed and friendly atmosphere. There were no messengers rushing in and out with breaking news for the president on the latest developments about the Soviet missiles in Cuba.

After Obote returned to Kampala, US ambassador Olcott Deming invited him to have dinner with the staff of the US embassy to receive his debriefing about the visit. During his presentation, Obote said: "I could not believe it. The radio and TV were full of ominous talk about a possible war between the United States and the Soviet Union, and there was President Kennedy and several U.S. officials calmly having lunch with me."[25]

After the crisis ended, it was revealed that President Kennedy wanted to give the impression to the American people that the US government was not in a state of panic and that normal governance was taking place. President Obote was asked to go through with the visit, despite the dangerous emergency situation facing the administration, as part of the effort to project an image of nonemergency "business as usual."[26]

6

Lyndon B. Johnson:
1963–1969

In the immediate aftermath of President Kennedy's tragic assassination on November 22, 1963, President Johnson had three main concerns:

- Complete the enactment of civil rights legislation that Kennedy had initiated.
- Decide what to do about the Vietnam War—escalate or get out.
- Prepare to be the Democratic candidate in the 1964 presidential election.

None of these issues directly concerned the newly independent African nations, but the African heads of state reacted with great enthusiasm after the enactment of the Civil Rights Act on July 2, 1964. This legislation made it illegal in the United States to discriminate against persons in public accommodations (restaurants, hotels, transportation) on the basis of race, color, religion, sex, or national origin.

As a result of the wave of African nations achieving independence between 1960 and 1964, African governments opened embassies in Washington and missions to the United Nations in New York. The African diplomats assigned to these diplomatic missions had an opportunity to view racial segregation and discrimination firsthand. In nearby Virginia, across the Potomac River from Washington, African diplomats saw signs on restaurants, hotels, and cinemas that said "Whites Only." When these same diplomats traveled by automobile between New York and Washington, they sometimes ran into discrimination themselves in some parts of rural Maryland. Thus, the enactment of the Civil Rights Act had a direct positive impact on highly placed Africans.

Just two weeks after the Civil Rights Act was signed into law, the Organization of African Unity held its annual summit conference in Cairo. In a memorandum dated July 21, 1964, the director of the US Information Agency, Carl T. Rowan, told President Johnson that the Civil Rights Act was the dominant theme of speeches at the meeting. Most of the African comments were highly favorable.

The president of Guinea (Conakry), Sekou Touré, the most Marxist, anticapitalist chief of state in Africa, told his fellow heads of state, "In America, the colored people engaged in the struggle for social progress and racial equality have just won a great victory."[1]

Some African leaders saw President Johnson's accomplishment in advancing civil rights as a straight-line precursor to a US initiative to get rid of racist regimes in southern Africa, namely South Africa and the Portuguese colonies. Others expressed skepticism because the Republican candidate for the presidency in the upcoming election of November 1964 was Senator Barry Goldwater of Arizona. Goldwater had voted against the civil rights legislation. Not surprisingly, African leaders unanimously welcomed Johnson's electoral victory over Goldwater.

Normal Africa Policy Review

With the majority of African colonial territories enjoying independence, the Johnson administration's review of US policy toward Africa was a normal exercise. During preparations for independence, most analysts were predicting a high level of instability, with Soviet agents running around the continent taking advantage of chaos. Toward the end of 1964, most observers in the US government were breathing a sigh of relief that Africa had not collapsed.

Averell Harriman, under secretary of state for political affairs, wartime US ambassador to England, and postwar chief of the Marshall Plan, provided a good example of this. In a memorandum dated October 28, 1964, Harriman told President Johnson that Africa was looking fairly good. Sure, there were some cases of violent instability, along with several military coups, but overall the outlook was positive.

In Ambassador Harriman's list of positive developments in self-governing Africa, he gave first place to the fact "that not a single new African nation [had] succumbed to Communist domination," despite many incentives provided by the Soviet Union and China. Harriman said that real-life experience had reinforced Africa's determination to remain "truly non-aligned and independent." That, in turn, reinforced the initial policy formulation of the Eisenhower administration to keep the Cold War out of Africa and to emphasize education, cultural exchange, and economic development.

Harriman also took note of significant economic growth in Liberia, Ethiopia, Sudan, and Nigeria. He saw the great potential for the development of crude oil production in Nigeria, Algeria, and Libya. There was also strong growth of minerals exports, including copper from Zambia and the Congo, iron ore from Liberia and Mauritania, manganese from Gabon, and bauxite from Guinea. What Harriman was observing turned out to be a ten-year commodities boom, with high prices for virtually every mineral exported from Africa for industrial use in the Western world. Harriman also noted increases in agricultural production in Côte d'Ivoire, Kenya, and Nigeria. He had substantive reasons to express optimistic expectations for the future.[2]

Independent Africa's Highest Priority: Liberate Southern Africa

As of early 1965, approximately 90 percent of colonized Africa had achieved independence. During the first two annual summit meetings of the Organization of African Unity, in 1964 and 1965, the dominant theme was: "We cannot begin to enjoy our self-determination until our African brothers in South Africa, Southern Rhodesia, Angola, Mozambique, and Guinea-Bissau achieve freedom."

The white minority governments of southern Africa found themselves in a less secure situation after their neighbors raised their flags of independence. All of southern Africa had indigenous African nationalist movements, most of which were residing in exile. Where newly independent African nations shared borders with white-ruled southern Africa, the nationalist movements moved in with their neighbors and started armed insurgencies, with the clandestine support of the African rulers. These anticolonial, antiracial wars began in 1964 and expanded steadily for the next two decades, burdening the Portuguese, South African, and Southern Rhodesian governments with rising financial and human costs.

In Portuguese Mozambique, the nationalist Front for the Liberation of Mozambique (FRELIMO) launched armed operations from independent Tanzania against the Portuguese administration. In Portuguese Angola, the nationalist National Front for the Liberation of Angola (FNLA) began making armed incursions against the Portuguese operating out of Congo (Kinshasa) to the north. In 1965, the nationalist United Front for the Total Liberation of Angola (UNITA) opened a second front against Portuguese rule, operating out of Zambia to the east. Armed insurgencies against Southern Rhodesia and the South African rulers of Southwest Africa (Namibia) did not begin until Portugal surrendered its African colonies in 1974, and guerrilla fighters began operating from Angola and Mozambique.

The US Policy Dilemma:
Protect US Interests or Support African Liberation

In view of Africa's own priorities, senior US officials began to examine options for US policy toward minority rule in southern Africa. They found significant obstacles to doing more to help the Africans than pay lip service to the ideal of liberation.

In the case of Portugal, the conventional wisdom was that as long as the United States needed the NATO air and naval base in the Azores, Washington had to go easy on the Portuguese regime, notwithstanding its corporatist, dictatorial configuration.

In the case of apartheid South Africa, the United States was able to take a juridical approach with respect to the mandated territory of Southwest Africa. The United States supported resolutions in both the UN General Assembly and the Security Council declaring that the United Nations, as a successor to the League of Nations, was the true "owner" of Southwest Africa. South Africa was therefore legally required to transfer power to a UN commission, which would bring about a transition to self-determination for the new nation to be called Namibia.

But what should the US policy be if South Africa politely ignored the UN resolutions and continued to plan the eventual annexation of Southwest Africa? There was significant pushback within the Johnson administration to any idea of inflicting sanctions against South Africa.

The US Defense Department made it quite clear that it had objections to doing anything to upset the South African government. Its most immediate concern was to preserve its extensive network of US Air Force satellite tracking stations. It pointed out that in addition to being good for satellite tracking, South Africa constituted "an optimum location for instrumentality supporting all unmanned lunar and planetary programs."[3]

On a strategic level, the Defense Department was still thinking in Cold War terms. It wanted to make sure that Africa's southern ports, and the sea route around South Africa, would be accessible by the US Navy in the event the Soviets blocked access to the Mediterranean and the Suez Canal.

Secretary of State Rusk was sympathetic to the liberation advocates, especially the new US permanent representative to the United Nations, Arthur Goldberg, who had accepted President Johnson's invitation to resign from the US Supreme Court to move to New York. Goldberg was asking Rusk to come up with policy positions that he could use during UN debates when the African delegations insisted on UN action against the white racists in southern Africa.

Rusk began a dialogue with Defense Secretary Robert McNamara, who understood the importance of the need for the United States to show support for the African position regarding the white regimes in southern Africa. He wanted to accommodate the State Department. With respect to the network of US Air Force tracking stations in South Africa, McNamara said that the entire system was in the process of being duplicated in Spain, but the work would not be completed before December 1966. As for the US air and naval station in the Portuguese Azores, McNamara said he was not convinced that the base was indispensable to US and NATO defense and promised to explore it further.

For the United Nations General Assembly meeting in October 1965, Ambassador Goldberg had to rely on what he called "unalterable opposition to the apartheid system" and US support for the transfer of control of Southwest Africa from South Africa to the United Nations trusteeship system. He was still unable to criticize Portugal for its stubborn refusal to consider self-determination for its African colonies.[4]

The Southern Rhodesia Crisis of November 1965

On November 11, 1965, the white minority regime governing the British colony of Southern Rhodesia declared independence from the United

Kingdom, in what became known as UDI (the Unilateral Declaration of Independence). The UK government called this an illegal act of rebellion and prepared to move against it. Needless to say, the United States was drawn into the crisis, which impacted the nations on Rhodesia's frontiers as well as the rebellious colony itself. The Rhodesian crisis was one about which the United States had no inhibitions with respect to its rhetoric. It was free to criticize the white minority and to express full support for the UK's actions against the white regime. In a way, the Rhodesian crisis diverted attention from South Africa, Southwest Africa, and Portugal, about which the United States was more or less tongue-tied due to conflicting interests.

How Did It Happen?

The Rhodesian crisis was several years in gestation. The white regime's rebellious action against UK rule did not happen overnight. The first group of white settlers had arrived in Rhodesia from South Africa in 1890, sponsored by the British South Africa Company. By 1923 the white population had grown considerably and had won wars against the indigenous Ndebele and Shona ethnic nations. As a result, the territory was granted self-governing status as a British Crown colony. From 1923, there was a British governor-general, representing the monarchy, who was always selected from the local white community.

After World War II, the white population was augmented by emigration from Britain. By 1955, the whites numbered about 250,000, compared to about 6 million Africans. At that time, the Rhodesian white political leaders developed the idea of establishing a federation uniting three adjoining UK colonies, Southern Rhodesia, Northern Rhodesia, and Nyasaland. The British agreed because of the expected economic benefits. The most visible entity of this federation was Central African Airways, a well-managed airline that transported passengers among the three federation members and to other destinations in South Africa and East Africa, with a weekly flight to London on an aircraft called the *Rhodesian Comet.*

The new entity was called the Central African Federation, based in the Southern Rhodesian capital of Salisbury. The first prime minister was Sir Roy Welensky of Southern Rhodesia. Welensky and his fellow white politicians fully expected that the federation would be granted independence from the British as a unit. But they failed to take into consideration the rise of black nationalism in the three colonies.

By the mid-1950s, a significant number of educated Africans at the university level considered white minority rule in Southern Rhodesia bad enough, demanding that it disappear. The idea of white minority rule controlling a federation of three UK colonies was totally unacceptable. The black nationalists organized and made a lot of noise, including in the UK press and at the United Nations. The most vocal African opponent of the federation idea was Hastings Banda of Nyasaland, who spent significant time in UK jails because of his "subversive" activities.

The work of the African nationalists persuaded the UK government that the three colonies would have to gain independence separately. Most important, the UK government decided that Southern Rhodesia could gain independence only after the colony's African citizens could vote in an election that would result in majority rule. This came as a shock to the whites of Southern Rhodesia, but they believed that there might be sufficient time before the granting of independence to persuade the UK government either to change its policy or to change its leadership through the election of a conservative parliament.

The UK Decision: The Fateful Years 1964–1965

In 1964, the UK granted independence to Northern Rhodesia, which became the Republic of Zambia, and to Nyasaland, which became the Republic of Malawi. When the UK served notice that Southern Rhodesia could attain independence only under black majority rule, white politics in the colony took a turn toward the extreme right. The Rhodesian Front Party, under UK war veteran Ian Smith, was elected in 1962, after the former ruling Federalist Party proposed to increase black representation in parliament to appease the British. Because of the UK decision on independence, Ian Smith put his government on a path toward unilateral action, with the full support of the white citizenry.

With the independence of Northern Rhodesia (Zambia) and Nyasaland (Malawi) in 1964, an increasing number of white Rhodesians bought into the idea of a unilateral declaration of independence from the UK. This sentiment was visible and palpable. Starting in early 1965, the UK Labour government under Prime Minister Harold Wilson started to prepare for the contingency, while engaging in a vigorous campaign to dissuade Ian Smith and his cohorts. Everyone remembered Assistant Secretary for African Affairs G. Mennen Williams's prediction after his first orientation visit to Africa in 1961: "Rhodesia is a volcano about to explode."[5]

The United States Becomes Involved

During a series of bilateral US-UK consultations, the State Department assured UK prime minister Wilson of full US support in the effort to prevent a unilateral declaration of independence. Joint contingency planning considered the idea of asking the UN Security Council to impose sanctions against the white Rhodesian regime, including a trade boycott against Rhodesian exports. During the first nine months of 1965, the United States made a number of demarches to Rhodesian prime minister Ian Smith in an effort to talk him out of a unilateral declaration of independence. President Johnson himself sent a personal message to Smith.[6]

Prime Minister Wilson Makes a
Last-Ditch Effort with US Support

UK prime minister Harold Wilson had no good options as he tried to manage the Rhodesian crisis. If Wilson agreed to grant independence to the white minority regime in Southern Rhodesia, he would be insulting the newly independent anglophone African nations in the British Commonwealth, as well as the other members of the Organization of African Unity. The UK would lose all credibility both in Africa and within the Non-Aligned Movement.

If the white regime in Rhodesia refused to listen to reason and accept the inevitability of black majority rule, then Wilson would have to engage in punitive action against 250,000 white British subjects, all of whom had relatives living and voting in England. Even the nonrelatives sympathized with their fellow UK citizens in Rhodesia. As the problem was described at the time, the UK government was unable to abandon their "kith and kin." Because of this dilemma, Wilson had to pull out all the stops to persuade both the white and black Rhodesians to agree to a compromise that would stave off an illegal unilateral declaration of independence.

The final effort to persuade Ian Smith and the black nationalist leaders to compromise took place during the last week of October 1965. At that time, I was a State Department Foreign Service officer assigned to the US consulate-general in Salisbury, Southern Rhodesia. Our entire staff were utterly astonished that the prime minister of England, with so many other things happening in England and the world, would spend four days in Southern Rhodesia in a last-ditch effort to prevent a political and diplomatic disaster.

Prime Minister Wilson spent most of his time in discussions with Rhodesian prime minister Smith and the rival black African nationalists, Joshua Nkomo and Ndabaningi Sithole. Nkomo was head of the Zimbabwe African Patriotic Union (ZAPU), and Sithole was head of the Zimbabwe African National Union (ZANU). "Zimbabwe" was the name slated to replace "Rhodesia" after independence under black majority rule.

Wilson proposed to create a royal commission that would bring in experts to study how to create a political transition in Rhodesia that would end in majority rule, while providing guarantees for the white minority in terms of their political rights and property. Neither Rhodesian side was willing to concede anything to Wilson. Smith refused to promise not to issue a unilateral declaration of independence, nor would he say that he would certainly support such a declaration. Smith even threatened that Zambia would suffer if the UK imposed sanctions against Rhodesia. The black nationalists demanded that Wilson absolutely refuse any concessions to the whites and that he maintain his policy of not granting independence except under conditions of majority rule.[7]

Wilson returned to London empty-handed. He knew that a unilateral declaration of independence was imminent, and so informed the United States.

Support for the UK in the Event of Southern Rhodesia's Independence

In Washington discussions took place on what US support for the UK should be after the inevitable announcement of a unilateral declaration of independence. The United States would certainly join in a boycott of all trade with Rhodesia, but it was wary of the idea of agreeing to help the UK make up for lost revenue as a result of a UK boycott of Rhodesia. For example, Rhodesia was the second biggest producer of Virginia tobacco in the world after the United States. The UK depended on Rhodesian tobacco for its cigarette industry. Would the United States provide access to surplus tobacco being stored by the US Commodity Credit Corporation, with appropriate subsidies? At first blush, US policymakers were negative about the idea of subsidizing the UK for prospective losses in Rhodesia. Support would be limited to the diplomatic and political.[8]

In a special national intelligence estimate dated October 13, 1965, the US intelligence community reached the conclusion that the white Rhodesians would be able to sustain themselves for several years under sanctions, as long as they had the support of neighboring South Africa and Portuguese Mozambique.[9]

The white Rhodesian government declared its unilateral separation from Britain on November 11, 1965, a holiday in the United States that recognized and remembered the nation's military veterans of all wars. Some of the language in the declaration was reminiscent of the American Declaration of Independence from the British Crown in 1776. The final sentence of the declaration was: "We have today assumed our sovereign independence."[10]

The UK Punishes Rhodesia, but Zambia Suffers Instead

Rhodesia had an oil refinery in the eastern city of Umtali near the Mozambique border. Umtali was connected to the Mozambique port of Beira by a crude oil pipeline. The Umtali refinery produced oil products, including gasoline for vehicles and trucks in Rhodesia and Zambia. The UK announced a naval blockade of Beira that would prevent all crude oil deliveries to the Umtali pipeline. This action shut down the Umtali refinery completely.

Rhodesia immediately switched to South Africa as a source of refined oil products. Zambia joined in the economic and trade boycott of Rhodesia and was immediately cut off from its only source of automobile gasoline and other refined oil products. This created an immediate transportation crisis in Zambia, with drastic gasoline rationing causing major hardship on citizens and businesses.

To make matters worse, Zambia's boycott of Rhodesia meant that it no longer used the Rhodesian railway system to ship its copper exports to the Mozambique port of Lourenço Marques. Thus, Zambia was faced with a major loss of revenue from its main export commodity.

The United States Responds to Rhodesia's Declaration of Independence

Immediately after the UDI announcement, the United States denounced the illegal action and declared its support of the economic boycott. In a conversation on November 12, 1965, President Johnson approved Secretary Rusk's checklist of immediate measures against Rhodesia:

- Embargo arms and ammunition.
- Suspend action on applications for US government loans and guarantees.

- Suspend Rhodesia's small sugar quota of 6,000 tons per year.
- Discourage US citizens from traveling to Rhodesia.[11]

Washington also ordered the US consulate-general in Salisbury to reduce its personnel complement to a minimum, leaving only a skeleton staff, with a middle-grade diplomat in charge, holding the reduced rank of consul.

I was one of the Foreign Service staff at the consulate-general ordered to depart. I was assigned to the US embassy in neighboring Lusaka, Zambia, as the economic-commercial officer. When I arrived in Zambia, I was informed that I would be limited to a ration of four gallons of gasoline per month for my automobile. I was thus required to travel to and from the embassy by bus, together with American colleagues living in my neighborhood.

The US embassy in Lusaka was plunged into crisis mode in an effort to help Zambia overcome its shortage of refined oil products and its inability to export its copper. Washington was sympathetic to Zambia's plight, which came about through no fault of its own, and was willing to spend some money to help alleviate the pain.[12]

Short-Term Fixes Found Through Air Transport

The United States chartered airfreight companies to airlift refined oil products from the Republic of Zaire (now Congo) across Zambia's northern border. This alleviated the gasoline shortage somewhat, especially for critical land cargo deliveries.

Regarding the transport of Zambia's copper exports, Washington found three C-130 cargo aircraft for sale from Alaska Airlines. The Zambian government purchased the aircraft and began using them to fly copper ingots to the Tanzanian port of Dar es Salaam. Needless to say, this had to be a temporary solution in view of the high cost. Copper is one of the heaviest elements on the periodic table.

The search for alternatives to the Rhodesian rail and road systems for Zambia's imports and exports had to concentrate on the Tanzanian port of Dar es Salaam. The State Department tasked USAID to compare the economics of constructing a railroad with that of building a regular truck and auto road from the Zambian copper region through Tanzania to Dar es Salaam.[13] The USAID study determined that the regular road option was the least costly and most efficient, and the US-financed construction project began in early 1977. It was completed prior to the end of the Johnson administration, thereby placing the United States squarely on the side of African democratic majority rule.

The one worrisome development was the entry of communist China into the middle of the crisis through its offer to finance the construction of a railroad from the Zambia copper region to Dar es Salaam. The Zambian government accepted the offer, and the Chinese built the railroad. In the long run, both projects contributed to Zambia's development, with no element of East-West competition playing any role.

The Johnson administration ended with the Rhodesian-UK crisis still ongoing. There was very little congressional or public interest in the issue. Washington, especially the State Department, could feel comfortable that the United States was on the right side of history.

The Congo Crisis Redux

The Democratic Republic of the Congo remained fragile but whole after the UN peacekeeping mission ended in 1964. Nevertheless, Lumumbist rebel activity continued in the eastern regions, and the central government appeared unable to deal with it. The challenge to the Johnson administration was to supply assistance without becoming directly involved.

The Rebel Takeover of Stanleyville (Kisangani)

The first crisis for Washington was not long in coming after the departure of the UN peacekeeping operation. In October 1964 the main rebel group, known by the Swahili name Simbas (Lions), captured the major regional city of Stanleyville at the source of the Congo River, about a thousand miles from the capital city, Léopoldville. The leader of this group, Christopher Gbenye, was a well-known radical anti-imperialist who saw the assassination of Patrice Lumumba as an attempt by the Belgians to continue their control over the Congo through "bought-off stooges" such as President Kasavubu and Prime Minister Moïse Tshombe, the former secessionist governor of Katanga province and friend of Belgian business interests. Gbenye was apparently able to obtain money and arms from sympathetic governments in Sudan, Ghana, and Tanzania.

Stanleyville constituted a major crisis for Kasavubu and Tshombe. The international community became involved because of the presence of 800 expatriates in the city, including thirty US citizens. There was also a US consulate in the city, with five US employees under Consul Michael Hoyt. In essence, all of the expatriate personnel in the city had effectively been taken hostage. Needless to say, both the US embassy in

Léopoldville and the State Department in Washington went into crisis mode as a result of this development.

The central government's response was to order a Belgian mercenary group it had hired to proceed to Stanleyville to take back the city. The government also offered to negotiate with Gbenye. The rebel response was to declare that all Americans and Belgians were considered "prisoners of war" to be placed under house arrest. This led to contingency planning by the Belgian and US governments for a military intervention. Joint discussions began on November 13, 1964.

Operation Dragon Rouge

On the US side, the combat command for the Middle East, South Asia, and sub-Saharan Africa was in charge. The agreed plan involved twelve US Air Force C-130 transport aircraft, borrowed from the US base in Evreux, France, to fly a battalion of 500 Belgian paratroops to drop into Stanleyville, after stops in the Ascension Islands and the Kamina base in Katanga province, about two hours' flying time from the target.

Because President Johnson faced increasing public criticism about his escalation of US involvement in the Vietnam War, he was not happy with the thought of US forces becoming engaged in combat in the Congo. Consequently, he was involved in every step of the planning process for the intervention in Stanleyville. His constant theme was that the Belgian troops would do all the work on the ground and that the US aircraft would be "in and out" quickly.

As the Belgian mercenary force neared Stanleyville, Christopher Gbenye began to threaten to kill Consul Michael Hoyt and Paul Carlson, an American medical missionary accused of being a CIA agent. In view of the deteriorating situation inside Stanleyville, President Johnson authorized the rescue mission, Operation Dragon Rouge, to proceed. To assist the troops in finding their way around the city, the State Department sent Foreign Service officer John Clingerman, a former consul in Stanleyville, to accompany the troops.

The aircraft arrived over Stanleyville at dawn on November 24, 1964. The troops from three aircraft parachuted next to the airport runway, quickly cleared the airport of rebels, and removed all obstacles that the rebels had placed on the runway. This allowed the remaining nine aircraft to land and discharge their troops.

Because the Belgian government informed the UN Security Council in advance of the operation, rebel leader Gbenye and his top lieutenants were able to flee Stanleyville before the troops arrived. The Simbas who remained were mainly youth, who proceeded to try to kill all of the expatriates. The Belgians and Americans burst out of their "house arrest" situations and made their escape. The final toll was two foreigners killed, including Carlson. The entire US consulate staff were saved from harm. The US aircraft evacuated about 200 wounded to Léopoldville.

The African Reaction to Dragon Rouge

The more radicalized governments in Africa, especially Ghana, Sudan, Egypt, and Algeria, still resented the assassination of Patrice Lumumba, considered the true leader of the Congolese independence movement. For this reason, some African regimes saw the US-Belgian military intervention in Stanleyville as an "imperialist act" designed to prevent Lumumba's heirs from rightfully returning to power.

On November 27–28, 1964, an ad hoc commission of the Organization of African Unity met to discuss the Stanleyville events. The result was a resolution condemning the US-Belgian military intervention as being totally unwarranted and a violation of the Congo's sovereignty. They announced this resolution despite President Kasavubu's written authorization for Operation Dragon Rouge.

The US "counterpropaganda" to this criticism was to plead that the operation was strictly for humanitarian purposes and that it saved Congolese lives as well as Belgian and American lives. The State Department knew that the OAU resolution was driven by a small group of anti-imperialist governments, and that the majority of African governments had no problem with the US-Belgian action.[14]

General Mobutu Takes Power in a Military Coup

Only two weeks after the white Southern Rhodesians illegally declared independence from Britain, the DRC army announced a military takeover of the government on November 25, 1965. The army's commanding general, Joseph Désiré Mobutu, declared himself president of the republic.

The military coup caused no panic in any of the Congo's communities. The Belgian expatriates were relaxed, including those in the Katanga mining complexes. Mobutu himself had become a close confidant of CIA station chief Larry Devlin during the political crisis that led to the assassination of Prime Minister Patrice Lumumba in 1961. That relationship remained strong at the time of Mobutu's coup four year later.

The US embassy and the CIA station wanted to make sure that the US government was not accused of orchestrating the coup. In a message to the State Department dated November 25, 1965, US ambassador McMurtrie Godley said: "We are following things closely, but I have told CAS (CIA), U.S. Military and Embassy personnel to be extraordinarily discreet. I believe we must avoid any impression that we had anything to do with this coup."[15]

Proof of US noninvolvement came the same day when Mobutu apologized to Station Chief Devlin for not giving him advance warning. Mobutu said that the coup was necessary because the Congo was in a never-ending political crisis. Something had to be done. Mobutu said that the coup had unanimous support among the senior military officers. Mobutu pledged continued close relations between the DRC and the US government and emphasized that communism had "no place in the Congo." Mobutu said that he expected to remain in power and that all existing governmental institutions would be maintained. Mobutu joked that the Kasavubu regime was so unstable that even former Katangan governor Moïse Tshombe had a brief stint as prime minister.[16]

On December 13, 1965, the CIA station expressed the view to Washington that "Mobutu's coup d'état represented the only feasible solution to the political crisis."[17] There was also a brief debate within the CIA station and the embassy as to whether or not Mobutu's regular payment should be continued now that he was head of state. The decision was to continue the payment for the time being.[18]

The major problem that Mobutu inherited from the Kasavubu regime was the rebel activity in Stanleyville and further east in Albertville (now Kalemie) and Fizi on Lake Tanganyika. The rebels were Lumumba adherents who were fighting to get rid of all Belgian and Western influence. They enjoyed safe-haven operating bases from tolerant, sympathetic governments in Sudan, Tanzania, and Burundi. It was particularly noteworthy that Kasavubu had hired 200 French and Belgian ex-military personnel as mercenaries. US embassy officers in Léopoldville reported encountering these individuals in bars, restaurants, and hotels. Several of them said that when the call for mercenaries came from the Congo, they quit their jobs, and in some cases their wives, for the attraction of high pay and adventure in Africa.

Power Goes to Mobutu's Head

Between the coup d'état in November 1965 and mid-1966, Mobutu was giving Ambassador Godley and his embassy team increasing heartburn.

The most important issue was the socioeconomic situation. Although copper export prices were quite high, nothing was being done in terms of investments in development, especially in health, education, and infrastructure. Unfortunately, Mobutu succumbed to family corruption. His uncle Litho was put in charge of stealing government money.

In addition, Mobutu was increasingly sensitive to accusations from intellectuals in Africa and Europe that he was just a lackey of the Americans and the Belgians. As a result, his public rhetoric started to emphasize anti-Western and anticapitalist themes. He launched his anti-Western activity by changing the names of the major cities from Belgian to Congolese. He changed the name of the Congo to Zaire, an ancient tribal name of the region. The name of the capital was changed from Léopoldville to Kinshasa, the name of a nearby village. Elizabethville became Lubumbashi. Stanleyville became Kisangani. And so on down the line.

He also abolished Western Christian names. Everyone was required to change his or her name to an "authentic" African name. Joseph Désiré Mobutu became Mobutu Sese Seko Nkuku Ngbendu wa za Banga. The name is translated as the "great warrior who vanquishes all enemies." And he instructed the men of Zaire (ex-Congo) to stop wearing Western suits, Western dress shirts, and Western ties. He established a new style of male outfit called the *abacos* ("down with the Western suit"). All of this would have been amusing to the US embassy community except for the portent of worse nationalism to come. His main Western scapegoat was Belgium, of course.

In October 1966, Mobutu demanded that Ambassador Godley depart. He was becoming fed up with Godley constantly nagging him to use the copper revenue to do some good for his people. He was also unhappy with the way that Godley was exercising tight oversight of CIA military support activities against the rebels in the eastern part of the country. Just before Mobutu's outburst, for example, the ambassador had turned down a request for CIA air strikes against the rebels in Kisangani (ex-Stanleyville).[19]

Nationalization of the Belgian-Owned Copper Mines Without Compensation

The big crisis came in December 1966, when Mobutu announced that the government of Zaire had nationalized the copper mines owned by the Belgian conglomerate UMHK. Mobutu had observed the rest of

Africa, and he saw that the governments owned most of the main economic production units. What better way to demonstrate to the rest of Africa that he was a real African and real anticolonialist anticapitalist?

What turned this particular action into a significant crisis was that Mobutu decided that Zaire would not pay compensation for the nationalized properties. Under international law, a government has the right to nationalize private property, but compensation must be paid.

Within the capital city, Mobutu's action was quite popular, especially among the university students. The students from Kinshasa (formerly Louvanium) University, located on high ground west of the capital city, came marching into the streets praising Mobutu. They were quite proud of Mobutu's blow against capitalism.[20]

Unfortunately for Mobutu, UMHK stopped transferring royalties from copper sales back to Zaire and the government central bank. Since copper sales were the major source of revenue for the government, it was not long before the regime was in deep financial trouble. In addition, 2,000 Belgian employees and their families in Zaire were without funding, not to speak of growing public animosity toward Belgians in general, 40,000 of whom resided in Zaire.[21] In Brussels, a number of politicians and business people were expressing the view that Katanga should have been allowed to secede.

Efforts at mediation between Mobutu and UMHK failed to produce results. In February 1967, Ambassador Godley had departed, and Deputy Chief of Mission Robert Blake was absent. As acting chief of mission, or chargé d'affaires, the Political Section chief (myself) tasked the Economic Section[22] and the USAID mission with finding a creative solution to the UMHK conundrum.

The proposed solution derived from the fact that the new owner of the copper mines, the Zaire government, did not have the people with the experience or management capability to run the mines. A long period of training would be necessary. In the interim, an external manager would have to be hired to run the mines under contract, until such time as a sufficient cadre of Zairian engineers and operators could be trained. Under these circumstances, the price of the management contract could have hidden in it compensation for the expropriated owners.

At about the same time, in February 1967, World Bank president Robert McNamara decided to visit the Congo to see what he could do to resolve the impasse between Mobutu and the owners of the Belgian copper mines. After all, it was not acceptable that one of Africa's most important countries should go bankrupt. His first act after arrival in

Kinshasa was to confer with the US embassy. As chargé d'affaires, I presented him with the proposed solution. McNamara liked it and, a few hours later, persuaded Mobutu to accept it. Mobutu was happy that the payment of compensation would be hidden and that royalty payments would be resumed. The management company that obtained the contract to run the mines was Société Générale des Minerais, a wholly owned Belgian subsidiary of UMHK.[23]

What was interesting, in terms of diplomatic practice in this case, was the embassy's action regarding such an important issue without any reference to the State Department in Washington. In Zaire, at that particular time in history, the US embassy was playing a proconsular role, and the State Department tolerated it.

The New US Ambassador Arrives

In June 1966, Robert McBride, the new US ambassador, arrived to assume command as President Johnson's personal representative. He had previously served as deputy chief of mission at the US embassy in Paris and spoke fluent French. His father had also been a career US diplomat who had served in the Congo many years earlier under Belgian colonialism as US consul in the port city of Boma, on the lower Congo River.

One of McBride's first challenges, a delicate one, was to decide whether or not the CIA station chief could be allowed to have regular contacts with President Mobutu. Mobutu had been accustomed to meeting regularly with the CIA station chief ever since Larry Devlin had befriended him when Mobutu was commander of the postcolonial Congolese army.

Ambassador McBride was inclined to uphold the classic rule that only the ambassador or his deputy chief of mission had the authority to meet with the head of state. After his arrival, however, McBride ascertained that Mobutu had become so accustomed to having access to the separate CIA channel that it would not be wise to shut that down. McBride's decision was to authorize the CIA station chief to meet with Mobutu, but only if he informed the ambassador ahead of time and agreed to carry any message the ambassador wanted to be conveyed.[24]

Here Come the Mercenaries

One month after Ambassador McBride's arrival, the nation of Zaire experienced a major shock. The group of mixed French and Belgian mercenaries, headed by the former Belgian major Jean Schramme, was based in two separate garrisons in the middle of hostile rebel activities—Bukavu, on Lake Kivu in the far east, and Kisangani, on the first upriver navigable point of the Congo River in the east-central region. Toward the end of June 1967, the security situation had greatly improved. The army, with mercenaries and CIA technical support, had virtually defeated the rebels in the east and forced them to depart Zaire for neighboring countries. The CIA had decided to pull out its covert military support apparatus and was in the process of doing so when a political bomb exploded. The two mercenary garrisons, serving under Zaire army command in Kisangani and Bukavu, mutinied and announced that they were in control of the two cities. Zairian foreign minister Justin Bomboko personally confirmed this to Ambassador McBride on July 6, 1967.[25]

The first action by the US embassy in Kinshasa after the announcement of the mutiny was to order the US consul in Bukavu, Foreign Service officer Frank Crigler, to evacuate the entire US staff and cross the Cyangugu Bridge into Rwanda next door. Crigler was able to accomplish this without interference from the mercenaries.

The Zaire government's official public reaction to this event was xenophobic, especially toward Europeans. Belgians living in Lubumbashi began to be attacked and beaten. Some Americans living in Kinshasa were also beaten. With the suspicion that the mercenaries mutinied on behalf of Moïse Tshombe, the governor of Katanga was arrested and put on trial for treason.

During an extremely intense month of curfews and aggression against Europeans and Americans, the US consul-general in Lubumbashi (ex-Elizabethville), Foreign Service officer William Harrop, worked day and night, using the prestige and favorable image of the United States to protect European expatriates from being harmed. He saved quite a few people from harm, and even death.

Mobutu Requests Three C-130 Aircraft

At a bilateral level, President Mobutu made a formal request to President Johnson to send three C-130 aircraft with full crews to Zaire for the purpose of aiding the army with logistics, and enabling them to fight the mercenaries and any lingering Marxist rebels in the east.[26] This created a dilemma for President Johnson, who was already under increasing criticism at home for his escalation of the war in Vietnam. Sending combat forces to Zaire, even in a small way, risked exacerbating his image as a controversial war president.

After listening to Ambassador McBride's argument, President Johnson agreed, under the condition that none of the aircraft and crews could come close to a combat situation. The missions were available purely to move Zairian troops and cargo around the country.

After the aircraft and American crews arrived in Kinshasa on July 10, 1967, Ambassador McBride told Mobutu that the aircraft would start operating only if anti-white, anti-Belgian, and occasional anti-American statements on radio and television stopped and if Mobutu agreed to promise that Tshombe would not be executed for treason. In addition to the flight crews, US paratroop personnel were stationed at the airport to provide security to the aircraft.

While preparations for the first flights were in process, the mercenaries in Bukavu suddenly evacuated the city and marched northwest to join their colleagues in Kisangani. Zairian troops moved in to retake Bukavu, and the staff of the US consulate returned as well.

The daily missions of the aircraft were requested by the Zaire high command and transmitted to the US embassy via the US defense attaché. As political counselor, I made the final decision as to mission acceptability. The mission description was then sent overnight to the Joint Chiefs of Staff in Washington for final approval. The key consideration was the need for certainty that the US flight personnel would be kept far away from potential physical harm. Despite these precautions, eighteen Republican members of Congress signed a letter to President Johnson demanding that he take US military units out of Zaire.

After three weeks of operations, the mercenaries were persuaded that whatever their original purpose, the Zaire regime had not disintegrated and there was nobody else available to join in the mutiny. Ambassador McBride persuaded Mobutu that he should not insist on arresting the mercenaries and putting them on trial. The fact that the US Air Force was assisting Mobutu's army probably had a psychological impact on the mercenaries' outlook as well. The mercenaries were evacuated through Rwanda in August 1967. The C-130 missions continued to December, in support of Zairian military efforts to quash the various rebel groups operating out of Tanzania, Sudan, Rwanda, and Burundi.

The Johnson administration's involvement in Zaire ended on a high note in 1968. In January, Vice President Humphrey went on an official tour of Africa, with a two-day stop in Kinshasa. He was given a sumptuous welcome, reflecting Mobutu's gratitude to the United States for saving his regime from rebels and mercenaries, as frustrating as the entire operation was for Ambassador McBride and the entire US embassy.

Even more important, Ambassador McBride and his embassy economic team were able to persuade Mobutu to make the reforms necessary to qualify for an International Monetary Fund (IMF) stabilization program, which began in 1968. The program brought financial and monetary stability to the country for the first time and set the stage for a period of noticeable development that lasted until 1975.

The Biafra Crisis in Nigeria: Part One

The Rise of Ethnic Tension Results in a Military Coup

The UK granted independence to the Federation of Nigeria on October 1, 1960. The new nation began with four geographic regions: northern, eastern, western, and midwestern. The Hausa-Fulani ethnic group dominated the northern region; the Yoruba group dominated the two western regions; and the Ibo group dominated the eastern region.

The Ibo, who are mostly Christian, were known for their entrepreneurship and love of education, and Ibo traders operated throughout Nigeria. Ibo traders and investors in northern Nigeria, which is mainly Muslim, became the object of discrimination and pogroms in the north, increasingly from 1960 to 1965. The year 1965 was particularly difficult, with many Ibo forced to return to the eastern region to escape persecution, including atrocities.

Ethnic tensions rose so high that younger officers in the Nigerian army overthrew the elected federal government in a coup on January 15, 1966. The elected president, Abubakar Tafawa Balewa, was assassinated. All political parties and the four federal regions were abolished. The new military ruler, Major-General Johnson Ironsi, was an easterner. The State Department's first reaction to the coup was that the issue of recognition did not arise. The United States recognizes states, not governments.

The fact that Ibo officers from the eastern region dominated the military hierarchy was not acceptable to the officer corps from the Hausa-Fulani ethnic group from the north. These northerners staged a second coup in August 1966, resulting in the death of President Ironsi. These northern officers wisely selected a Christian officer from the middle belt between Christian south and Muslim north, Lieutenant-Colonel Yakubu Gowon, to take over as chairman of the Supreme Military

Council. Previously the army chief of staff, Gowon as chairman of the Supreme Military Council, was effectively head of state.[27]

Threats of Secession Should Nigeria Not Become a Loose Confederation

The second coup made matters a lot worse in the eastern region. The military governor of the eastern region, Lieutenant-Colonel Chukwe-meka Ojukwu, an Ibo, saw the second coup as a sign that the northern Muslim military officers were continuing the pattern of discrimination, persecution, and atrocities against his people. In conversations with US consul John Barnard in Enugu, his capital city, Ojukwu said that domi-nation of Nigeria by northern military officers was unacceptable to the Ibo. He pointed out that the federal capital city of Lagos was under the control of northern troops. He believed that all other ethnic groups were ganging up on the Ibo. If the other Nigerians would be unwilling to negotiate a new constitution that would establish a loose confederation, the eastern region would have no choice but to declare its independence as the new state of Biafra.[28]

The US embassy in Lagos and the Africa Bureau in the State Department reacted to Ojukwu's threats of secession with a unanimous recommendation that Nigerian unity be the highest priority for US pol-icy. Secretary of State Dean Rusk reacted to this recommendation with impatience. He took time off during a visit to Manila in the Philippines, on October 27, 1966, to fire off a message to the Africa Bureau and US embassy in Lagos, admonishing them to be careful about rushing into a "keep Nigeria unified" mode. Rusk pointed out that the West Indian and East African federations both broke up very early. Maybe the United States should let nature take its course.[29]

In view of Rusk's warning, the State Department issued a tepid statement of support for the maintenance of Nigerian unity in order to maintain good relations with the federal military government. The high priority for US policy between November 1966 and May 1967 was to work hard to prevent violent hostilities between the eastern region (Biafra) and the central government. In short, the United States wanted to try everything to prevent Nigeria from "going over the brink."

Despite its hard work, the Africa Bureau was becoming increasingly pessimistic during the first quarter of 1967. The State Department sent a message to the US embassy in London on March 11, 1967, that said:

"Recent developments have led the Department to the reluctant conclusion that if Nigeria is to retain unity in any form, a loose confederation with virtually autonomous powers residing in the regions is realistically the most that could be hoped for."[30]

By late May 1967, the highest levels of the US government decided to just sit back and "sweat it out." There was little the United States could do to help the Nigerians reach a compromise. The Ibo in the eastern region were insisting on a loose confederation with regional autonomy. The Hausa-Fulani in the northern region were adamant in their demand that there be a strong, northern-controlled central government, and they were willing to fight the east to achieve that.[31]

The Eastern Region Declares Secession

On May 30, 1967, the State Department sent a circular telegram to all US embassies in Africa and to several embassies in Western Europe: "On May 30, the Military Governor of Eastern Nigeria formally proclaimed Eastern Nigeria to be the sovereign independent Republic of Biafra."[32] The federal military government immediately declared a state of emergency, and a war situation was effectively under way.

The initial US reaction was to be noncommittal on recognition of Biafra and to tell the federal military government that the United States must suspend all military sales. Needless to say, the federal military government was unhappy with the US attitude of neutrality and evenhandedness.

On the basis of US national interests in Africa, it would have been wise for Washington to express support for Nigerian national unity and to denounce the Biafra secession right from the beginning. But there was an emotional aspect that could not be swept under the rug. Many Americans, including US diplomats, sympathized with the Ibo because of the suffering they endured in their efforts to lead normal lives in northern Nigeria. As a thoughtful communication from the US embassy in Lagos, dated March 7, 1968, said: "Our approach to the conflict between the [federal military government] and Biafra has been colored by our revulsion against the brutalities inflicted on the Ibos in 1966. Sentiment beclouds our policy."[33]

In mid-April 1968, as war combat was unfolding, the State Department advised Assistant Secretary of State for African Affairs Joseph Palmer on what US policy should be:

• Noninterference in internal affairs.
• Promote a peaceful solution.
• Avoid an increase in US commitments.
• Be cautious in dealing with representatives of Biafra.[34]

In the Johnson administration's final month, December 1968, a consensus grew that providing aid to the suffering civilians inside Biafra had become the highest priority for the United States. The United States could do very little else by way of influencing a solution. The incoming Nixon administration would inherit this difficult challenge with respect to one of Africa's most important independent nations.

Is the United States Condemned to "Take Charge" in Africa?

At an early juncture in postcolonial African history, the Johnson administration's experiences with crises in Southern Rhodesia, Zaire, and Nigeria constituted a test of the basic US policy that, in Africa, the former colonial powers should remain in front and in charge of crisis management in their former colonies. Those three experiences demonstrated that in some crisis situations, the United States would have no choice but to take charge, or at least to play a major supporting role. The option that "this is not a US problem" appeared to be henceforth unavailable in Africa.

7

Richard M. Nixon:
1969–1974

President Richard Nixon was the first politician elected to the White House after World War II who had significant knowledge of Africa. A thirty-day visit to Africa in 1957 prepared him to dominate President Eisenhower's initial policy meetings concerning the newly independent African nations.

Nixon made a second tour of sub-Saharan Africa in early 1967, traveling as a private citizen. In preparing for his trip, Nixon informed President Johnson and the State Department and requested assistance from US embassies to make appointments with government officials and other leading personalities. At that point, Nixon had been out of government for four years after having been defeated in the 1962 California gubernatorial election.

Johnson responded graciously to Nixon's request. He sent an instruction to every US embassy on Nixon's itinerary to give the former vice president the highest level of VIP treatment.[1]

Less than two years after his second tour of Africa, Nixon was sworn in as the thirty-seventh president of the United States. Right from the first day, January 20, 1969, his top two priorities for US foreign and national security policy were ending the war in Vietnam and managing continuing tensions in the Middle East generated by the June 1967 Six Day War. Nevertheless, African issues kept dropping into his inbox throughout his five and a half years in office.

In his second year in office, on February 18, 1970, Nixon sent a special report to Congress titled "U.S. Foreign Policy for the 1970s: A New Strategy for Peace." The report's section on Africa demonstrated his consistent view about the continent ten years after the great wave of independence of the 1950s and early 1960s:

> We have two major concerns regarding the future of Africa:
>
> • That the Continent be free of great power rivalry or conflict in any form. This is even more in Africa's interest than in ours.
> • That Africa realize its potential to become a healthy and prosperous region in the international community. Such an Africa would not only be a valuable economic partner for all regions, but would also have a greater stake in the maintenance of a durable world peace.

Nixon then went on to list the three major challenges facing Africa in the future:

> • Economic Development: Through the harnessing of human and natural resources.
> • Nationhood: How to weather the strains of internal diversity, especially ethnicity.
> • Southern Africa: Tensions caused by the racial policies of the white-ruled regimes. The problems must be solved, but they will take time.

Nixon concluded that in assisting Africa in the search for solutions to these challenges, the United States would be guided by the principle of noninterference in internal affairs.[2]

The Biafra Crisis in Nigeria: Part Two

The Nigerian civil conflict between the federal military government (FMG) and the breakaway "Biafra" eastern region was at its height as Nixon took office. As of January 1969, the Biafran war in Nigeria was more or less at a stalemate. The rebel army was fighting valiantly and preventing the federal military from advancing into Biafran territory. In addition, there was no sign that the federal military government would accept the rebel demands to change the Nigerian government into a loose confederation, with most power belonging to the individual states. The high cost of continuing the war did not seem to motivate the FMG to compromise, because they knew that they would eventually prevail, given their overwhelming advantages in manpower and military equipment.

The Nixon administration continued the Johnson policy toward the war: maintain strict neutrality; support Nigerian unity; and give priority to humanitarian relief. What changed over the course of a year was the growing public sympathy in the United States for the Biafran cause. Journalists' reporting had emphasized the Ibos' history of persecution and discrimination. The idea of an independent Ibo state was appealing to those Americans who were following Africa and Nigeria. Senator Edward Kennedy was among the opinion leaders on this subject. The astute Biafran rebel regime sent articulate Ibo intellectuals to the United States to talk to the press and to universities.[3]

Within the US government, sympathy for Biafra was growing. The senior director for Africa on the National Security Council staff, Roger Morris, was clearly pro-Biafra. Throughout 1969, he was constantly sending notes to National Security Adviser Henry Kissinger complaining about the State Department's alleged refusal to adhere to the "strict neutrality" policy established by President Johnson and confirmed by President Nixon. Senator Kennedy had become quite vocal in insisting that the United States do something to mediate an end to the war, which was causing so much hardship to Ibo civilians trapped behind the battle lines. He was an active supporter of an organization called Americans for Biafra Relief.[4]

Even the usually dispassionate analysts in the US intelligence community were succumbing to emotion and sympathy about Biafra. Their reports gave some encouragement to those who believed that if only Biafra could hold out a bit longer, they could force the federal government to make concessions.[5]

The diplomats in the State Department's Bureau of African Affairs, led by Assistant Secretary of State David Newsom, correctly saw that there was no possible way for Biafra to force the federal government to accept its demands. It was a war of attrition, and one that the government was likely to win. Newsom was motivated mainly by the idea that it would be disastrous for African nations to start breaking up into independent ethnic states. Hence the State Department was constantly emphasizing, "Keep Nigeria unified."

The more that US political leaders such as Senator Kennedy expressed sympathy for their cause, the more the Biafran leaders were motivated to continue to hold out. A second and crucial source of support was the government of France. As of early 1969, the government of French president Charles de Gaulle was airlifting arms at night from their former colony of Gabon directly into airfields within the Biafra enclave.

Senior officials of the French Ministry of Foreign Affairs were quite frank in their discussions at the State Department in explaining President de Gaulle's rationale for supplying arms to the Biafran secessionists. They explained that France had had two large federated colonies in west and central Africa: French West Africa based in Dakar, Senegal, and French Equatorial Africa, based in Brazzaville, Congo. In the mid-1950s, after extensive consultations with African political leaders, the French concluded that the existence of two very large francophone independent states in Africa was not politically sustainable. The existence of so many ethnic states within states would cause instability and probably lead to the type of civil war that Nigeria was suffering. On that basis, France gave independence to fifteen states rather than two.

The French explained that they sincerely believed that the British had made a grave mistake in bringing the gigantic territory of Nigeria to independence as one state. They should have created at least three states, and possibly five. Hence, President de Gaulle had decided to assist the secessionists in Nigeria's eastern region. Cynics among US analysts said that de Gaulle's underlying main concern was to prevent a powerful anglophone state from dominating their former colonies in West Africa and thereby to protect French economic interests.[6]

Under its policy of "strict neutrality," and without any sign that mediation was possible, the State Department worked zealously to maintain the flow of humanitarian relief to the people of the eastern region. Even this effort caused friction on both sides.

Although the federal government argued that air shipments of humanitarian relief would prolong the war and the suffering, it agreed to authorize such flights for the benefit of the people living under "Biafran" control, who were, after all, Nigerians. There was a major problem, however. The government wanted the flights to take place during daylight hours so that it could make sure there were no arms shipments mixed in. The Biafrans allowed flights to come in only at night so that arms deliveries could take place under the cover of relief deliveries. The State Department instructed the International Committee of the Red Cross (ICRC), which was running the humanitarian airlift with US financing, to operate only at night. The government objected strongly but nevertheless pledged not to shoot down the relief flights.

Until the end of the war in early 1970, the government complained regularly to former ambassador to Nigeria Elbert G. Mathews about the US policy of neutrality, about the constant US admonitions regarding the importance of not seeking revenge against the Ibos, about the United States granting visas to Biafran intellectuals coming to plead the rebel cause, and about the US government's regular public use of the term "Biafra" instead of "secessionists" or "rebels." The government wanted to make sure that the US government would resist efforts by Americans who sympathized with Biafra to take up the rebels' cause.

The war ended in early 1970 with the army of the federal government finally overwhelming Biafran defenses. Roger Morris's earlier prediction to National Security Adviser Henry Kissinger that the troops would commit genocide against the Ibo people proved totally unfounded. President Yakubu Gowon fulfilled his earlier pledges of amnesty and total reintegration of the eastern region into the federal fold. The Biafran commander, Lieutenant-Colonel Odumegwu Ojukwu, escaped to Côte d'Ivoire, but even he was later allowed to return to Nigeria and live in peace among his Ibo people.

The significant interest in the Biafran war within American public opinion was a precursor to even more private citizen involvement in the making of Africa policy as communications continued to expand and improve in subsequent years. This phenomenon grew to explosive proportions in 1986, when the broad American public loudly exclaimed that it had become fed up with apartheid in South Africa.

Unfinished Business in Southern Africa

When the Nixon administration looked at southern Africa in early 1969, they found that nothing much had changed since Kennedy-Johnson:

- The white minority in Southern Rhodesia were still running the country, and were quite resilient in the face of international sanctions, economic boycotts, and a total absence of any recognition of their declaration of independence from Britain.
- South Africa continued to refuse to recognize UN resolutions and International Court of Justice decisions that the territory of Southwest Africa belongs to the United Nations and should be handed over for trusteeship.

- The Portuguese continued to tell anyone who would listen that their African colonies were actually part of "greater Portugal," and that any talk of self-determination did not make constitutional sense.
- The South African system of racial separation, known as apartheid, was increasingly repressive toward the nonwhite races. In view of civil rights legislation enacted in the United States during the Lyndon Johnson administration, US–South African relations could no longer be considered "normal" and posed a challenge to US policymakers.

Problems for Portugal

This "not much had changed" checklist notwithstanding, there was one significant development in the southern African equation that was brought in by the wave of newly independent states during the decade of the 1960s. The overseas Portuguese territories of Angola, Mozambique, and Guinea-Bissau were no longer protected by friendly colonial powers on their borders. Mozambique had the Republic of Tanzania on its northern border. Angola was surrounded by the Congo (Kinshasa) and Zambia. Guinea-Bissau had the former French colonies of Guinea (Conakry) and Senegal on its borders.

Because Portugal was so intransigent against the idea of self-determination for its African territories, nationalist movements with armed guerrilla fighters established themselves for all of the Portuguese African territories, with the support of the Soviet Union, communist China, Egypt, and several African governments. When the neighboring countries became independent, they opened their doors and provided safe havens for the insurgent groups. Thus, by 1964, Portugal was faced with guerrilla armies in all three of its mainland territories. This required the Portuguese government to increase its induction of young men into the armed forces, most of whom were sent to Africa to engage in warfare.

Portugal's two island colonies, Cape Verde and São Tomé, had nationalist movements, but armed resistance was not possible because connections with independent African nations were not available. However, anti-Portuguese guerrilla fighters from Cape Verde did participate in the armed resistance in Guinea-Bissau and later participated in that nation's independent regime.

Between 1965 and 1975, virtually every Portuguese family had sent at least one of its members to fight in Africa. Needless to say, this changed the domestic political calculus for the Portuguese government and had a major economic impact on an already poor nation with a corporatist-fascist dictatorship regime.

Recommendations to President Nixon

The State Department's Bureau of African Affairs reviewed every case file on southern Africa and made recommendations to President Nixon through Secretary of State William P. Rogers and National Security Adviser Henry A. Kissinger. As Kissinger told Nixon in a memorandum dated April 3, 1969: "We need to review policy toward southern Africa. The guerrilla wars in Mozambique and Angola are drawing in the Chinese and the Soviets. Southern Rhodesia looks like it is becoming a drawn-out race war. In South Africa, the United States is facing conflicts of interest between its economic and military interests and its opposition to that nation's racial politics."[7]

One complicating factor was the change of government in the United Kingdom, an essential diplomatic partner for the United States in southern Africa. The fiercely anti–white minority Labour government of Harold Wilson had been replaced by a more relaxed Conservative government under Edward Heath in 1970.

Southern Rhodesia

In a memorandum dated February 19, 1969, the director of the State Department's Bureau of Intelligence and Research, Thomas Hughes, told Secretary of State Rogers that Southern Rhodesian prime minister Ian Smith was developing new constitutional proposals that would bring black Africans into parliament, but that there was no hope that the whites would eventually accept black majority rule. For that reason, no UK government could grant independence to Southern Rhodesia.[8]

In terms of trade with Southern Rhodesia, the United States had implemented the mandatory UN sanctions against the white regime in December 1966. However, because the issue was dragging on, with no hope of resolution in sight, some US domestic interests were beginning to look for exceptions to the sanctions. Particularly important was Rhodesian chrome, which was important for a great variety of industries. The only other source was the Soviet Union, and US business was becoming nervous about its dependence on a Cold War adversary. Union Carbide Corporation was particularly busy lobbying for an exception in order to import Rhodesian chrome.[9]

There was also the issue of the US consulate remaining in the Rhodesian capital of Salisbury with a skeleton staff of three Americans. The British had requested that the consulate be closed because it gave the impression that the United States was recognizing the illegal Rhodesian regime. In July 1969, Nixon accepted Kissinger's recommendation that the consulate be kept open as a useful listening post. That decision was confirmed on January 28, 1970.[10]

On March 6, 1970, the new Rhodesian constitution was promulgated declaring a total break with the UK as an "independent republic." The UK made another high-level request that the United States close its consulate in Salisbury. This time, President Nixon agreed. All US personnel were transferred out of Salisbury.[11]

In July 1970, the issue of Rhodesian chrome came to a head. Secretary Kissinger recommended that President Nixon grant a waiver for the import of Rhodesian chrome to Union Carbide Corporation on "hardship grounds." On August 7, 1970, President Nixon signed a memorandum granting the hardship exemption for Union Carbide while promising to "continue to fully implement the UN Security Council resolutions regarding trade with Rhodesia."[12]

Congress got into the act by enacting the Byrd Amendment on September 24, 1971, exempting chrome from the embargo on Rhodesia for all companies, on the grounds that the only other source was the Soviet Union and, therefore, a security risk.[13] The State Department opposed the Byrd Amendment because of the image it conveyed that Congress was no longer opposing the white minority regime in Southern Rhodesia.

South Africa and Southwest Africa

The Africa bloc at the UN, with the assistance of the Soviet Union and the Non-Aligned Movement, made sure that the Southwest Africa issue was on every meeting agenda. For example, UN Security Council Resolution 269 of August 12, 1969, with the United States voting in favor, declared: "South Africa's continued occupation of Namibia is a violation of territorial integrity and an encroachment on the authority of the UN. The Government of South Africa must withdraw from Southwest Africa by October 4, 1969."[14]

In addition to the Security Council, the World Court decision in 1966 stated that the original League of Nations mandate that gave South Africa control of the former German Southwest Africa was no longer valid, and control over the territory should pass from the League to the

UN. The African bloc wanted the UN to enact sanctions against South Africa in view of that government's refusal to comply with the World Court decision.

The challenge to US policy toward South Africa was to walk a fine line between public rhetoric that denounced apartheid and the government's repressive racial policies on the one hand, and the values of US trade with South Africa and US private investments in South Africa on the other. Each was valued at $850 million in 1969 dollars, which would be the equivalent of several billion in the year 2019.

On December 9, 1969, the National Security Council's Interdepartmental Group for Africa issued a paper titled "U.S. Interests in Southern Africa." The paper elaborated a "balanced policy" toward southern Africa, stating: "The aim of our present policy is to try to balance our economic, scientific and strategic interests in the white states by disassociating the United States from the white minority regimes and their repressive racial policies." The measures to be implemented included:

- Assigning nonwhite US diplomats to the US embassies and consulates in the region.
- In dealing with the public, treating blacks as equal to whites.
- Accepting UN responsibility for Southwest Africa.
- Implementing the UN arms embargo against South Africa.
- Neither encouraging nor discouraging US investments.[15]

Throughout the year 1970, the United States was constantly tinkering with its policy toward South Africa, with the hope of keeping the forty African UN members satisfied that the United States was on their side, while protecting US economic interests.

On January 28, 1970, President Nixon signed a memorandum that added to the list of authorizations and prohibitions with respect to South Africa.[16] The list included:

- Limiting US naval visits to South African ports to emergencies only. In addition to this symbol of opposition to racism, the prohibition on port visits was designed to avoid the embarrassment of South Africa prohibiting African American naval personnel from going on shore leave in that country's ports.
- Trying to "play down" debates on Southwest Africa in the United Nations in order to avoid having to veto extremist resolutions.[17]

With respect to Southwest Africa, the president signed National Security Decision Memorandum 55 on May 22, 1970, that:

- Restricted official visits to Southwest Africa as well as overflights by official aircraft.
- Prohibited EXIMBANK loans and guarantees to the private sector in Southwest Africa.
- Ruled out guarantees to US investors in Southwest Africa against claims of future lawful Southwest Africa governments.[18]

In July 1970, the Conservative government in the UK decided to resume arms sales to South Africa, thereby breeching the key Western sanction against the apartheid regime. In a public statement, the United States dissociated itself from the UK decision.

On August 17, 1970, President Nixon signed a memorandum[19] concerning the implementation of the UN arms embargo against South Africa and the Portuguese African territories. While confirming previous decisions to adhere to the UN arms embargo, the memorandum introduced the idea of selling "non-lethal dual use items on a case-by-case basis." Thus, the sale of Lear Jets and Cessna dual-engine 401 and 402 craft to the South African Defense Forces was allowed. But the Cessna single-engine 180 and 185 aircraft remained on the prohibited list. As time went on, the list of allowed and prohibited items continued to expand.[20]

In terms of United States–South Africa trade, the administration wanted to protect the lucrative sales of nuclear technology, equipment, and enriched nuclear fuel to South Africa's electric power system by General Electric and other US companies.[21]

One interesting and quite innovative idea that came out of the continuous stream of policy discussions and papers was to encourage US companies operating in South Africa to engage in nondiscriminatory employment practices. Assistant Secretary for African Affairs David Newsom raised the idea in a memorandum to Secretary of State Rogers on February 17, 1971. Under Newsom's proposal, there was nothing to prohibit US companies in South Africa from elevating black employees to management status and treating everyone equally in the workplace. This concept was to become highly important in US policy a decade later, in the 1980s, when the American public became increasingly aware of and concerned with the continuing tragedy of South African apartheid.[22]

As a significant symbol of US opposition to apartheid, the State Department assigned an African American Foreign Service officer,

James Baker, to the US embassy in Pretoria, South Africa, on July 6, 1971. The South African government expressed its disapproval through diplomatic channels, but accredited Baker nevertheless.[23]

Walking the fine line in southern Africa between opposition to racism and support for US economic and security interests continued to drive US policy toward South Africa and Southwest Africa to the end of President Nixon's tenure in 1974. It is interesting to note that the president spent significant time on African issues despite the much higher and more pressing priorities of Vietnam and the Middle East.

A Tragic Genocide in the Republic of Burundi Happens Virtually Unnoticed

Historical Note

Burundi and its northern neighbor, Rwanda, are small countries situated on Lakes Tanganyika and Kivu, respectively, along East Africa's Great Rift Valley. For about thirty years prior to the end of World War I, both countries were colonies of Germany, part of German East Africa that included the current nation of Tanzania.

Burundi and Rwanda are situated on rich volcanic soil at an altitude of about 5,000 feet. Because of their good agricultural potential and healthy climate, they attracted African migrants starting in about the sixteenth century. Migrants coming from the west, identified as Hutu from the Bantu language group, were agricultural. Migrants coming from the north, identified as Tutsi from the Nilotic language group, were pastoral.

Over time, the population mix stabilized at about 85 percent Hutu and 15 percent Tutsi. They also evolved a common language called Kirundi in Burundi and Kinyarwanda in Rwanda. Politically, the Tutsi tended to dominate with a system of monarchical rulers called *mwamis*.

Under German colonialism, the Tutsi ethnic group was considered more advanced intellectually. On that basis, the German administrators tended to favor the Tutsis for civil service jobs and for higher-level education. After the Germans lost their colonies at the end of World War I, the Belgian government took control under a mandate from the League of Nations. The Belgians followed the same practice as the Germans in favoring the Tutsis for advancement in government and education. People were identified as either Hutu or Tutsi in their official documents.

As the time came for Belgium to grant independence to the two countries, it was expected that the Hutus would come to power on the basis of majority rule. At independence, the Hutu majority took power in Rwanda. In Burundi, on the other hand, the Tutsi elite, with the assistance of Belgian friends, managed to control the newly independent government.

In 1972, twelve years after independence, and after a series of coups, Burundi was under the control of the country's military, led by Colonel Micombero as head of state. In early May 1972, violence broke out, led by Hutu insurgents who wanted to replace the minority Tutsis and take their rightful place as majority rulers. It was this action that led to a government-sponsored genocide against the Hutus.

The Hutus Attack and the Tutsis Respond with Overwhelming Genocidal Force

In early May 1972, the State Department began receiving reports from the US embassy in Bujumbura, Burundi, about terrible atrocities being perpetrated by the government. Members of the Hutu ethnic group, especially males with fifth-grade educations or higher, were being systematically rounded up and murdered. Tutsi civilians were participating in the killings.

US ambassador Thomas Melady, a noncareer Nixon supporter and Republican Party stalwart from Washington, had long experience working in Africa with various charitable foundations. His deputy chief of mission (DCM) was career Foreign Service officer Michael Hoyt. Together, Ambassador Melady and DCM Hoyt sent graphic descriptions of the many ways that Tutsi officials and private citizens were systematically murdering Hutus. For the Tutsis, keeping the majority Hutus suppressed was the only way to remain in power.

When the reports came in, I was directly concerned because I was director for Central African affairs in the State Department, with responsibility for Burundi, among others. What surprised us at first was the total lack of reaction on the part of other African governments. For them, it was a matter of "the internal affairs of other countries." Our first reaction was to make sure US citizens were safe. We also looked for ways to provide humanitarian assistance to victims.

The incoming messages from the US embassy in Bujumbura were not highly classified and thus had widespread distribution within the US government. Since the State Department was not making any public statements, other branches of the government were finding out about the tragedy through their copies of the messages. The office of Senator Edward Kennedy of Massachusetts took a particular interest in the matter. In addition, the *New York Times* had obtained copies of the embassy messages.

In a memorandum dated June 26, 1972, National Security Council staff member Melvin H. Levin told National Security Adviser Henry Kissinger that Senator Kennedy was highly critical of the administration for not doing anything about the tragedy and for "suppressing information about events in Burundi." At about the same time, Senator John Tunney of California asked me to brief him about Burundi. After listening, he said he would make a statement of outrage on the floor of the Senate. When he made his statement, no other senators were there to listen.

Levin told Kissinger that with very little leverage, the United States had supported a diplomatic initiative led by the Papal Nuncio, together with the Belgians, West Germans, Swiss, British, Dutch, and Zairian ambassadors. Unfortunately, the initiative had no effect. Levin said that he expected the issue to "break more sharply into the public view."[24]

On August 18, 1972, the National Security Council staff sent a message to Kissinger in Tokyo: "Burundi tribal slaughter goes on: The extermination of Hutu males with any semblance of an education seems to be continuing in Burundi. None of the Africans are doing anything, including neighboring Rwanda, which has a Hutu government."[25]

In mid-August, 1972, there remained one neighbor of Burundi who had not been approached about the genocide unfolding there, namely President Julius Nyerere of Tanzania. We instructed the US ambassador in Dar es Salaam to discuss the genocide with him. Nyerere then communicated to the president of Burundi that he had cut off all rail transport between the port of Dar es Salaam and the Burundi border and would not reopen it until the killing stopped.[26]

Nyerere's action was effective. The killing ended. It was a pyrrhic victory, however, since as many as 80,000 to 100,000 Hutus had already been murdered.

Ironically, President Nixon became emotional about the Burundi genocide just when it was ending. In a telephone conversation with Kissinger, Nixon said: "I want to know what the hell happened. What is the matter with the State Department, Henry? They've killed one hundred thousand people. Are we callous about it? Don't we care? You know the trouble is, State just wants to play to these goddamn African leaders."[27]

The essence of President Nixon's unhappiness was his belief that the career specialists in the State Department's Africa Bureau had a double standard. They expressed horror at what white South Africans were doing to the black majority, but they were ready to tolerate the atrocities that African leaders were committing against their own peoples in some cases.

Later, academic studies about the Burundi genocide, including critiques of the US response, were published. The most critical, a report issued in 1973 by the Carnegie Endowment for International Peace, said that the State Department failed to take the only action that might have stopped the genocide earlier—stopping all US imports of Burundi coffee. US coffee companies had been importing 100 percent of Burundi's coffee production. To the best of my knowledge, no one ever raised this proposal.[28]

But there was one important person in the US government who did not let the Burundi genocide be forgotten, Congressman Donald Fraser of Minnesota. During August 1973, the House of Representatives Subcommittee on International Organizations held a short hearing on the Burundi genocide, as part of a broad study on the relationship of human rights to US foreign policy. Congressman Fraser was in the chair. I was the main State Department witness. The committee accepted my review of what the State Department did, or failed to do, without criticism. But at the end, Chairman Fraser accused National Security Adviser Henry Kissinger of being insensitive, not only to the Burundi tragedy but also to a number of situations in other parts of the world. The subcommittee report said: "The prevailing attitude of the administration favored power politics at the expense of human rights."[29]

Genocides occurred in Rwanda in 1994 and in the Congo in 1996. As we will see, the US government proved unable to act in these as well.

8

Gerald Ford: 1974–1977

There was smooth continuity in foreign policy between the Nixon and Ford administrations. The main reason for this was the continuation of Henry Kissinger as secretary of state. With respect to Africa, President Ford sincerely believed in the key policy of all his predecessors since the end of World War II: the United States should emphasize economic and cultural development and should make every effort to prevent the introduction into Africa of great power rivalries, especially the Cold War's US-Soviet competition for the hearts and minds of African nations. Unfortunately for President Ford and Secretary of State Kissinger, US-Soviet great power competition forced its way into US Africa policy as a major challenge, much to the secretary's frustration.

In the final moments of the Nixon administration, on April 25, 1974, a coup by midlevel army officers overthrew the fascist dictatorship in Portugal. As Secretary Kissinger described it, "The virtually bloodless coup was triggered by Lisbon's African policies, and the divisions within the military to which they gave rise." In other words, the Portuguese people and military could no longer bear the burden of three guerrilla wars in Africa.[1]

Nineteen months later, Kissinger and his US government national security team had to stand by helplessly while they watched an offshoot of the once clandestine Portuguese Communist Party, the Popular Movement for the Liberation of Angola (MPLA), take power in the newly independent African colony of Angola.

Across the continent, in the Horn of Africa, America's best friend in all of Africa, Emperor Haile Selassie of Ethiopia was deposed in a coup on September 12, 1974. It took a while for the US embassy in Addis Ababa and the State Department to determine who the real perpetrators of the coup were. When the Ethiopian army officers who emerged as the new power group made themselves known as the Provisional Military Administrative Council (the Derg), it was clear that the US situation in this strategically located country was bound to deteriorate. By 1977, Soviet military advisers and equipment, as well as Cuban troops, were flowing to the Ethiopian armed forces, much to the detriment of US influence.

The Portuguese Revolution and the Rapid Independence of Portugal's African Colonies

The midlevel officers who overthrew the Portuguese dictatorship called themselves the Armed Forces Movement. Their two main objectives were to establish democracy in Portugal and find a solution to Portugal's African colonial problem. For leadership, they sought out General Antonio de Spinola, who had written a book calling for a political solution to the anti-Portuguese insurgencies in Africa. Spinola also agreed that Portugal should have a democratic form of government.[2]

The new regime moved quickly to enable the African colonies' transition to independence. This action necessarily required dialogue and negotiations with the armed insurgent movements that had been fighting the Portuguese since the independence of their neighboring countries. In Angola, the insurgents were receiving assistance from Zambia and the Congo and Zaire republics. In Mozambique, Tanzania helped the insurgents. Guinea-Bissau rebels were operating out of neighboring Guinea (Conakry).

Needless to say, the Portuguese settlers who had emigrated to Africa with the understanding that they would be living in Portuguese-owned territory indefinitely were frightened about their futures and angry about what was happening in Lisbon. In Mozambique and Guinea-Bissau, the transfer of power to the African nationalists was relatively easy, because each had only a single rebel movement. In Mozambique, the Front for the Liberation of Mozambique (FRELIMO), a Marxist movement, replaced the Portuguese administration on June 25, 1975. In a routine fashion, Secretary Kissinger requested President Ford's approval to raise the status of the US consulate-general in Mozambique's capital, Lourenço Marques, to an embassy, and to propose the formal opening of diplomatic relations to the president of Mozambique, Samora Machel.[3]

The same situation applied in the mainland colony of Guinea-Bissau and the island colony of Cape Verde, where the Party for the Independence of Guinea and Cape Verde (PAIGC) took power in both nations. In the tiny Portuguese island colony of São Tomé and Príncipe, located on the Atlantic Ocean due west of Gabon, independence came easily on June 12, 1975, with the Movement for the Liberation of São Tomé and Príncipe taking power without opposition.

Angola and the Potential for Communist Control of the New State

The big challenge for US policy in Portuguese Africa arose in Angola, where there were three insurgent movements fighting the Portuguese. Before they departed Angola definitively on November 11, 1975, the Portuguese regime tried to bring the three rebel movements together to forge a peace agreement and set the stage for the election of a new independent government. The parties reached an agreement in the Portuguese town of Alvor in January 1975, but it was quickly forgotten as the three movements resumed fighting soon thereafter.

As is true with all insurgencies anywhere in the world, each of the three rebel groups in Angola had outside partners who supplied them with arms and advice. The Marxist MPLA was supplied from the Republic of Congo (Brazzaville) to the north, which in 1975 identified itself as Marxist. The centrist National Front for the Liberation of Angola (FNLA) was based and supplied from Zaire to the north. The Union for the Total Independence of Angola (UNITA) was supplied from the east by Zambia, and from South Africa through the border with Southwest Africa (Namibia).

A meeting of the National Security Council's Interdepartmental Group on June 13, 1975, reached a consensus that the highest priority for the United States in Angola would be to prevent the MPLA from taking power. That particular issue became one of the most frustrating problems of Kissinger's entire tenure as secretary of state.[4]

The war among the three insurgent groups unfolded slowly during 1975, as the Portuguese prepared to depart. Independence for Angola was scheduled for November 11, 1975. For the first half of 1975, the UNITA movement was doing well. It captured a number of towns in central Angola, with the main prizes being Huambo, a substantial city in the high plateau region, and the strategic port of Lobito on the southern Atlantic coast.

The FNLA, however, showed very little fighting ability. Its leader, Holden Roberto, was based in the Zaire capital, Kinshasa, and refused to go into the field to lead his troops. It was no surprise, therefore, that the MPLA was able to force the FNLA to retreat from their operational area to the north of the Angolan capital city Luanda.

During this period, the United States was providing financial assistance to both the FNLA and UNITA in an official CIA covert action project.[5]

Here Come the Cubans

In late September and early October 1975, Cuban troops started to arrive in Luanda, first by ship and then by airlift. The Portuguese, who were in the last stages of departure, did nothing to interfere with the Cubans. Since the 1974 Portuguese revolution, the MPLA had been receiving various forms of assistance from its sister communist government, Cuba, mainly in the form of military training. But even before the arrival of Cuban troops, Cuban military advisers had been in the field with the MPLA fighters and had incurred casualties.[6]

The Castro regime in Cuba justified its military intervention in Angola by proclaiming, in the United Nations, that the "imperialists" were trying to stop the only legitimate Angolan liberation movement from taking power on behalf of the Angolan people. Therefore, the Cubans had no choice but to intervene.[7]

That troops from a communist country had come in to support the MPLA was bad enough; but the fact that they were Cuban caused a major shock in Washington. The Castro regime in Cuba remained a total political pariah in the United States, especially among the Cuban exiles living in Florida.

The first thing that the State Department did upon the arrival of the Cubans was to order the closing of the US consulate-general in Luanda. The order went out from the State Department on November 2, 1975, indicating that the closure should take place no later than November 11 and that all American personnel should be evacuated to Lisbon.[8]

On the diplomatic front, under Cuban protection, the MPLA controlled Luanda. It was not unexpected, therefore, that on Independence Day, November 11, 1975, the MPLA declared itself the legitimate government of the Republic of Angola. Recognition came immediately from the Soviet Union, Cuba, East Germany, Poland, Mozambique, Mali, Guinea-Bissau, Cape Verde, São Tomé, Somalia, Romania, and Brazil. However, the fighting among the three liberation movements continued, and there were many voices calling for a ceasefire. The Organization of African Unity continued to recognize all three movements as legitimate and started to work for a ceasefire. The South Africans let it be known that they had ceased all assistance to UNITA, so that other Africans would not be tempted to consider UNITA as a puppet of the white minority regime.[9]

On November 10, 1975, Secretary Kissinger responded to two questions on Angola during a press conference. With respect to Soviet and Cuban involvement in Angola, the secretary pointed out that the Soviets had introduced a substantial amount of military equipment into Angola and that Cuba had sent fighters and advisers. He said: "We consider both of these steps by extra-continental powers a serious matter and really, as far as the Soviet Union is concerned, not compatible with the spirit of relaxation of tensions." The secretary also pointed out that the United States supported the OAU call for a ceasefire and for negotiations among the three factions. He said that the United States had no other interest to pursue in Angola beyond support for Angola's territorial integrity.[10]

Behind the scenes, Secretary Kissinger was quite upset about the Cuban-Soviet intervention in Angola. Looking at the big picture, he saw their initiative as a major blow to the image of the United States as the world's leading great power. In a meeting with his senior associates in the State Department and the National Security Council on December 18, 1975, Kissinger described the likely takeover of power in Angola by the MPLA as a "U.S. collapse." In almost hysterical language, Kissinger said: "A U.S. collapse will have the profoundest effect in Africa. In Europe, it will prove that the collapse in Vietnam was not an aberration."[11]

In the same meeting, Kissinger expressed annoyance with the career Foreign Service officers in the Africa Bureau who had not grasped the larger worldwide damage to America's image caused by the Cuban expeditionary force in Angola. The Foreign Service officers were thinking mainly about possible Soviet control of Angola's oil resources, as well as Soviet use of Angola's airfields for ocean surveillance. But they failed to recognize, according to Kissinger, the broader strategic significance of the Cuban-Soviet action.

Kissinger's Response to the Cuban-Soviet Military Initiative in Angola

Keep the War Going

Despite the MPLA takeover of Angola's capital city, Luanda, Kissinger wanted to continue supporting the other two rebel groups still fighting the MPLA in various places in Angola. His method was to use the Angola Covert Paramilitary Program, run by the CIA, to supply arms and money to UNITA and the FNLA, who had become allied. Some of the material was transferred via the government of Zaire. The secretary wanted to keep the fighting going until such time as the MPLA would decide that there was no alternative to negotiation. He also sought to prevent further recognition of the MPLA as the legitimate government of Angola.[12]

But the CIA covert action program was not to last long. In a nation deeply traumatized by the war in Vietnam, very few members of Congress were willing to see the United States become embroiled in a new third world conflict in a remote country in Africa. So, several Democratic members of Congress, including Senator Dick Clark of Iowa, Senator John Tunney of California, and Representative Ron Dellums of California, began attaching amendments to various bills to prohibit the expenditure of appropriated US funds for the provision of arms and equipment to any group engaged in fighting in Angola. Senator Clark's amendment became law as part of the Arms Export Control Act of 1976. From that point, until 1986, the Clark Amendment was continually cited as the symbol of US impotence in Angola.

Within a matter of months, the MPLA government received sufficient recognitions to give it the legitimacy it needed to enter the United Nations. For the US government, the fight to prevent the MPLA from taking power was effectively over.

Chide the Soviets over Their Violation of Détente

Both President Ford and Secretary Kissinger considered the Soviet-Cuban action in Angola a violation of the relationship of détente forged between President Nixon and Soviet president Brezhnev between 1972 and 1974. US-Soviet détente comprised a series of agreements related to arms control, nonproliferation, and the Helsinki Accords, on human rights. Basically, détente was an understanding between the United States and the Soviet Union that they would not deliberately seek to undermine each other's key interests around the world. The Soviets were particularly interested in détente with the United States as a further impediment to Chinese expansion in the Far East, after Sino-Soviet relations began to deteriorate in the early 1970s.

Ford and Kissinger decided to complain to the Soviets that their Angola adventure was very annoying because it violated the spirit of détente. In a conversation with Soviet ambassador Anatoly Dobrynin on December 9, 1975, Ford and Kissinger complained that the massive Soviet arms buildup in Angola was way out of proportion for that small country and that the Soviets were making a bad security situation worse. Ford ended the conversation by remarking, "I am for détente, but this is difficult for me to explain."[13]

Written exchanges between Washington and Moscow followed the exchange with Dobrynin. Washington complained of Soviet interference in the domestic affairs of Angola. The Soviets said that they were assisting the only legitimate Angolan liberation movement, which had become the legitimate government of Angola. Their intervention was, therefore, perfectly justifiable. The Soviet Angolan operation was just one of several actions that were to accelerate the decline of US-Soviet détente between 1976 and 1979.[14]

In 1975, the US Congress prohibited the administration from becoming involved in the Angolan civil war in any way. From that point on, the only support for anti-MPLA rebels came in the form of arms and equipment South Africa supplied to UNITA across the Namibian border. As a result, UNITA continued harassment operations against the MPLA regime without interruption until May 1991, when the Angolan civil war finally came to an end.

Will Southern Rhodesia Become the Next Domino?

The Portuguese revolution of 1974 completely changed the security scenario for Southern Rhodesia and Southwest Africa (Namibia). With Mozambique's rapid independence, its long border with Southern Rhodesia became open to guerrilla fighters of the Zimbabwe African National Union (ZANU), led by Robert Mugabe. At the same time, the northern border of Southwest Africa opened to guerrilla fighters of the Southwest Africa People's Organization (SWAPO), with Cuban support.

After being frustrated by the US Congress on his objective of keeping the Angolan war going, Kissinger's thoughts shifted to Southern Rhodesia. What would prevent the Cubans, Kissinger reasoned, from sending military forces to Mozambique to help the nationalist insurgents defeat the white Rhodesian antiguerrilla fighters? With that hypothesis in mind, Kissinger inaugurated a sustained major diplomatic offensive to persuade the white leaders of Southern Rhodesia that the time had come to initiate a negotiated transition to black majority rule. At the same time, he exerted pressure on South Africa to move Southwest Africa toward legality and independence under UN auspices.

The Kissinger Plan for Southern Rhodesia

Secretary Kissinger did not limit his activities to applying diplomatic pressure on Prime Minister Ian Smith of Southern Rhodesia. He also proposed concrete solutions. In a meeting with South African ambassador R. F. Botha in Washington on April 16, 1976, Kissinger unveiled his comprehensive strategy to bring an end to the crisis and lead Rhodesia to majority rule.

Kissinger proposed a package of incentives for both the black majority and white minority. In the political realm, he proposed guaranteed representation for the white minority in both the executive and legislative branches, with super majorities needed to pass certain laws. He proposed compensation for any white Rhodesian who wanted to just pack up and go home to the United Kingdom. He also proposed economic development financing for an eventual majority-rule regime. Kissinger proposed that, during the transition period, the UK would resume its colonial rule and appoint a UK governor to preside during a two-year interim timeframe.[15]

Kissinger showed his plan to South African prime minister B. J. Vorster, Southern Rhodesian prime minister Ian Smith, and UK prime minister James Callaghan. All considered the plan truly comprehensive and fair to all sides.

On September 24, 1971, Ian Smith addressed the nation. He announced that the Rhodesian cabinet had decided to accept the proposals put forth by Kissinger and the UK government. He put it in terms of their having no choice. It was either accept the "package deal" or Rhodesia would be left to fight "terrorism" and "communism" by itself. He listed all of the safeguards and financial guarantees designed to keep the confidence of the white minority. He said that there would be a two-year interim period, at the beginning of which all sanctions would be lifted and insurgent warfare would cease. He also listed the financial incentives proposed for whites who wanted to leave and for those who wanted to remain. During the interim period, Smith envisaged, there would be negotiations with political representatives of the black majority.[16]

The Geneva Conference Does Not
Follow the Playbook

The official negotiating conference to hammer out the details of the transition to majority rule in Southern Rhodesia began in Geneva on October 27, 1976. Before that date, the Organization of African Unity held meetings in Lusaka, Zambia, to discuss the Rhodesian issue. The rhetoric at those meetings was militant, rejecting all ideas of special guarantees for the whites. For the independent African governments, it was "one man, one vote." There was no need for guarantees. The Rhodesian whites were "Africans" just like anyone else.

At the Geneva conference, the Rhodesian Africans were not unified. The Zimbabwe African National Union–Patriotic Front (ZANU-PF), led by Robert Mugabe, were extremists. They demanded independence and majority rule immediately. The Zimbabwe African Patriotic Union (ZAPU), led by Joshua Nkomo, was slightly more moderate, and willing to have an interim regime under British rule. Ndabaningi Sithole of the original Zimbabwe African National Union (ZANU), from which Mugabe had broken away, was willing to accept a white veto during the transition.

This militant activity frightened the white Rhodesians, who started to have second thoughts. Some wanted to take their money and return to the UK even before independence.[17]

In essence, the Geneva conference was really two conferences. One involved a discussion among the British, the white Rhodesians, and the black Rhodesians about the methodology for achieving independence with majority rule. The second conference was among the different black factions competing for leadership of the black community.[18]

The UK chair of the Geneva conference was Ivor Richard, the British permanent representative to the United Nations. His highest priority was to achieve a consensus about the date of independence. The whites wanted to make sure that all preliminary arrangements for their guarantees were in place before independence. The black political leaders wanted early independence and immediate black majority rule. Chairman Richard could not persuade the conferees to agree on a date for independence.[19]

During the conference, the US presidential election took place, and Governor Jimmy Carter defeated President Ford. Everyone knew that Secretary Kissinger would have to leave no later than January 20, 1977.

His leverage decreased considerably upon the announcement of the election results.

The Geneva conference failed, finally, because the participants could not agree on a date for independence. The white delegates, watching the black politicians arguing among themselves, threw up their hands and said, "We told you so!"[20]

What was essentially a civil war was deemed likely to continue. Peace would have to wait until 1980. During that period, the war increased greatly in intensity. The white Rhodesian army conducted commando raids into Mozambique to destroy rebel bases, kill rebels, and destroy ammunition stocks. The rebel insurgents came into Rhodesia at night and destroyed white farms.

Meanwhile, Kissinger worked hard to persuade the South Africans to arrange a negotiating conference comprising the white political leaders and the representatives of SWAPO. As Kissinger's time in office was fading, the South Africans decided to relax on this issue. The Namibia issue would be settled only in 1988.

In East Africa, US Interests Are Placed in Jeopardy

Historical Perspective

Ethiopia was the first nation occupied by the Nazi-Fascist Axis during World War II. In 1941, British South African troops ousted the Italian military. In that year, in addition to their occupied territory in Ethiopia, the Italians lost all of their holdings in East Africa, including their colony in Eritrea and their colony in Somaliland.

When Emperor Haile Selassie was restored to his throne in 1941 and afterward, the United States gave him very friendly treatment, especially through the supply of arms for his military. The emperor was sufficiently grateful that he sent a battalion of troops to fight alongside the US Army during the Korean War (1950–1953). He also gave the US Navy a place in the city of Asmara to house a communications facility serving the Indian Ocean region, called the Kagnew Station.

By the mid-1960s, the emperor and his government were starting to face some serious problems. Internally, the province of Eritrea was in a state of rebellion, with a guerrilla war being waged against the central government from the Nakfa Mountains. In addition, the emperor was presiding over a feudal economic and social system that favored his Amhara ethnic group. His elites controlled most of the land, and the farmers were essentially serfs. This situation was causing considerable social unrest.

With respect to arms sales, Ethiopia was one of two African countries, along with Zaire (Congo), eligible to receive sophisticated weapons from the United States. Under US legislation known as Conte-Long, the administration was, and still is, required to certify to the Congress that selling sophisticated military equipment to a developing country is in the best interest of the United States and will not harm the recipient country. Under Conte-Long, Ethiopia received F5A fighter jets equipped with Sidewinder missiles.

Major Changes in US-Ethiopian Relations During the Ford Administration

In mid-1972, significant political changes began to take place in Ethiopia. Persons described as "radical Marxist students" were pushing out the emperor's administration. It was a silent revolution, with the emperor kept in place as a figurehead.

On September 12, 1974, the Ethiopian army announced that a certain group of officers calling themselves the Provisional Military Administrative Council (the Derg) had taken power under the leadership of Major Mengistu Haile Mariam. Information emerged that the Derg had engaged in widespread executions of political adversaries, including other military officers. Their action became known as the Red Terror. The Derg was also reputed to be Marxist in orientation.

Throughout the transition period, 1972–1974, the revolutionaries informed the US embassy that their action was not aimed at the United States and that they wanted to continue the military-equipment supply relationship with the United States. In response, President Ford and Secretary Kissinger decided to wait. As the stories of mass executions became public in late 1974, they were reluctant to be seen delivering arms to an Ethiopian military engaged in particularly heinous human rights violations. The memory of the United States doing little to nothing in response to the Burundi genocide of 1972 was still fresh. So, they adopted a wait-and-see posture.

Ethiopia Wants Normal Relations with the United States and Fears Somali Aggression

On January 27, 1975, the Ethiopian foreign minister, Kifle Wodajo, visited Secretary Kissinger. He said he wanted to make clear that the internal changes in the Ethiopian power structure had nothing to do with external relations. Those internal changes were made in order to bring social justice and economic advance to the Ethiopian people. In other words, please do not be frightened by our Marxist, anticapitalist rhetoric, which was aimed against the now-overthrown emperor's feudal system.[21]

Minister Kifle said that the military junta was particularly concerned about the weak state of their armaments and readiness. He was particularly worried about the military advantage held by neighboring Somalia, whose military dictator, President Siad Barre, was threatening to invade Ethiopia's Ogaden region, just across the border, where most inhabitants were Somali-speaking. Siad Barre accused the British of transferring the Ogaden from Somali territory to Ethiopia in 1941 to punish the former Italian colonial power for joining the Nazi Germans in the war against the Western Allies, and he insisted that the population of the Ogaden wanted to return to Somalia.

Somalia had long been the scene of major disputes among the different pastoral clans. Siad Barre's emphasis on external irredentism, seeking to gain sovereignty over Somalis living in Ethiopia, Kenya, and Djibouti, was a convenient way to divert attention from these internal squabbles. When he came to power in a coup in 1969, Siad Barre proclaimed that Somalia would be a "Marxist socialist" state. This attracted the attention of the Soviet Union, which was quite willing to supply arms such as heavy tanks and MiG fighter aircraft. In return for their generosity, Siad Barre gave access to every part of the country to the Soviets, who were particularly interested in the northern port of Berbera, where they placed cruise missiles.[22]

As of May 1975, the situation of instability in the subregion continued.[23] The Eritrean insurgency against the Derg regime had become stronger. There were reports of assistance coming from the Arab nations via Sudan. A May 1975 intelligence community assessment of the situation in Ethiopia described the military junta in charge of Ethiopia as "an unstable coalition of disparate military figures, with anti-DERG dissidence increasing." As further elements of instability, the assessment listed Somali irredentism and Arab support for the Eritrean independence movement. It noted that the Soviet government was not encouraging Somalia to attack Ethiopia.

The report also emphasized the dangers to the US military's communications center in Asmara, the Kagnew Station, right in the heart of Eritrean insurgency.[24] The station was vulnerable to attack, so Washington started to think about closing it down. In any event, Washington was planning to transfer the facility to a combination of satellite communications and a new station on the island of Diego Garcia in the middle of the Indian Ocean.

The State Department continued to tell the US embassy in Addis Ababa that the United States wanted to maintain good relations with the Ethiopian regime. On September 30, 1975, Secretary Kissinger met with Ethiopian foreign minister Kifle and expressed the desire to have good relations, saying, "Ethiopian internal issues are none of our business." Kissinger also announced that the United States would sell sixteen F-5 jet fighters to Ethiopia.[25]

At the same time, the United States informed the Somalis of its intention to resume regular development aid. Despite this friendly gesture, the US embassy in the Somali capital, Mogadishu, reported that Siad Barre was still totally in the Soviet camp on all issues and recommended stopping all assistance, including humanitarian.[26]

Throughout 1976, President Ford's last year in office, US-Ethiopian relations were marked by wide variations due to internal power struggles within the ruling military group in Ethiopia. It was a period marked by intense conflict, with many executions within the midlevel officer corps that was in power. When extremely radical persons were in control, relations with the United States tended to be tense. When the moderates came back, relations improved. The United States remained calm throughout, with an emphasis on not burning any bridges. And in Somalia, where Soviet influence was at its peak, the US embassy continued to observe and report, while maintaining important contacts within the Siad regime.

Hurt by lingering bad feeling from President Nixon's Watergate scandal and resignation and the subsequent presidential pardon, Gerald Ford lost his bid for reelection to Georgia governor Jimmy Carter in November 1976. Looking back at eight years of US policy toward Africa, Secretary Kissinger had few reasons to be happy. The US "collapse" in Angola, his failure to bring the Southern Rhodesia crisis to closure despite a major diplomatic effort, and most important, the decline of US-Soviet détente must have hurt.

The war between Ethiopia and Somalia, which most observers expected imminently during the Ford administration, later exploded during the Carter administration.

9

Jimmy Carter: 1977–1981

As President Jimmy Carter entered office on January 20, 1977, his main African interest was to finish the work of bringing majority rule to Southern Rhodesia that President Ford and Secretary Kissinger had started. But tensions in the Horn of Africa were at a boiling point and distracted the Carter administration away from southern Africa at the outset.

The Horn of Africa Crisis Boils Over

Because President Mohamed Siad Barre of the Republic of Somalia was a self-proclaimed "Marxist socialist" and thus a willing partner of the communist bloc, the Soviet Union was generous to Somalia with military equipment, both lethal and nonlethal.[1]

At the same time that they were providing arms to Somalia, the Soviets were warning it not to invade the Ethiopian province of the Ogaden, which had a majority population of ethnic Somalis. This province has the shape of a large bird's beak pointing directly into the heart of Somalia. When the British ended the Italian occupation of Ethiopia in 1941, they arbitrarily included the Ogaden as part of Ethiopia, rather than Somalia. Since Somalia gained independence from the Italians and British in 1960, it had been the policy of every Somali government to reunite all ethnic Somalis living in neighboring Ethiopia, Kenya, and Djibouti. President

Siad Barre had the temperament and political will to try to make unification happen, by force of arms if necessary.

During the first half of 1977, President Mengistu Haile Mariam of Ethiopia was not in a strong position. Though he had consolidated his power by eliminating rivals through brutal force, he was also dealing with a growing insurgency in the coastal province of Eritrea. The rebel group there, the Eritrean People's Liberation Front (EPLF), was receiving direct assistance from Arab governments across the Red Sea, via neighboring Sudan. In the capital city of Addis Ababa, plotters continued to seek Mengistu's overthrow. And Somali irredentism, seeking the transfer of the Ogaden to Somali control, was looming as Mengistu's most important security challenge.[2]

On July 23, 1977, the Somali army launched a full-scale invasion of Ethiopia's Ogaden region. The invasion had been preceded by the infiltration of guerrilla fighters, who organized Ogadeni Somalis into fighting units. Within two weeks, the Somalis had taken control of two-thirds of the Ogaden region, although they did not control the major towns.

Toward the end of August 1977, the Soviets made a momentous decision. Ethiopia, they decided, was more important to Soviet interests than Somalia. After all, Ethiopian president Mengistu had proclaimed his regime to be Marxist. So they decided to help Ethiopia resist the Somali invasion with a massive airlift. By mid-December 1977, the Soviets had delivered to Ethiopia $7 billion worth of military equipment, 16,000 Cuban fighting troops, and two brigades of troops from South Yemen. In short, the Soviets had switched sides.[3]

The Soviet-Cuban intervention stopped the Somali advance, and the Ethiopian army, with Cuban assistance, pushed the Somalis back to the point, in January 1978, where they controlled less than 20 percent of the Ogaden. The situation then turned into something of a stalemate, while the two sides prepared their next steps. In this context, it is worth noting that the US F-5 fighter jets, sold to the Ethiopian regime in 1975, were far superior in combat to the MiG fighter jets the Soviets had provided to Somalia.

US policy toward the conflict evolved on August 25, 1977, during a Policy Review Committee meeting chaired by Deputy Secretary of State Warren Christopher. The first consideration was to provide support and assurances to two friends of the United States, Sudan and Kenya, which risked becoming caught up in the war. The committee then decided to appeal to African leaders to urge outside powers to refrain from supplying arms to either side. The committee also decided that the United

States would refrain from supplying arms to either side and call for a total boycott, thereby calling attention to the fact that the Soviets alone were fueling the war. Thus, the United States adopted a policy of neutrality. As further evidence of neutrality, the United States decided not to accede to Ethiopia's request to send a new ambassador.[4]

Having lost their main source of arms (the Soviets), the Somalis either had to withdraw from the Ogaden or find a new arms supplier. They naturally turned toward the United States. On October 13, 1977, Somali ambassador Abdullahi Ahmed Addou delivered a proposal to Under Secretary of State for Political Affairs Philip Habib. In it the Somalis proposed to end all military ties to the Soviet Union, including ending the 1974 Soviet-Somali friendship treaty, and request the withdrawal of Soviet military and civilian advisers. As for the US-Somali relationship, the proposal called for the signing of military, political, and economic agreements with the United States, including the lease of port facilities to the US Navy.

Habib's response was to decline the proposal politely. He said that the United States had to maintain a position of neutrality and thus could not engage in military cooperation so long as Somali troops were in Ethiopian territory. He also said that agreements were not needed for cooperation in the economic and political sectors. Habib urged the Somalis to seek a political solution through the Organization of African Unity.[5]

Subsequently, in December 1977, Secretary of State Vance decided that neutrality did not mean boycotting Ethiopia. So, he advised President Carter to name an ambassador to Ethiopia in order to maintain access and to demonstrate that the Ethiopians had alternatives to dependence on the Soviets.[6]

Continued instability within the Mengistu regime in Addis Ababa was demonstrated when the Ethiopian ambassador in Washington informed National Security Adviser Zbigniew Brzezinski that he was resigning and requesting asylum in the United States because he was afraid to return to Ethiopia. He said that the "Red Terror" situation in Addis Ababa was like the terror of the French Revolution of 1789.[7]

Persuading the Somalis to Withdraw and the Ethiopians Not to Invade

During the first three months of 1978, US diplomacy was focused on persuading the Somalis to withdraw from the Ogaden and persuading the Ethiopians not to invade Somalia after the Somali withdrawal. Visitors to

Addis Ababa, including National Security Council Adviser David Aaron, were able to engage President Mengistu in conversations about cross-border activity. Mengistu pledged that his forces would not invade Somalia and that the Soviets and Cubans would not be allowed to use Ethiopia as a base from which to undermine other African nations.[8]

With respect to the US dialogue with Somalia, a National Security Council meeting in February 1978, with President Carter presiding, decided to offer Somalia defensive arms if they withdrew from Ethiopian territory. The NSC also decided to encourage Organization of African Unity mediation rather than United Nations mediation, wherein great power politics would probably cause problems.[9]

In a presidential directive, NSC-32, issued on February 24, 1978, the US Information Agency was ordered to "publicize more widely the Soviet and Cuban role in Ethiopia," especially the overall responsibility of Soviet General Petrov, who had all military forces under his command, including Soviet, Cuban, and Ethiopian. A key element of this propaganda offensive was to show that the Soviets and Cubans were not just helping to defend Ethiopia against the Somali invasion, but also helping the Ethiopians fight the Eritrean insurgency.[10]

The Decline of US-Soviet Détente Accelerates

Up to the end of February 1978, the US approach to the Somali-Ethiopia dispute was somewhat clinical. As an officially neutral party, the United States was providing its good offices to uphold territorial integrity and bring about an end to conflict. This was in sharp contrast to the almost hysterical reaction of former secretary of state Henry Kissinger to the massive presence of Cuban forces and Soviet advisers in Angola in 1975 after the precipitous withdrawal of the Portuguese colonial power.

Nevertheless, National Security Adviser Brzezinski, who shared the same worldview as Kissinger, found it important to interject the subject of overall US-Soviet relations as a subset of the Soviet-Cuban operation in Ethiopia. In a memorandum to President Carter on March 3, 1978, he complained that the Soviet action in Ethiopia was a symptom of a wider problem in which Moscow was applying détente selectively, to the detriment of US influence in the world: "The Soviet Union is pursuing deliberately a policy, on which they embarked some fifteen years ago, to structure a relationship of stability with the United States in those areas that are congenial, while pursuing every opportunity to promote Soviet influence."[11]

Two months later, on May 27, 1978, during a meeting with Soviet foreign minister Andrei Gromyko in the Oval Office, President Carter presented a full list of worldwide grievances that supported Brzezinski's thesis of Soviet perfidy in the application of détente. Needless to say, Gromyko rejected the charges. Regarding Africa, Gromyko said that the Soviet Union did not have a single fighting soldier on the continent. Furthermore, Gromyko pointed out that the Soviets had advised Siad Barre not to invade Ethiopia, as they were advising Ethiopia not to invade Somalia in the months ahead. The bottom line, according to Gromyko, was that Ethiopia had been the victim of aggression, and the Soviets had a perfect right to help them reject the Somali invaders. In this context, Carter warned Gromyko to stay out of Ethiopia's internal Eritrean insurgency. Gromyko's response was to call for Eritrean autonomy within Ethiopia, a return to the peaceful situation that existed between 1952 and 1962.[12]

The Soviet action in Ethiopia was a variant of the Brezhnev Doctrine, announced by Soviet president Leonid Brezhnev in November 1968. Brezhnev claimed the right of the Soviet Union to intervene in the affairs of communist countries to strengthen communism. Ethiopia under the rule of a Marxist military group appeared, in Soviet eyes, to have embarked on the road toward communism.

On March 7, 1978, President Carter sent a message to Somali president Siad Barre informing him that, in view of the Cuban-Soviet intervention, Somalia was facing defeat in the Ogaden region and that the United States was prepared to furnish defensive weapons after Somali withdrawal from Ethiopian territory. Two days later, the Somalis responded that they would withdraw, and on March 14, Secretary of State Vance was able to inform President Carter that the withdrawal was complete. Two days later, Assistant Secretary of State for African Affairs Richard Moose visited Siad Barre and informed him that the United States would be offering a "non-lethal package to help meet legitimate defense needs."[13]

On April 7, 1978, a special NSC Coordinating Committee meeting decided that if Siad Barre promised not to send his forces across any borders, he would be offered a package worth $10 million for nonlethal equipment and $5 million for lethal defensive items. After this event, the Somali-Ethiopian border remained relatively quiescent until 1991, when the Ethiopians finally achieved their revenge against Siad Barre.[14]

After the Somali withdrawal, the one element of crisis in the Horn that remained was the insurgency in Eritrea, also known as the War for

Eritrean Independence. The war resulted from Emperor Haile Selassie's abrogation of a UN decision in 1952. Under that decision, the former Italian colony of Eritrea merged into a loose confederation with the Empire of Ethiopia and had virtually complete autonomy within the confederation, except for foreign policy, defense, and monetary matters. Ten years later, in 1962, the emperor made a unilateral decision to abolish the confederation and transform Eritrea into an Ethiopian province under total central government control. This gave rise to the birth of an insurgent Eritrean independence movement that by 1978 had grown into a significant asymmetrical conflict.[15]

The US analysis of the Eritrean conflict was that ending the war required a political solution. The Mengistu regime was not likely to negotiate unless it came under pressure. The United States believed, therefore, that it was necessary to help the insurgents maintain their pressure. The United States could not assist the rebels, so a decision was made to encourage the Arab governments in the region to furnish assistance to the Eritrean rebels. The Arab governments agreed and maintained a flow of arms through neighboring Sudan until the war was finally terminated in May 1991.[16]

Somalia Up and Ethiopia Down

The Ethiopians knew that Arab neighbors were supplying the Eritrean rebels through Sudan, and they suspected, correctly, that the United States was encouraging this assistance. Consequently, the Mengistu regime became increasingly cool toward the United States, and increasingly warm toward the Soviets. On July 26, 1980, the Ethiopians declared Ambassador Fred Chapin unwelcome in Ethiopia and demanded that he be recalled within two weeks in lieu of being declared persona non grata. The United States complied with this request and prepared a public declaration explaining that "the decline in U.S.-Ethiopian relations is due to Ethiopia's systematic defense of Soviet positions, its dismal human rights, and its refusal to pay fair compensation for expropriated properties."[17] From that date, the United States would not again name an ambassador to Ethiopia until 1991.

On the other side of the border, Somalia became more important to the United States because of national security issues. The French Territory of the Afars and Issas (TFAI) became independent on June 27, 1977, as the nation of Djibouti, the same name as the country's main port overlooking the Bab el Mandeb at the mouth of the Red Sea.

The US Navy had been using the seaport and airport of Djibouti as its main base for surveillance and operations in the Indian Ocean. With French colonial control removed, the Navy was looking for alternative facilities in the event of instability in Djibouti. The Somali ports of Berbera and Mogadishu were considered to be good fallback sites. Thus, on August 28, 1980, the United States and Somalia exchanged notes that expanded US access to Somalia's airport and seaport facilities.[18]

The US Defense Department's budget for fiscal year 1981 included a plan for military construction in Somalia. Thus, within a period of five years, the United States had lost its best friend in Africa (Ethiopia) and gained a new lukewarm friend, Somalia.

Rescuing Zaire's President Mobutu from His Own Rebels

One relatively small incident in May 1978 demonstrated how US interests could be directly troubled by events in southern Africa. On May 23, a column of about 2,000 armed troops crossed the northern border of Angola into the Katanga province of southeastern Zaire. They attacked the city of Kolwezi, one of Zaire's main mining towns, where several thousand expatriates, mostly Belgians, resided.

The regular Zairian army was unable to cope with this invasion, causing President Mobutu to call for international assistance. The French government responded, saying that troops from its Foreign Legion, based in Corsica, were ready and available. But the French lacked the necessary airlift. They appealed to President Jimmy Carter, who responded, without hesitation, that the United States would supply the aircraft. Within twenty-four hours, three gigantic US C-5M Super Galaxy transport aircraft were on their way to Corsica, followed by a refueling stop in Dakar, Senegal, where a company of Senegalese troops came aboard. Within a week, the invading force was defeated, but the city of Kolwezi had suffered significant damage.[19]

Troops of Zairian origin from Katanga province had carried out the invasion. These troops had been part of the Katangese secessionist movement of Governor Moïse Tshombe, who had taken refuge in Angola after UN peacekeepers defeated their movement in 1961. After congressional action in 1975 prohibited the Ford administration from furnishing assistance to armed groups in Angola, President Mobutu continued to send matériel to the UNITA and FNLA fighters who opposed the Soviet- and

Cuban-supported MPLA regime in Angola. The Cubans had organized the 1978 invasion in retaliation for Mobutu's continued support for the rebels.[20]

It is interesting to note that the Carter decision to support President Mobutu in 1978 was in direct continuity with the Nixon-Ford Africa policy. In view of Carter's more "leftist liberal" political orientation, he might well have abandoned corrupt human rights violator Mobutu to his fate. Mobutu's army was refusing to fight. But in geopolitics, Mobutu was America's loyal ally in the defense of independent Africa against Soviet-Cuban predators. This was the key element of continuity in US policy in Africa at that moment in history.

Tackling the Problem of White Minority Rule in Southern Africa

When the Carter-Mondale administration took office in January 1977, they found the southern African landscape significantly changed from the situation eight years earlier when the Nixon-Ford administration had come to power. The guerrilla wars against the white minority regime in Southern Rhodesia and the Southwest Africa (Namibia) territory administered by South Africa that began during the Ford administration had intensified. The cost to Rhodesia and South Africa in money and manpower had increased greatly.

Maintaining Pressure on the White Minority Rhodesian Regime via South Africa

The Carter administration came into office determined to make progress on Southern Rhodesia and Namibia. Secretary of State Cyrus Vance said as much in a conversation with African nationalist leader Joshua Nkomo in London on May 6, 1977. Vance said the United States wanted independence for the future Zimbabwe under majority rule in 1978. He believed that the path to majority rule went via consultations on a new constitution. Nkomo cautioned Vance that the United States should not play a direct role in order to avoid "bringing in big power politics." Vance agreed.[21]

President Carter named a strong team to help him deal with the southern Africa issues. Secretary Vance, a left-of-center attorney from New York City, headed the team. To the position of US permanent representative to the United Nations, Carter named Andrew Young, a former congressman from Atlanta, Georgia, veteran of the civil rights struggle, and close associate of the Reverend Martin Luther King Jr. Young's deputy permanent representative, Donald McHenry, was a prominent African American intellectual associated with corporate boards and various think tanks.

Ambassadors Young and McHenry had as their main objective the liberation of Southwest Africa (Namibia) from the illegal control of South Africa. They also planned to use the UN forum to demonstrate to the independent African nations that the United States was on the right side of history in opposing both South African control of Namibia and the repressive apartheid regime in South Africa itself. With respect to South Africa, the United States had to be careful about calling for UN sanctions against the regime before the liberation of Southern Rhodesia could be achieved. South Africa had the only leverage over the white Southern Rhodesian regime, because all of Rhodesia's imports and exports transited through South Africa. Of particularly vital importance was the steady flow of refined petroleum products. Thus, at the outset, the United States limited its treatment of South Africa to demands that it implement UN resolutions ordering the transfer of authority over Namibia to the United Nations.

Vice President Walter Mondale was also active on the southern Africa question. At a meeting on May 19, 1977, Mondale told South African prime minister B. J. Vorster that the United States expected South Africa to put pressure on Rhodesian prime minister Ian Smith to accept elections leading to majority rule. Vorster responded that Smith had accepted the idea in principle but needed to know that the rule of law would be maintained, especially with respect to land and property rights. Confiscations must be ruled out. Vorster also said that elections should produce an African leader who would negotiate a new political system with Smith. They both agreed to support UK foreign secretary David Owen's effort to negotiate a new constitution leading to elections.[22]

Inside Southern Rhodesia, the regime faced increasing costs in meeting the challenge of nationalist guerrilla forces making hit-and-run cross-border raids from Mozambique and Zambia against white communities. In an analytical memorandum dated September 16, 1977, the Central Intelligence Agency said that Rhodesia was "experiencing a serious drain on its limited white manpower." The net emigration rate for whites had been averaging more than a thousand per month from a white population of fewer than 270,000, compared with six million blacks. It was becoming increasingly difficult to maintain an army of 20,000 in view of the steady white exodus.[23]

The Complications of Internal Rhodesian and Nationalist Politics

Competition and conflict among the black nationalists complicated and slowed the negotiation process. The external nationalist guerrillas were doing all the fighting and believed they should be considered the only legitimate representatives of the Zimbabwean people. In a meeting with Secretary Vance in Washington on March 12, 1978, nationalist leaders Robert Mugabe and Joshua Nkomo, speaking respectively for the Zimbabwe African National Union–Patriotic Front and the Zimbabwe African Patriotic Union, argued that only they should negotiate a cease-fire and control the interim process. They said they would not participate in any negotiations that included the so-called internal African political leaders, who were willing to share power with whites.[24]

A month later, on April 17, 1978, Vance met in Pretoria, South Africa, with Rhodesian prime minister Smith, accompanied by the internal Rhodesian black leaders Abel Muzorewa and Ndabaningi Sithole, who insisted that they commanded majority support among the black population. Smith said that failure to reach an agreement would open the door to Soviet and Cuban involvement. Muzorewa and Sithole's expressions of black majority support bolstered Smith's feelings that he might be able to pull off a majority-rule "internal" settlement working with them alone, while ignoring the external fighters. Both Britain and the United States kept telling him that such an "internal" settlement would not end the warfare.[25]

The rest of 1978 went by without any progress, because the external and internal black Zimbabwe leadership could not agree on an "all-parties" solution. Nor could they even agree to an "all-parties" conference proposed by UK foreign secretary Owen.

On March 6, 1979, Secretary Vance informed President Carter that Prime Minister Ian Smith had run out of patience and was planning an election with the internal black leaders that would lead to black majority rule on his terms. Vance told Carter there was no way such an election would result in the end of the war. An election was desirable, Vance said, but it had to be under UN supervision, with all parties represented. He also said that an escalation of the war could result in a similar fate later on for South Africa. He told Carter that the United States and the

UK would continue to press for a UN-supervised election. In a decision dated April 20, 1979, President Carter stated that US policy on Rhodesia would remain unchanged. It continued to require an internationally supervised election.[26]

The Conservatives Come to Power
in the UK and Bring a Solution

In the May 1979 UK election, the Conservatives replaced Labour in power. In a conversation with Secretary of State Vance in London on May 21, 1979, Lord Peter Carrington, the new foreign secretary, said that Britain's Rhodesia policy might change. The UK was seriously considering recognizing an "internal solution" with Bishop Abel Muzorewa as prime minister. Vance responded that the United States could not join in such a policy. This was the first indication of a possible separation between Britain and the United States on the Southern Rhodesia issue. In effect, Vance was warning Carrington that the United States would not lift sanctions in the event of an "internal settlement."[27]

On May 24, 1979, Vance met with Prime Minister Margaret Thatcher, who said that the UK would encourage African governments to establish a dialogue with Muzorewa. She believed that "continued dialogue would lead to *de facto* recognition of Muzorewa." Thatcher's hopes were effectively dashed when all other governments in the Commonwealth said they would reject any election that excluded nationalist movements engaged in insurgency against the white regime.[28]

Following the Commonwealth rejection of the Muzorewa solution, the Organization of African Unity summit conference on July 21, 1979, voted to recognize the Patriotic Front of Mugabe and Nkomo as the "sole legitimate and authentic representative of the people of Zimbabwe."[29]

The final blow to the Conservatives' inclination to recognize the "internal solution" of a Muzorewa government came from a meeting of the Commonwealth Heads of Government in Lusaka, Zambia, August 1–7, 1979. The meeting decided that there should be an all-parties constitutional conference at Lancaster House in London, to begin on September 10, 1979. The purpose was "to reach agreement on the terms of an Independence Constitution, to agree on the holding of elections under British Authority, and to enable Zimbabwe Rhodesia to proceed to lawful and internationally recognized independence, with the parties settling their differences by political means." The Lancaster House Conference continued until December 15, 1979, with all objectives achieved. All parties signed the document, including the UK government, the Muzorewa "Government of Zimbabwe-Rhodesia," and the Patriotic Front of Mugabe and Nkomo.[30]

The US government recognized the legitimacy of the Lancaster House agreement and lifted all sanctions upon the arrival of the UK governor. The subsequent election brought the Patriotic Front to power, with Robert Mugabe named prime minister. His government represented majority rule, with guarantees for the white minority. The process and the outcome were major successes.

The Carter administration played its assigned role by providing close support to the UK, mainly by maintaining pressure on the government of South Africa to use its leverage over the Southern Rhodesian minority government. It was an exercise in excellent diplomacy in complex circumstances. It is also important to recognize the important role played by Secretary of State Kissinger during the Gerald Ford administration. His proposals for a balanced set of guarantees for both the majority blacks and the minority whites eventually constituted the core of the final Lancaster House Agreement.

Ending South African Control over Southwest Africa

The Carter administration was intensively active in negotiations to end South Africa's control over its League of Nations–mandated territory of Southwest Africa (the future Namibia) for its entire four years in power. The administration had a choice between two approaches to the Namibian issue.

The first would have been to unleash Andrew Young and Donald McHenry, Carter's two African American permanent representatives to the United Nations. They could have denounced the repressive apartheid regime in South Africa and demanded that Namibia be handed over to UN control by a certain date, failing which severe sanctions would be imposed.

The second approach was to view Namibia as a UN issue and work patiently through diplomacy within the UN to persuade South Africa to transfer authority over the territory to the world body. The key element of the diplomatic effort was to assure South Africa that the objective was to bring about independence for Namibia, not to undermine the apartheid regime itself. Being naturally disposed to paranoia, the South

Africans felt threatened from many directions, especially from Ambassadors Young and McHenry at the US mission to the UN in New York.

President Carter and Secretary Vance chose the second approach. One of their first decisions was to form the Namibian Contact Group, made up by the five Western governments on the Security Council: the United States, France, the United Kingdom, Canada, and West Germany. The group worked together in making a large number of demarches and proposals during the next four years.

The Carter administration also decided to focus on the implementation of UN Security Council resolutions pertaining to Namibia. The main ones were Resolution 385, enacted January 30, 1976, and Resolution 435, enacted September 29, 1978. The United States had voted for both, through Republican and Democratic administrations.

The main points of the Security Council resolutions were that the South African "occupation" of Namibia was illegal; that South Africa was legally obliged to transfer control over Namibia to the UN; that power should be transferred to the people; and that the Southwest Africa People's Organization was a legitimate representative of the Namibian population. The UN General Assembly, where the independent African nations have a very large voting bloc, had earlier declared SWAPO to be the "sole legitimate representative of the Namibian people."[31]

In addition to being a political organization, SWAPO was also a military force that was waging an insurgency against South African entities in Namibia. The insurgency operation became increasingly relevant after Angola achieved independence from Portugal in 1975, and SWAPO was allowed to set up bases on Namibia's northern border. SWAPO received arms and training from Cuban forces assisting the Angolan government. Needless to say, the Cuban connection caused the South Africans to do everything possible to prevent SWAPO from taking power in an eventual independent Namibia.

South Africa Seeks an Internal Solution

Early in the Carter administration, the South Africans started to send signals that they intended to transition Namibia to independence without the UN through an internal procedure, providing majority rule without SWAPO. They organized their internal solution in the form of the two-year-long, multiracial Turnhalle Constitutional Conference, held from 1975 to 1977. "Turnhalle" referred to the historic building where the conference took place in Namibia's capital, Windhoek. The purpose of the conference was to write a constitution for an independent Namibia.[32]

In various conversations, Secretary Vance and Assistant Secretary of State for Africa William Schaufele told the South Africans that the Turnhalle process would not be recognized internationally as being legitimate, because SWAPO was excluded and because the UN was not presiding, notwithstanding South Africa's declared intention to bring about Namibia's independence under "majority rule." The black majority, of course, would comprise carefully selected political actors deemed compatible with the white minority community of Namibia. As South African prime minister Vorster told US ambassador William Bowdler on April 7, 1977, "We want to end our administration in Namibia." Bowdler noted that Vorster had been heavily influenced by former secretary of state Kissinger's failure, just prior to the end of the Ford administration, to persuade SWAPO's president, Sam Nujoma, to stop the guerrilla war.[33]

Meanwhile, the UN began to gear up for its assigned role as transitional administrator. Secretary-General Kurt Waldheim named Under Secretary Martti Ahtisaari to be the UN administrator of Namibia. Waldheim also decided to create a UN Transitional Advisory Group (UNTAG) to provide temporary administrative services, pending the democratic election and training of a new Namibian government. UNTAG would also have UN peacekeeping military forces, UN internal security police, and UN civil servants on temporary duty to help the new Namibian government become established.

Endless Negotiations on the Future of Namibia, 1977–1980

From early 1977 to the end of 1980, the Western Contact Group engaged in detailed, painstaking negotiations with the South African regime at the highest levels. The Contact Group continued to press for an internationally supervised election and transition to independence for Namibia. The South Africans kept holding out for an internal transition based on South African supervision, leading to an independent Namibia on the South African model.

The discussions covered all sorts of details, such as the phased departure of South African forces from Namibia, and whether or not some South African military units would remain in remote areas just in case of trouble. Would SWAPO be allowed to have units inside Namibia during the transition? Would there be monitoring of SWAPO bases outside of Namibia? Would elections held inside Namibia under the authority of the South African administrator be recognized? All of these discussions took time and tended to stretch out the duration of South African administration. At all times, the Contact Group insisted on a solution that would be compatible with Security Council Resolution 435.

On April 29, 1977, the Contact Group decided on its "final talking points":

- An internationally acceptable settlement must be consistent with UNSC Resolutions 435 and 385.
- There should be elections under universal suffrage for a constituent assembly.
- The UN must participate in the elections.
- All Namibians living in exile should be allowed to return.
- The South African government should plan its withdrawal.
- The South African government is put on notice not to implement the Turnhalle constitution.[34]

Negotiations continued through 1977, with the South African government making concessions on noncontroversial issues. For example, it accepted a major UN presence during the transition.[35] However, it said it would not begin a phased withdrawal of its troops until SWAPO completely stopped fighting, but it insisted on having a small contingent of South African government troops remain.[36] At one point, South Africa introduced, then quickly removed, a demand that all Cuban troops depart from Angola before Namibia could be granted independence. This demand was later destined to become crucial as the negotiations continued under the Reagan administration (1981–1989).[37]

On February 1, 1978, the Western Five (the Contact Group) issued a "final text" of their proposal for a Namibian settlement:

- The UN special representative will ensure the fairness and impartiality of the election.
- The election will choose representatives for a constituent assembly.
- All political prisoners will be released. All refugees will return.
- There will be a complete ceasefire and a phased withdrawal of South African government forces.[38]

On September 26, 1978, after several months of fruitless talks about details, Prime Minister Vorster said that a UN solution was not acceptable and that the South African government would hold its own election in Namibia. At that point, the Western Five began to think about possible coercive action against South Africa. A month later, the Western foreign ministers reached the conclusion that "South Africa wants to perpetuate white rule in independent Namibia." In other words, independent Namibia would be a clone of apartheid South Africa.[39]

On November 16, 1978, the United States started to take a hard line with the South African government on the Namibian question. Secretary of State Vance sent a message to Foreign Minister Pik Botha, stating: "Western resolve should be taken seriously. Don't take for granted that sanctions are not possible. If the [South African government] goes through with its threat to hold an election in Namibia for a constituent assembly December 4–8, it will be totally against the international consensus. The interim government will be illegal."[40]

President Carter followed up Secretary Vance's admonition with a letter to the new South African prime minister, P. W. Botha, on December 11, 1978, immediately after the "illegal" Namibia election. He told Botha, "You must implement resolution 435." The letter was written in a stern tone that Botha characterized as "a threat." On April 6, 1979, Carter was more explicit: "Should the UN plan fail to receive South Africa's support, I believe that UN measures against your country, under Chapter VII, would be inevitable."[41]

On May 14, 1979, the South African administrator of Namibia proclaimed the formation of a national assembly based on the election of a constituent assembly in December 1978. This interim regime received no recognition and was considered illegal by the international community.

Throughout the rest of 1979 and 1980, the South African government kept complaining that it was being "trapped by the UN" and that the UN wanted to send hostile African forces into Namibia. At the same time, it was clear that the United States was not about to fulfill its earlier threats to invoke sanctions under Chapter VII of the UN Charter. At the UN, Ambassador Andrew Young had left his position after only two years, because he had violated the policy that the United States did not talk to the Palestine Liberation Organization. That greatly weakened the American will to get into a diplomatic conflict with South Africa.

In the White House, National Security Adviser Zbigniew Brzezinski was well aware of the Soviet and Cuban presence in Angola and was in no hurry to change Namibia's status and thereby enable the communist armed menace to reach the northern border of South Africa.

The stalemate on Namibia continued into the Reagan administration, concluding only at the end of December 1988.

The Soviet Invasion of Afghanistan and Its Impact on Africa

Massive Soviet military forces invaded Afghanistan starting on December 27, 1979. This action constituted a major shock and challenge to the Carter administration. As US ambassador Thomas Watson in Moscow said in his first communication to Washington following the invasion, "The Soviet installation of a regime of its own choice outside of the Warsaw Pact constitutes a dangerous and unprecedented change in Soviet policy." Immediately afterward, President Carter sent a personal message to President Leonid Brezhnev stating that the invasion was a clear violation of the "Basic Principles on Relations that you signed in 1972."[42]

One result of the Soviet action was a major exercise in Washington designed to make life difficult for the Soviets. Consideration was given to every aspect of the US-Soviet relationship, especially the economic aspect. Two resulting decisions affected the United States–Africa relationship: Carter's decision to boycott the Summer Olympic Games scheduled to be held in Moscow in 1980; and Carter's decision that the United States needed to obtain military facilities in the Middle East in order to oppose a potential Soviet military thrust south into the region from Afghanistan.

Boycott of the Moscow Summer Olympics

President Carter asked the US Olympic Committee to boycott the 1980 Summer Games in Moscow. The US committee complied. Carter ordered a worldwide diplomatic campaign to persuade every government to follow the US example. Africa, with fifty independent states, was a major target of the boycott campaign.

In planning for the boycott effort in Africa, the White House decided to send as its emissary an American who was immensely popular on the continent, World Heavyweight boxing champion Mohammed Ali. The champion took on the assignment with enthusiasm. The State

Department provided a full professional escort and arranged for Ali to meet the head of state in every country he visited. Ali made a strong case for the boycott and took advantage of his visits to appeal to crowds who came to see him.[43]

The problem with an appeal for an Olympic boycott in Africa was related to the previous Summer Olympic Games in Montreal in 1976. At that time, the Organization of African Unity called for an Olympics boycott because the international community had done nothing to end white minority rule in Southern Rhodesia. The US response, and that of other Western countries, to that appeal was that the Olympics should not be the subject of political considerations. When Mohammed Ali made a boycott appeal, most of the Africans repeated what they had heard from the United States four years earlier. Nonetheless, in terms of United States–Africa relations, the Ali tour was a huge success.[44]

The US Need for Military Facilities in or near the Middle East

About a month after the Soviet invasion of Afghanistan, the United States received reliable intelligence that the Soviet High Military Command was engaged in planning for a military thrust south from Afghanistan, through Iran to Kuwait, on the Persian Gulf. While military commands engage in constant planning, this does not mean the plans will be implemented. But in this particular case, immediately after the invasion, planning for a military thrust through Iran to Kuwait on the Gulf had to be taken seriously.[45]

Assuming that such a southward thrust could take place, President Carter decided that the United States should seek to obtain facilities in the Middle East where arms and equipment could be pre-positioned, in order to counter such an action. Emissaries were sent to Saudi Arabia, Kuwait, and Syria to request appropriate facilities. The responses were negative, along the lines of: we want you to be close by, in case we need your help, but we prefer that you remain "over the horizon."

As a result of the negative responses from Middle Eastern friends, the United States began looking to African countries near the Middle East that might be cooperative. And the Africans were ready to be helpful.

As noted, during the Ford administration Somalia had offered to share the port and the airfield in the city of Berbera. After the Soviet invasion, the United States spent more money than previously planned, about $50 million, on contract work to upgrade both the port and the airfield.

To respond to a potential attack against Iran and Kuwait, the United States focused on Kenya's airport in Nairobi and its naval facility in the port of Mombasa. The Kenyan government was most supportive, giving the US military unlimited access to both. This led the State Department to open a consulate in Mombasa to serve naval personnel. And the government of Sudan authorized the United States to pre-position arms and equipment in Port Sudan on the Red Sea.[46]

The Soviets never did carry out military plans for a southward thrust through Iran to the Gulf. When the United States needed to operate militarily in the Middle East in 1990 to counter Iraq's invasion of Kuwait, Saudi Arabia and other Arab nations opened their doors to the US military. In the event, the facilities obtained in East Africa ten years earlier were not used.

Looking at the bigger picture, the United States had gained the experience of working with African nations in preparing for military action in the Middle East. It was an experience that served both sides well in subsequent crises.

10

Ronald Reagan:
1981–1989

The Carter administration addressed the Southern Rhodesia and Namibia issues simultaneously, ending with a win in Southern Rhodesia. But a positive outcome for Namibia remained elusive. Indeed, the nature of the Southern Rhodesia solution made the quest for a Namibia solution even more difficult.

In virtually all of the conversations between US government officials and South Africans during the Carter years, the South Africans almost always said something along the following lines: "Please do not allow Robert Mugabe to come to power in Rhodesia-Zimbabwe. Please do not let the Southwest Africa People's Organization come to power in Namibia." In the eyes of the South Africans at all levels, Robert Mugabe and SWAPO were Marxist radicals with strong leanings toward communism. From the South African point of view, the worst outcome happened in Zimbabwe. Under UK supervision, the country's first democratic election before independence in 1980 resulted in the election of Robert Mugabe as president.

The Reagan administration's first key decision with respect to Namibia involved the presence of Cuban troops in neighboring Angola. As Assistant Secretary of State for African Affairs Chester A. Crocker stated in a speech in Honolulu in August 1981, the South Africans could not be expected to give up control of Namibia if the Cubans in Angola would then proceed to position African National Congress (ANC) fighters on the northern South African border.[1]

The mission of the ANC, since its founding in 1912, was to ensure political rights for the nonwhite majority in South Africa. As the white minority apartheid regime became increasingly repressive, the ANC became increasingly militant. The government outlawed the ANC in 1960. As a result, the ANC decided that it had no alternative but to form an armed wing, which they called Umkhonto we Sizwe (Tip of the Sword). Between 1960 and 1990, when the ANC once more became legal, its armed wing staged acts of sabotage in white residential and business areas.[2]

Thus, the presence of Cuban troops in Angola had to be taken into consideration in any diplomatic process designed to bring Namibia to independence, as required by UN Security Council Resolution 435 and previous declarations of the world body.[3]

Crocker's Policy of "Linkage"

Assistant Secretary Crocker's policy recommendation was that the United States should establish a policy of "linkage" between the implementation of Resolution 435 by the Republic of South Africa and the departure of Cuban troops from Angola. His recommendation was accepted initially by Secretary of State Alexander Haig and subsequently confirmed by Secretary of State George Shultz.[4]

Needless to say, the community of independent African nations, speaking through the Organization of African Unity, was decidedly unhappy with the concept of "linkage." They insisted that South Africa had the legal obligation to transfer sovereignty over Namibia to the United Nations. What the sovereign state of Angola decided to do with respect to its own security, including the continued presence of Cuban forces on Angolan soil, had nothing to do with the Namibian issue, according to them.

The government of Angola had its own security apprehensions with respect to South Africa. The ruling party in Angola, the MPLA, had come to power in 1975, as the Portuguese colonial forces were pulling out, in the midst of an internal war against two other Angolan nationalist fighting groups, the UNITA and FNLA movements. Cuban forces were airlifted to Angola to make sure that the MPLA controlled the capital city of Luanda and were therefore in a position to declare themselves the legitimate government of Angola. The Cubans also made sure that the other two nationalist groups were driven away from the capital city.

Between 1975 and the beginning of the Reagan administration in 1981, the internal conflict in Angola continued. The UNITA movement, based in the southwestern region of Angola, was receiving support from South African military forces. The FNLA movement, based in neighboring Zaire, had essentially faded away. When the United States informed all interested parties that there could be no implementation of UN Resolution 435 without a parallel schedule of departure of Cuban troops from Angola, the majority of African governments strongly criticized the Reagan team, especially Assistant Secretary Crocker, for having inserted the linkage factor into the process.

During the period 1981–1985, the Angolan regime was still not sufficiently confident that it could contain the UNITA insurgency without the backing of Cuban forces, the support of Soviet military advisers, and the regular flow of Soviet military equipment. The Angolans could not endorse a schedule of Cuban troop departures without receiving some security assurances of their own.

Crocker could have just tossed out the linkage bomb and sat back, while the Angolans, Cubans, and South Africans sorted things out on their own. But he knew that such a complex set of relationships and related apprehensions and hidden agendas needed a mediator and that only the United States could fill that role. He therefore launched a marathon negotiation that lasted, remarkably, for eight years before achieving its objectives. In the final month of the Reagan administration, a tripartite agreement, signed in New York at the United Nations on December 22, 1988, codified those objectives: the departure of all Cuban troops from Angola; the departure of all South African troops from Angola; and the implementation of UN Resolution 435, leading to the independence of Namibia in 1990, after a relatively short and highly productive UN administration.

The departure of South African forces from Angola provided assurances to the Angolan regime that their military operations against the UNITA insurgency in southwestern Angola would not be met as in the past by South African military units with arms, equipment, and fighter aircraft. There was no stipulation in the final agreement, however, that South Africa would stop supplying arms to UNITA. This issue was determined to be one of "national reconciliation" among Angolans.

Vestiges of the Cold War

Why did negotiations among Angola, South Africa, and Cuba take so long under US mediation? It was not a given that Angola would accept the United States as a mediator when the United States continued to refuse to recognize or have relations with the Angolan government. During the final six months of the Carter administration, in anticipation of engaging the Angolans on the issue of Namibia, the president was given the option of formally recognizing the MPLA regime as the legitimate government of Angola. Carter's notation on the options document was, "Let's wait on this one."[5]

The Carter decision to delay indefinitely the recognition of the Angolan regime reflected his view that the Cuban and Soviet presence in that country was the primary factor in potential US-Angolan relations. In other words, Carter, along with National Security Adviser Brzezinski, saw the Soviet-Cuban presence in Angola primarily as a violation of the US-Soviet détente agreements reached between Presidents Nixon and Brezhnev in 1971–1973.

Chester Crocker, however, had the more pragmatic view that the Soviet-Cuban presence in Angola was primarily an impediment to regional peace and stability in southern Africa. Unfortunately, the Carter decision not to recognize the Angolan regime made it difficult for Crocker to identify authentic Angolan decisionmakers willing to go out on a limb and trust the United States to play an impartial role. Hence, it took a long time for the negotiations to become truly substantive.

The South Africans, too, did not have a fully unified view of Crocker's mediation effort. The South African military and intelligence communities breathed a sigh of relief when Ronald Reagan defeated Jimmy Carter in the 1980 presidential election. Reagan tended to view South Africa first as a "bulwark against communism," and only secondarily as a repressive racist regime. It was not surprising, therefore, that the conservative South Africans saw an advantage in delaying the negotiations, giving their US counterparts time to downplay independence for Namibia and emphasize the Cuban-Soviet presence in Angola.

The Rise of US Domestic Political Opinion on South Africa

After four decades of relative public indifference in the United States toward the racial situation in South Africa, the issue began to generate significant public concern around the middle of the 1980s. Press reports from South Africa told the world that police bullets were killing black South African students as they demonstrated against the apartheid system. The police also used lethal force against students demonstrating over the ridiculous requirement that they learn the Afrikaans language in addition to English. Seen on television, these repressive actions ignited US public opinion at many levels. Indignation was far more widespread than in the African American community alone. Throughout the United States, Sunday sermons in churches were telling white Americans that South Africa had become a new nucleus of evil. In May 1986, anti-apartheid demonstrations interrupted scores of graduation ceremonies at major US universities.

In Washington, organized demonstrations took place almost daily at the South African Embassy during the first half of 1986. Members of the social elite were chaining themselves to the embassy fence and demanding to be arrested. Organizers were keeping lists of times for individuals to demonstrate. A standard greeting was, "Have you been arrested at the South African Embassy yet?"

At the same time, the implementation of the Brezhnev Doctrine in Angola caught the attention of the American political right, with Cuban troops and Soviet advisers propping up a regime born of the Portuguese Communist Party. Among all the communist regimes in the world at the time, the Castro regime in Cuba wielded the biggest "red flag" for the Americans. It was no surprise, therefore, that conservative members of the US Congress raised the visibility of the Cuban-Soviet presence in Angola to demonstrable political levels.

A decade earlier, with the memory of the US "collapse" in Vietnam still fresh, the US Congress enacted legislation, known as the Clark Amendment, that prohibited US support to any group in Angola. This cut short Secretary Kissinger's plan to provide covert support to the armed UNITA movement fighting the Angolan regime. In 1986, with the memory of Vietnam fading, and because of the visceral reactions to the Cuban projection of force into southwestern Africa, Congress repealed the Clark Amendment. Shortly thereafter, President Reagan authorized a CIA covert action designed to assist the UNITA insurgency in Angola.[6]

Since UNITA had demonstrated strong military capabilities and had resisted repeated offensives on the part of Angolan heavy tanks and aircraft bombers, the repeal of the Clark Amendment caused the professional anticommunists in some intelligence agencies and the Defense Department to salivate at the thought that the UNITA movement might

actually defeat the Angolan regime with the additional, newly authorized US military assistance.

On the American political left, public sentiment against apartheid in
South Africa had reached such high decibel levels by 1986 that both
Republicans and Democrats in Congress felt that the United States
should start getting tough with that regime. Congress enacted strong
economic sanctions against South Africa, including the prohibition of
all new private investments and bank loans. Under the advice of a sen-
ior assistant, Patrick Buchanan, President Reagan opted for the "South
African bulwark against communism" view and vetoed the legislation.
He had not counted on the strength of anti-apartheid sentiment that led
Congress to take the rare step of overriding his veto. Thus, the United
States had spoken, and South Africa took notice.

Needless to say, the congressional action imposing significant economic sanctions on South Africa in 1986 was disturbing to the apartheid
government in Pretoria. Sanctions struck a blow to the very heart of
South Africa, against its core principle of separation of the races, but
they did not affect the disposition of the territory of Namibia.

In Angola, the MPLA regime and their Cuban military protection
force had failed to eliminate the UNITA insurgency movement over the
previous ten years, despite the massive delivery of Soviet arms and
advisers. With the congressional lifting of its 1975 embargo on any US
covert assistance to persons and groups in Angola, the MPLA-Cuban-
Soviet team was suddenly faced with the possibility of an even stronger
UNITA insurgency. Did that mean the internal Angolan war would go
on indefinitely?

The Namibian Negotiations: To Be or Not to Be?

The US government's actions threatened to undermine, if not termi-
nate, the negotiations about Namibia. South Africa and Angola could
have decided to circle the wagons and tell mediator Chester Crocker
to "drop dead." Indeed, for this very reason, Crocker had opposed both
the imposition of sanctions and the repeal of the Clark Amendment. In
the event, both South Africa and Angola suddenly saw the successful
end to negotiations about Namibia as important to their respective
security situations.

Above all, South Africa wanted to stop the surge of US and Western
opinion against the homeland apartheid system. Cooperation in the

transfer of Namibia to UN jurisdiction was one way to divert attention, at least temporarily, from apartheid itself. As for the Angolans, their highest priority was the departure of South African military forces from Angola and the resultant weakening of the UNITA insurgency.

What about the Cubans and the Soviets? After a decade of rotating military units between Cuba and Angola, the Cubans were becoming tired. Above all, individual Cuban personnel were contracting HIV/AIDS at an above-average rate. These individuals were repatriated to Cuba and placed in quarantine, without treatment, and left to die. This did not contribute to the popularity of the military operation in Angola. In addition, the Angolans were quite laggard in their expense payments to the Cubans.

As for the Soviets, their new president, Mikhail Gorbachev, with his innovative policy of glasnost, or transparency, was starting to look carefully at the costs of the Brezhnev Doctrine. Was it cost-effective to be spending the equivalent of a billion dollars a year supporting a so-called Marxist regime in Angola? Gorbachev was inclined to support an end to the Angola–South Africa–Namibia crisis in order to end the drain on Soviet resources. During 1987 and 1988, the Soviet foreign ministry had one or more of their diplomats present on the fringes of the negotiations, and on several occasions, they took important initiatives with the Angolans and Cubans to keep the talks on the rails.

The net result was that the US mediation effort on Namibia suddenly took on new life. From January 1987 to December 1988, Assistant Secretary Crocker and his team were able to negotiate two key documents. Covering Namibia and Angola, they satisfied South Africa, Angola, and Cuba to the point of signing them on December 22, 1988.

Several of the earlier negotiating sessions had taken place in Brazzaville, Republic of the Congo. The negotiators gathered in Brazzaville for up to one week at a time. The meetings were so frequent that each delegation was assigned a floor in the Pullman Hotel, with its name at the elevator. Needless to say, President Denis Sassou Nguesso of the Republic of the Congo was quite proud of his role as host of many of the negotiating sessions. He was equally proud of the Brazzaville Protocol, signed by the parties on December 13, 1988, in which the parties agreed to recommend the details of their agreement on Namibia to the Secretary-General of the United Nations.[7]

While the December 22, 1988, agreements resulted in the departure of Cuban and South African troops from Angola, they did not deal with Angola's internal conflict between the MPLA regime and the UNITA insurgency. In his remarks a day before the signing ceremony in New

York, Assistant Secretary Crocker said, "Washington will continue arming the rebel group (UNITA) and reject full diplomatic ties with Angola until it makes peace with its opponents."[8]

Crocker's statement, as a Republican appointee, was needed to reassure American conservatives that the United States had not abandoned the UNITA freedom fighters resisting the "Marxist" government of Angola, and that the United States continued to consider the Angolan government to lack legitimacy until such time as it made peace with the important and large element of Angolan society represented by UNITA.

It remained for the next administration, under President George H. W. Bush, to midwife a resolution of the Angolan civil war.

President Reagan Takes an Interest in Mozambique

The other important African nation that received independence from Portugal in 1975 was Mozambique, on Africa's southeastern coast. Unlike Angola, the newly independent government of Mozambique required neither Cuban military forces nor Soviet advisers to consolidate its power. The colony had only one anti-Portuguese insurgent movement, the Front for the Liberation of Mozambique. When the Portuguese administration departed in 1975, FRELIMO took over power smoothly. The FRELIMO government rapidly achieved worldwide recognition, including from President Jimmy Carter, who ordered that the US consulate-general in the capital city of Lourenço Marques (now Maputo) be elevated to the status of US embassy.

President Reagan's first contacts with the FRELIMO leadership were positive. When his daughter Maureen visited Mozambique as a member of a visiting US official delegation, she was given high VIP treatment because of her father. Later, Mozambique's first president, Samora Machel, visited the White House and made a favorable impression on President Reagan.

Nevertheless, Mozambique became a nation of special interest to US foreign policy during the Reagan administration, based on FRELIMO's extremist internal policies. The regime started out with an ideology of pure Marxism designed to wipe out "reactionary" tribal culture, Catholic Church doctrine, and all elements of capitalism. Harsh methods, such as the public execution of tribal chiefs, the confiscation of Catholic Church properties, and the nationalization of private business, caused quite a bit of resentment within the general population.

FRELIMO's early extremist internal policies, which lasted from 1975 to 1980, saw the rise of an armed opposition group, the Mozambican National Resistance (RENAMO). This antigovernment insurgency was based in the country's central provinces of Inhambane and Sofala. RENAMO's founder and president, Afonso Dhlakama, continued to lead the movement as a legal political party until his death in July 2018.

RENAMO constituted a major problem for the FRELIMO regime during 1975–1980, when insurgents fighting to bring about majority rule in neighboring Southern Rhodesia were launching sabotage raids from Mozambican territory. Rhodesian intelligence discovered the existence of RENAMO and started to send arms to these insurgents in central Mozambique, causing a major internal security problem for the FRELIMO regime.

After the United Kingdom, with US support, negotiated majority rule in Rhodesia in 1980, Rhodesia changed its name to Zimbabwe. Cross-border military activity between Mozambique and Zimbabwe came to an end. But the long border between Mozambique and South Africa enabled African National Congress military units to attack the apartheid regime from Mozambique. Needless to say, South African intelligence services continued the support for RENAMO begun by Rhodesian intelligence.

In the United States, conservatives also discovered RENAMO. Think tanks such as the Heritage Foundation and conservative members of Congress viewed RENAMO as the Mozambique equivalent of UNITA in Angola. UNITA was fighting the Marxist regime in Angola and receiving US covert assistance. RENAMO was fighting a similar Marxist regime and thus deserved US recognition as "freedom fighters" against communism. The obvious major difference was the presence of Cuban forces and Soviet advisers in Angola, while Mozambique had no such Soviet-Cuban presence.

In early April 1987, President Reagan requested a briefing on Mozambique from his National Security Council staff. As special assistant to the president and senior director for Africa on the NSC staff, I was assigned to do the briefing.

President Reagan began the conversation with a report that "many of my friends in Orange County (Southern California) are urging me to give support to RENAMO in Mozambique in the same way that we are helping UNITA in Angola." He asked for my reaction to that.

I reminded him that United States–Mozambique relations were very good. I emphasized the Mozambique government's efforts to discourage cross-border insurgent activity against South Africa. Most important, I told him that RENAMO had a terrible human rights record. Anyone in their geographic region of operations who opposed them, or refused to cooperate with them, was murdered. Also, RENAMO used human slaves to carry their arms and other cargos on long marches. I pointed out that US covert assistance in Angola was not unanimously accepted within the US Congress and that there were growing demands that it be stopped. I suggested that US aid to UNITA was a high priority in US efforts to persuade the Cuban troops to depart and the Soviet Union to remove their military advisers. If the United States then started arming RENAMO, it would put US aid to UNITA in jeopardy.

After listening to the presentation, President Reagan said that he agreed with the recommendation that the United States should not begin a relationship with RENAMO. However, he said that he wanted the State Department to start working to bring about peace in Mozambique. Clearly, RENAMO's people were Mozambicans, not men from Mars. So there must be a way of reconciling Mozambicans.

The State Department started to work on a peace process for Mozambique, enlisting President Reagan's participation for discussions with Mozambique's second president, Joaquim Chissano, and his most important advisers. This effort carried over into the George H. W. Bush administration with the signing of a final peace treaty between the Mozambique government and RENAMO in Rome in early 1992. President Reagan deserved significant credit for this good outcome in southeastern Africa.[9]

The United States as a Conflict Mediator in Africa

The insertion of US domestic politics constituted probably the most significant new element in the long and difficult, Soviet-supported US mediation effort leading to the independence of Namibia, as described by Paul Lewis in the *New York Times*.[10] Certainly, Cold War anticommunism had been baked into US politics since the end of World War II, but the popular reaction to the conflict in southwestern Africa during 1986 represented something new in US politics. It was the beginning of a new emphasis on human rights and democracy in foreign policy, as defined by US public opinion.[11] Assistant Secretary Crocker's remarkable achievement also reflected an international reality. For complex conflict negotiations, especially in Africa, the expertise, neutrality, and credibility of US diplomacy has been virtually indispensable. Is this description as valid today as it was in 1987? A review of what has taken place in Africa since 1988 would indicate that the United States remains an indispensable party, either as a direct intervenor, as in South Sudan (George W. Bush) or Libya (Obama), or as a facilitator, as in Ethiopia and Angola (George H. W. Bush).

"Tell Me How to Hurt Libya"

While the southern Africa marathon mediation occupied most of Assistant Secretary Crocker's time during his eight-year tenure, other interesting things were happening in United States–Africa relations during that period.

President Reagan's first secretary of state, retired general Alexander Haig, had considerable experience in the National Security Council and in the White House during the Nixon administration. While preparing for his confirmation hearings before the Senate Foreign Relations Committee, Haig received briefings from the State Department's many bureaus.

One of those was the Bureau of Intelligence and Research (INR). Its briefers informed him that he would be receiving every morning, very early, an intelligence summary of main developments in foreign affairs that had taken place during the previous twenty-four hours. The summary would also contain two or three brief analyses of the most important events. In addition, the INR briefers described the bureau's relationship to the entire US intelligence community, comprising fifteen separate agencies. They told him that INR provided foreign policy guidance to the entire community, thereby helping the various agencies focus their collection priorities.

After listening to the briefing, Secretary-Designate Haig thanked the INR team, and then said: "I have an assignment for you. Tell me how to hurt Libya."[12]

Brainstorming the Libya Conundrum

As of early 1981, the Libyan Arab Jamahiriya of "Brother Leader" Muammar Qaddafi was in full revolutionary mode. Qaddafi's policy was to support revolution wherever it was taking place. Thus he sent assistance to the Irish Republican Army of Northern Ireland and to the Islamist insurgents in southern Philippines. He was annoying all the other Arab governments by accusing them of being reactionary and doing very little against Israel. State's Bureau of African Affairs was concerned about Qaddafi's project to subvert moderate governments in sub-Saharan Africa, using his vast financial resources derived from oil.[13]

The INR team took Secretary-Designate Haig's request seriously and put their heads together to determine where the Libyans might be most vulnerable. They reached consensus on the African nation of Chad, immediately south of Libya's border.

In 1981, Chad was in the midst of a civil war among several armed factions representing different regions and ethnic groups. As of 1978, Qaddafi had occupied a narrow band of northern Chad, the Aouzou Strip, because it had an airfield that his air force could use against enemies to the south. Qaddafi was an active intervenor in Chad's civil war, supporting one warlord or another, depending on his immediate strategic views. He was also using the airfield to bomb various factions in Sudan.

Because of the civil war in Chad, the United States could not start a project there to "hurt Libya" until the war ended in 1985, when African governments brokered a general peace. The peace agreement called for all foreign forces to depart, but Libya maintained its occupation of northern Chad, equal to about one-third of the entire country.

The Anti-Libya Covert Action in Chad

Libya's continued occupation of northern Chad was a violation of international law. The United States thus had no problem persuading Chad's president, Hissène Habré, to agree to a project that would arm and train his military to drive the Libyan army back across the border to their own territory. The Chadian army's chief of staff, Idris Deby, informed President Habré that he was enthusiastic about the project.

The project began in late 1986 and quickly demonstrated that the Libyan army was capable only when there was no real opposition. The Chadians, driving Toyota vehicles armed with heavy machine guns, quickly destroyed the Libyan units, driving those who were not killed across the northern border. Qaddafi and his army were humiliated.[14]

President Reagan was sufficiently impressed by the success of the Chad operation that he invited President Habré to make an official visit to Washington, which took place in April 1987. During the official luncheon, President Reagan asked President Habré to provide his analysis as to why Qaddafi interfered in neighboring African countries.

Habré said Qaddafi did not believe that the end of the slave trade was justified. Qaddafi considered the black Africans still worthy of slave treatment. That is why the Libyans operated in sub-Saharan Africa as if they had ownership rights over the black peoples living there. Habré's statement delighted President Reagan, reinforcing his anti-Qaddafi prejudices.[15]

Revolutionary Change in Liberia

Starting in 1822, hundreds of freed American slaves began emigrating to the west coast of Africa under the auspices of the American Colonization Society (ACS), which collected funds from people who believed that former slaves would be better off living in Africa, their ancestral home. The ACS called the western African territory Liberia, which remained under its control until 1847, when the former slaves in Liberia declared themselves the independent nation of Liberia.

Because of their more advanced technology and education, the former slaves who settled in Liberia were able to dominate the indigenous population they found there. The new settlers called themselves Americo-Liberians and designated the indigenous inhabitants "country people."

Between 1847 and 1980, the Americo-Liberians ruled Liberia, although they constituted only 5 percent of the population. On April 12, 1980, the political situation changed dramatically. Five drunken Liberian army enlisted men went to the mansion of President William R. Tolbert Jr. Finding no security personnel, they entered the mansion and assassinated President Tolbert. The next morning, the newly empowered enlisted men pulled leading Americo-Liberian politicians from their homes and took them to the beach, where they executed the politicians by firing squad.

Suddenly, enlisted army personnel found themselves governing Liberia. They designated one of their own, Sergeant Samuel Doe, to be the provisional president of Liberia. This coup by enlisted men was very popular among Liberia's "country people," who constituted over 90 percent of the population. The US government had no problem with the change in Liberia's political power.[16]

Unfortunately for Liberia, the "country people" were divided into sixteen different ethnic groups, and President Doe ruled on behalf of only one of them, the Krahn tribe. It did not take long for the majority of the Liberian population to turn against Doe when they saw the bulk of government resources reserved for the Krahn.

Doe decided to organize a presidential election in 1985, which all observers agreed that he lost. But he arranged to rig the final count to give him the victory. This election was blatant theft on Doe's behalf.

The Reagan administration took note of the fact that the election lacked credibility but did nothing to protest Doe or attempt to revise the result. An informal explanation the State Department later gave effectively stated that rigged elections are the rule in sub-Saharan Africa, so why pick on Liberia?

Secretary Shultz's Visit to Liberia

In January 1987, Secretary of State George Shultz made his first trip to Africa, visiting five countries in West, East, and Central Africa. The Liberian capital, Monrovia, was his first stop.

During his meeting with President Doe, Shultz was treated to a presidential tirade, replete with screaming and yelling. Doe's message was that Liberia was America's best friend in Africa and received virtually nothing in return. The reason for America's policy was that Doe and his political cohorts, many of whom were Americo-Liberians, were stealing Liberia's considerable revenue from its worldwide ship registry service and from the Firestone rubber plantation.[17]

In response to Doe's "appeal," Secretary Shultz asked Peter McPherson, administrator of the US Agency for International Development, who was in the delegation, to take a new look at Liberia. A few months later, McPherson sent a team to Liberia to assist the Doe government in developing fundamental institutions such as budget and auditing systems to ensure that national revenues went into appropriate channels. After the first two months, US ambassador James Bishop had to request that the team be recalled, because Doe was refusing to change his ways.

In late 1989, at the beginning of the George H. W. Bush administration, an insurgency sponsored by neighboring Côte d'Ivoire resulted in Doe's death and seven years of highly destructive civil conflict. Thinking back to 1985, some US officials wondered whether a timely US demand that the election result be revised might have averted the disastrous civil war of 1989–1997. In any event, the subsequent civil conflict in Liberia was destined to challenge US diplomacy in the administrations of George H. W. Bush and Bill Clinton.

11

George H. W. Bush:
1989–1993

More than in any previous administration, Africa policy under
President George H. W. Bush* was derived substantially from higher-
priority interests in other regions and sectors. Major changes in the
Soviet Union leading to the decline of the communist system and an
opening to democracy drew the United States and the Soviet Union
closer together. President Bush and Soviet Premier Mikhail Gorbachev
developed a strong personal relationship that opened the door to several
bilateral arms reduction treaties. Because President Bush had confidence
in Premier Gorbachev, he issued a directive in June 1989 to his national
security agencies to find ways to react positively to any requests for
assistance from Gorbachev and his close associates.[1]

In July 1989, I was contacted by my Soviet counterpart, Anatoli
Adamishin, vice minister for Africa and human rights. He said that
Prime Minister Gorbachev had issued a directive that the Soviet government should find an honorable way to stop its support for Marxist
regimes in Ethiopia and Angola. The Soviets were spending $1 billion a
year in each country on arms deliveries and military advisers. Gorbachev no longer considered these expenditures to be in the best interest of the Soviet Union. Adamishin said that his government would

---

*I was assistant secretary of state for African affairs for the entire four years
of the Bush administration.

appreciate US assistance in ending the internal conflicts in Ethiopia and Angola. The end result would be peace in the two countries and a perfect reason for the Soviets to end their commitments.

I pointed out that the United States had no diplomatic relations with Angola and that US relations with Ethiopia were at a very low level. The United States had not had an ambassador accredited to Ethiopia since 1978, and had hardly any bilateral communications. An assistant secretary of state for African affairs had not visited Ethiopia in over fifteen years.

Adamishin asked if I would accept an invitation to visit the Ethiopian head of state, Mengistu Haile Mariam. Before I could answer, I had to request an authorization from higher levels in view of conservative animosity toward the Ethiopian regime. After I consulted the White House, Secretary of State James Baker told me that my proposed travel to Ethiopia was not popular with conservatives in the White House; but in view of the president's determination to help Gorbachev, I was authorized to travel there.

Conversation with the Ethiopian Head of State

When I arrived in the Ethiopian capital, Addis Ababa, in August 1989, I found that the regime was fighting two insurgencies. In the province of Eritrea, the Eritrean People's Liberation Front (EPLF) had been fighting for independence for twenty-seven years, since 1962. The other insurgent group, based in northern Ethiopia, was the Tigre People's Liberation Front (TPLF), which was fighting to overthrow the Mengistu regime. Both movements were receiving assistance from Sudan and, through Sudan, from Arab regimes. In an act of retaliation, the Mengistu government was sending arms to the Sudan People's Liberation Movement (SPLM), African Christian rebels in southern Sudan fighting the Arab regime in Khartoum. The geographic subregion known as the Horn of Africa was in a state of chronic instability.

President Mengistu asked me what could be done to improve relations between the Ethiopian and US governments. I was ready with a checklist:

- Enter a peace process with the two rebel insurgencies.
- Allow the departure to Israel of approximately 20,000 Ethiopian Jews who desired to emigrate.[2]
- Reduce the level of "total socialism" in the economy to allow for the growth of a private sector.

- Find a way to eliminate gross human rights violations, especially extrajudicial executions and the large number of political prisoners.

Mengistu found our requirements reasonable. He said that he was already talking to the Israeli government about organizing the departure of the Ethiopian Jews. He asked if we could recommend a mediator. When I suggested former president Jimmy Carter, Mengistu asked if we could arrange for Carter to be the mediator and if we could determine if the EPLF would be willing to accept him.

We had contact with the president of the EPLF, Isaias Afwerki, via our US embassy in Khartoum. After Isayas agreed to Carter, we were able to recruit the former president to take charge of the mediation.

As for the TPLF, the government of Italy volunteered to handle the mediation, with Mengistu and TPLF leader Meles Zenawi both accepting. A key element of these dual mediations was that the fighting continued. Ceasefires were not acceptable to any of the protagonists.

Behind the Mediations: Mengistu's Hidden Agenda

In October 1990, we received intelligence reports that the Mengistu regime had no real interest in making peace with the two insurgent groups. They had received notice from the Soviets that military assistance would soon be suspended and that they should seek a peaceful outcome with the assistance of the United States. Instead of concentrating on peace, the Mengistu regime was busy looking for alternative sources of assistance to replace the Soviets. Their first target was Israel. The plan was to release the Ethiopian Jews for emigration to Israel in return for Israeli arms. Their first request to Israel was for cluster bombs, one of the most destructive weapons to be used against large concentrations of people. They had already succeeded in purchasing a small number of cluster bombs from Chile during their worldwide search.

When the Israelis approached the United States about the Ethiopian "arms for Jews" project, the United States recommended that the Israelis not refuse outright but instead start by furnishing lower-level arms as a sign of willingness to cooperate. In the meantime, the negotiations might possibly make progress.

In November 1990, the EPLF decided that they no longer had confidence in former president Carter as a mediator and demanded a change. The result was a joint request from the Mengistu regime and the

EPLF for the State Department to take charge of the mediation. The State Department's Bureau of African Affairs accepted the mediation responsibility and held the negotiating sessions in Washington.

The Ethiopians Start to Lose the War

Starting in February 1991, a major change in the two battlefield situations began to appear. For many years, the Ethiopian military had kept the rebels bottled up in their mountain safe havens. The rebels could make raids but could not capture anything. Their major accomplishment was to remain active and undefeated. But during the first quarter of 1991, both rebel groups started to capture territory, pushing the Ethiopian army back. This new development began to be reflected at the negotiating table, with the Ethiopians making substantive concessions for the first time, and they expressed a willingness to schedule elections and to share power before elections. They also proposed the organization of a loose confederation that would give significant power to the provinces while maintaining the Ethiopian nation intact.

In late April and early May 1991, the rebels were showing signs of possibly winning the two wars. By the second week in May, the EPLF rebels had captured the Eritrean provincial capital, Asmara, and the TPLF rebels were at the gates of the national capital, Addis Ababa. On May 21, President Mengistu boarded an air force plane and flew into exile in Zimbabwe. Vice President Tesfaye Debre Kidan took over and asked us for advice. As a first step, we asked the TPLF not to enter the capital city until we could organize talks about the future. We scheduled a conference in London for May 25, with the assistance of the UK Foreign and Commonwealth Office. We told the vice president that we could not sponsor a peace conference until he released the 18,000 Ethiopian Jews waiting in a camp near Addis Ababa for emigration to Israel.

Vice President Kidan agreed. On May 24 a round-the-clock Israeli airlift began taking the 18,000 Jewish Ethiopians on the three-hour flight to Tel Aviv, with completion on May 27.

The London Conference: Bringing the War to an End with a Soft Landing

As the London conference was getting under way, the US chargé d'affaires in Addis Ababa, Robert Houdek, issued a distress call. Ethiopian army personnel had fallen back to Addis Ababa and were not under any control. He feared pillaging and violence in the capital. Since the TPLF force had demonstrated good discipline in the cities and towns they had captured, we requested that they enter Addis Ababa to make sure the city remained calm. This is what they did.

For the Ethiopian government, Foreign Minister Tesfaye Dinka headed the delegation in London. The president of the TPLF, Meles Zenawi, headed his delegation. President Isaias Afwerki of the EPLF headed the Eritrean delegation.

Since the EPLF had already taken control of Asmara, the main question was the future of the province. Since the secession of Eritrea would constitute a major psychological blow to the majority of the Ethiopian people, the conference decided that the Eritreans would exercise self-government for a three-year cooling-off period, followed by a referendum in which the Eritrean people would decide whether to remain part of Ethiopia or become an independent state.

As for the capital city of Addis Ababa, TPLF president Meles Zenawi said that his group would take temporary charge of the interim government and plan an all-parties conference in July 1991 to prepare for a democratic future for the nation.

Ethiopian foreign minister Tesfaye Dinka issued fruitless objections to these decisions on behalf of the virtually nonexistent Ethiopian government. He then requested political asylum in the United States, which was granted, and went on to have a brilliant second career working as a senior adviser on African governance for the World Bank.[3]

As the conference mediator, I held a press conference at the US Embassy on May 28, 1991, to announce the results of the discussions. The press wondered why the United States would acquiesce in the breaking up of an African nation, contrary to US rhetoric over the three previous decades. I said that Eritrea constituted a special case in that the Eritrean people never had an opportunity to exercise self-determination and deserved to do so after many years of struggle.

Later, in my final meeting with Meles and Isaias, I expressed the expectation that the Eritreans would certainly vote for independence three years later. It would be important, therefore, for the two independent nations to maintain a common economic unit, with the same currency, free cross-border trade, and continued Ethiopian use of the Eritrean ports of Masawa and Aseb. This outcome would guarantee maximum economic opportunity for both countries and would minimize the disadvantage of Ethiopia becoming landlocked. Meles and Isaias agreed in principle. And they actually continued their common market after Eritrean independence in 1993, until they went to war in 1998 during the Clinton administration, thereby destroying every institution they had built together.

After the London conference, the US State Department's representatives felt proud. They had assisted the Soviets in ending their expensive commitment to the Ethiopian regime, organized the departure of the Ethiopian Jews to Israel, and brought an end to Ethiopia's internal wars with a soft landing.

Why Did the Ethiopian Army Fall Apart So Rapidly?

After ending its work in mediating the Ethiopian wars, the Bureau of African Affairs wanted to know why the Ethiopian army collapsed so rapidly, starting in February 1991, after having kept the rebels totally in check for so many years. It concluded that the Ethiopian military had decided as a group that the war would soon be over, once the State Department took over the mediating role, and most of the troops decided they did not want to be the last Ethiopians to die just as the war was ending. The rebels did not think that way at all. They kept fighting at full throttle, while the government troops fell back to the capital city and safety.[4]

And Now to Angola

The Soviets also wanted the United States to help bring about a solution to the Angolan civil war so that they could return home and end Moscow's expensive assistance program in support of the Angolan army. As of August 1989, the United States had no diplomatic relations with Angola. How to make contact to begin a peace process was not evident. Nevertheless, as a result of US leadership in the negotiations leading to the December 1988 accords on independence for Namibia and the departure of Cuban troops from Angola (see Chapter 10), the Bureau of African Affairs had valuable personal relationships within the Angolan elite.

President Mobutu's Aborted Mediation Attempt

In June 1989, an earlier African attempt to bring about peace in Angola had occurred. President Mobutu Sese Seko of the Republic of Zaire (now Democratic Republic of the Congo) brought together Angolan president Eduardo dos Santos and UNITA insurgent leader Jonas Savimbi. Mobutu organized a summit conference with eighteen African heads of state on June 22, 1989, in his home village of Gbadolite, in northern Zaire. Mobutu's view was that national reconciliation among Angolans was the only way to bring about peace. There should be neither winners nor losers.

During the Gbadolite meeting, a peace agreement was written and signed by the protagonists and by all of the heads of state as witnesses. The key element of the agreement was a merger between the two parties. Savimbi agreed to join the government as vice president. UNITA agreed to become an official political party within the existing Marxist political system. The Angolan government agreed to forgive and forget the rebellion.

A few days later, on Sunday, June 26, 1989, it became clear that Savimbi had signed the agreement because he felt intimidated by all the heads of state present. He also wanted to please President Mobutu, who was allowing international arms shipments to transit Zaire en route to UNITA's base in southwestern Angola. Savimbi clearly did not like the agreement, because he wanted the Angolan people to decide on their leadership through free and fair elections. Joining a "Marxist" regime that he had been fighting for so many years was totally unacceptable to him. His mentor, President Houphouët-Boigny of Côte d'Ivoire, was negative about the agreement as well.

On that Sunday, June 26, I was at the State Department for the purpose of drafting a press statement expressing US support for the Gbadolite agreement. At the same time, Savimbi's US lobbyist, Paul Manafort of the firm Black, Manafort, and Stone, arrived at the department to meet with Secretary of State Baker. After their conversation, Secretary Baker called and instructed me to draft the press statement to express disappointment with the agreement because it did not provide for a democratic election. I issued the statement as directed, and braced myself for the wrath of President Mobutu.

During the first week of August 1989, my wife and I were in Basel, Switzerland, about to board a cruise boat on the Rhine heading toward Amsterdam in the Netherlands. I received a call from the State Department directing me to travel to Rabat, Morocco, to meet with Jonas Savimbi. My wife boarded without me, and I flew to Rabat to meet with Savimbi, hoping to catch up with the boat somewhere in Germany.

Savimbi explained that he could not comply with the Gbadolite agreement. His combat against the Angolan MPLA regime was designed to compel a free and fair democratic election. The idea of UNITA joining a Marxist regime under a Marxist constitution was totally unacceptable. He asked what the US reaction would be if UNITA went back to their insurgency in violation of the agreement that Mobutu and eighteen other African heads of state had sponsored. I responded that the United States would understand his decision and would continue to support UNITA. I was not reticent about making this commitment, because I had heard negative comments from Secretary Baker when the news of the Gbadolite agreement first came in. It was clear at that point that the entire US conservative political movement remained fully behind the UNITA cause in Angola.

When President Mobutu heard about Savimbi's decision, he became furious and decided to stop the transit of arms shipments through Zaire. This placed UNITA in grave danger, because the insurgency had no other way of replenishing its arms. By October 1989, UNITA's weapons stocks were dwindling, and the Angolan army was beginning to make significant gains on the ground.

That same month, President Bush asked both Mobutu and Savimbi to visit him in Washington. Bush made a personal appeal to Mobutu to allow the weapons deliveries to resume. Mobutu responded that he could not refuse a personal request from the president of the United States. In addition, to mark his reconciliation with the head of UNITA, he was inviting Savimbi to his sixtieth birthday party at his villa in southern France. As a result of President Bush's initiative, UNITA regained its ability to keep the Angolan army in check, while maintaining its ability to carry out hit-and-run harassment attacks throughout Angola.

The Soviets Continue to Need US Help to Get Out of Angola

The first opening for US-Angolan engagement took place in Windhoek, Namibia, at that nation's independence festivities in March 1990. Secretary of State James Baker headed the US delegation. The architect of Namibia's independence, former assistant secretary of state Chester Crocker, was Secretary Baker's special guest in the US delegation.

In Windhoek, there was no problem in arranging a meeting between Baker and Angolan president Eduardo dos Santos. To put dos Santos at ease about US intentions, Baker explained that US assistance to the UNITA insurgency was not designed to overthrow the Angolan government. Rather, the purpose of US assistance was to prevent the defeat of UNITA by a much more powerful government military machine, and nothing more. It was only logical, therefore, that peace negotiations be initiated to end the conflict.

President dos Santos easily accepted Baker's logic, but then wondered how negotiations might get started. Because of its relationship with UNITA, the United States could not serve as the mediator. Before the conversation ended, it was agreed that Portugal would be in the best position to run the negotiations.

Immediately after the Windhoek talks, Baker flew to Kinshasa, the capital of Zaire, where he met with Jonas Savimbi. The UNITA leader was delighted to learn that dos Santos had agreed to a negotiation that could lead to the democratic election that Savimbi had consistently designated as his highest priority. Savimbi felt confident that he would win an honest election, because he considered himself to be the true African, while dos Santos and his cabinet included no one who could even speak an African language. They were considered "black Portuguese."

By mid-1990, the negotiations had begun under Portuguese mediation in the resort city of Bicesse, about thirty-five miles from Lisbon. The United States and the Soviets were invited to be official observers. The US delegation included diplomats, legal advisers, and military officers. With a wealth of expertise, the US delegation could not fail to have major influence on the discussions. This was especially true with respect to the informal talks during breaks, meals, and evening hours.

The Soviets Intervene to Break a Long Impasse in the Negotiations

Angolan peace negotiations in Portugal, under the chairmanship of José Durão Barroso, Portugal's vice minister of foreign affairs, lasted from June 1990 to late November 1990. Despite the considerable help available from the Portuguese foreign ministry and the observers, the negotiations were totally stalemated for five months. UNITA made an initial concession by expressing its recognition of the MPLA regime as the legitimate government of Angola, and President dos Santos as the legitimate head of state. They also dropped their demand for a transitional government during elections preparations. What they had been fighting for was the installation of democracy. Nevertheless, the government side continued to insist on the status quo with respect to the existing regime, while inviting UNITA to become a legitimate political party within the existing system.

At the State Department, we were somewhat relaxed about the lack of progress in the negotiations, expecting that a breakthrough would take place at some point. But we had not anticipated the wrath of an extremely impatient Soviet foreign minister, who reminded us that the Soviets were in a hurry to rid themselves of their Angolan financial burden.

At the Houstonian Hotel in Houston, Texas, on December 9–10, 1990, Presidents Bush and Gorbachev dealt with the issue at one of their periodic summit meetings. After listening to a briefing on the limited progress made in the Angolan negotiations, Soviet foreign minister Eduard Shevardnazde took the bull by the horns. He instructed his director for Africa, Yuri Yukalev, and me, to go off by ourselves and pretend we were the Angolan government and UNITA respectively and write a balanced agreement. We then spent three hours together and came up with the main lines of a peace agreement, including the writing of a new constitution, the merging of the armies, UN supervision of the election, the encampment of the armies during the transition to an election, and ending all arrivals of arms from all sources.

Shevardnazde then instructed us to invite the two parties to Washington for a meeting on December 12. At that gathering, at the State Department, both parties reviewed and accepted the draft agreement in principle. Both said they would recommend acceptance to their principals, which was finalized in a matter of days. It was clear that Soviet impatience had forced the hand of the Angolan regime. The next step was to return the talks to Minister Barroso in Portugal in order to fill in all the necessary details. This process was completed by early May 1991, and a formal signing ceremony took place in Lisbon on May 30, just a few days after the London conference, which under US auspices had resulted in an end to the protracted Ethiopian civil war. During that last week in May 1991, the Africa Bureau of the State Department had the right to feel good about itself.

The Angolan Election and Its Tragic Aftermath

The Angolan presidential election was set for September 1992. During the transition, the State Department had several priorities: ensure that UNITA leader Savimbi and his team had the tools to protect their interests in the election; ensure that the troop encampments were completed before the election; and open a new US embassy in Luanda so that US diplomats could view preparations for the election firsthand.

Savimbi was naturally concerned about obtaining a fair count in the election. Secretary Baker introduced him to a US company that assisted in the preparation of elections. The company made it possible for UNITA to monitor the vote tallies from each polling place.

The movement of troops from various operational bases to camps was a logistical nightmare, given the poor state of the roads. The State Department was able to enlist the support of the Arizona Air National Guard to conduct their annual exercises in Angola instead of Arizona. The Arizona team did a remarkable job of moving different military units, as well as election materials, around the country.

The State Department was given a space in one of the most elegant residential neighborhoods of Luanda to install an embassy. With the help of a US company that could erect a prefabricated structure in one week, the US embassy opened expeditiously by August 1991. Edward Dejarnette was named the first US ambassador to independent Angola.

During the election campaign, the difference of style between UNITA's Savimbi and the government's dos Santos could not have been more pronounced. Dos Santos hired a Brazilian public relations firm that made him look like a fatherly figure who spent a lot of time playing soccer with children. He represented the Angolan family. Savimbi, meanwhile, presented himself as the warrior who was going to liberate the Angolan people from tyranny. Most of his public statements were warlike and bellicose.

Early in the campaign, polls favored Savimbi because of his true African roots, as opposed to the "black Portuguese" in power. In addition, the vast corruption of the regime, with its immense oil wealth, was well known to the people. Savimbi was so far ahead at the outset that some of the regime's top officials decided to send their families to live outside Angola, mainly to Portugal.

During the second half of the campaign, sentiment began to change. Savimbi was seen more and more as a war lover seeking revenge. He appeared menacing. At one point, he declared that all those who bought and sold on the black market would be punished. Considering the sorry state of the economy, virtually everyone resorted to the black market to survive. Savimbi's rhetoric started to frighten people.

The election took place as scheduled, and dos Santos was declared the winner with 48 percent of the vote to Savimbi's 35 percent. Since dos Santos did not win with more than 50 percent, a runoff was called for under the constitution. Savimbi's first reaction was to state that the election must have been rigged because he did not win. He produced some evidence that the tallies for several minor candidates were identical in some of the voting stations.

Savimbi requested that the US government support his claim that the election was rigged. On behalf of the US government, I told him there was no basis for such a conclusion. That was the end of our once friendly relationship. Back in Washington, virtually all of UNITA's political supporters agreed that Savimbi and UNITA had obtained their demand for a free and fair election and needed to accept the result. Some diehards demanded that the US government uphold UNITA's claim of rigging, but Secretary of State Baker and the key committee chairpersons in Congress agreed that the election results were valid.

The tragic aftermath of the election was that UNITA decided to revert to their guerrilla war, with much greater death and destruction than earlier, because the movement then had access to most of Angola rather than just the southwest, where they had been hiding before the peace agreement. Without assistance from either South Africa or the United States, UNITA sustained itself with sales of diamonds and other minerals from mines that they occupied, working mainly through intermediaries in Rwanda.

The guerrilla war continued until Savimbi was killed in combat on February 22, 2002, ten years after the presidential election. Efforts to end the war earlier had continued throughout the Clinton administration and the first years of the George W. Bush administration.

Both the United States and the Soviet Union were relieved of their financial and political burdens as soon as the United Nations declared the September 1992 election valid.[5]

The Portuguese Also Needed Help in Africa

The day after the Angolan peace agreement was signed in Lisbon during the final week of May 1991, Secretary of State Baker had a conversation with Portuguese prime minister Aníbal Cavaco Silva. Baker was expecting a difficult discussion because he was planning to announce that the United States would no longer be paying rent for its military base in the Portuguese Azores archipelago in the eastern Atlantic Ocean.

It turned out that Cavaco Silva's main concern was not the Azores, but Mozambique. At that point in time, the Mozambique peace process had been ongoing for about a year, centered in Rome. Unlike the Angolan peace negotiations, which took place in Portugal under Portuguese control, the Mozambique negotiations had absolutely zero Portuguese participation. Cavaco Silva explained that with several million Portuguese citizens having lived in, and fled, Angola and Mozambique, the government had a political problem. The Portuguese government's absence from the Mozambique peace process was seen by the exiles as an abandonment of Portugal's national interests. Could the United States do something to help?

Relieved that the Azores issue had not annoyed the prime minister, Secretary Baker said that he was sure the United States could find a role for Portugal in the Mozambique negotiations. It was an easy assignment. The United States arranged for the Portuguese government to become an official observer at the talks and, subsequently, as an official external participant in the implementation of the agreement, as stipulated in the Rome accord.[6]

The First Mozambique Peace Initiative Is Short-Lived

As previously noted, President Reagan launched the Mozambique peace process in April 1987, when he agreed that the United States would not support the RENAMO insurgent movement as some of his conservative political friends in southern California had recommended. Instead, President Reagan instructed the State Department to find a way to bring about political reconciliation between RENAMO and the FRELIMO government.

A brief period of ceasefire resulted from the Reagan initiative, but RENAMO was not invited to operate as a political party. The FRELIMO hierarchy insisted that under their system only a single Marxist vanguard party could be allowed to exist. Thus, for RENAMO, nothing had changed, and they decided to return to insurgency. While assistance from the white Rhodesian government had ended in 1980 when Rhodesia became Zimbabwe under black majority rule, the African National Congress's anti-apartheid insurgency conducted from Mozambique constituted an incentive for South African intelligence to provide arms and other assistance to RENAMO, thereby picking up where the white Rhodesians left off.

During Reagan's first term, Assistant Secretary of State for Africa Chester Crocker brokered a "nonaggression" agreement between Mozambique and South Africa. This agreement, known as the Nkomati Accord, was signed on March 16, 1984, on their common border. In essence, South

Africa agreed to stop supporting RENAMO, and Mozambique agreed to stop all ANC operations against South Africa from its territory.[7]

The Nkomati Accord was more easily signed than implemented. Strong forces opposed it on both sides. For the Organization of African Unity, ending apartheid in South Africa was black Africa's highest priority. The independent African governments did not appreciate the idea that the African National Congress would lose its main base of operations. On the white South African side, the intelligence and military communities and the mainstream political conservatives did not trust Mozambique's ability to prevent the ANC insurgency from operating out of its territory. After all, the FRELIMO party in Mozambique was Marxist to the core, and the South African conservatives could not believe anything they said.

Probably just as important for Mozambique was the deep bitterness of the Portuguese community that had to flee after Portugal granted the colony independence on June 27, 1975. The newly empowered FRELIMO party, in their early period of extreme Marxist ideology, confiscated everything owned by the Portuguese, including the properties of the Roman Catholic Church. The bitterness of the Portuguese community was so great that they did everything possible to sabotage and destroy whatever they could on their way out, such as filling plumbing with cement. The Portuguese exiles from Mozambique went to Brazil, South Africa, and the United States, as well as Portugal. This group did everything they could to support RENAMO against the FRELIMO government.

President Bush Restarts
the Mozambique Peace Process

A strong admirer of President Reagan, President George H. W. Bush did not want his predecessor's initiative aimed at ending the civil war in Mozambique to end in failure. Bush accepted the State Department's recommendation to invite Mozambique's president Joaquim Chissano and his key policy advisers to visit the White House. The meeting took place on March 12, 1990.

Bush's main argument was that the international community could not be counted upon to take care of the RENAMO problem. The RENAMO-FRELIMO conflict was an internal Mozambican problem that had to be settled on the basis of internal reconciliation. The FRELIMO government was in a state of denial if it believed that it could carry on as usual and just wait for RENAMO's collapse, while large populations in central

Mozambique were suffering from the guerrilla war. It was not going to happen. In addition, for Chissano to argue that FRELIMO had to remain the only legitimate political party was unworkable. That would amount to telling RENAMO to surrender. Three years after President Reagan made a similar argument, President Chissano and his key advisers finally agreed with Bush's thesis.

One of the main civil society actors in Mozambique was the Catholic lay order St. Egidio, based in Rome, which agreed to host the negotiations in Rome, with financial and technical support from the Italian government. The United States was invited to be an official observer. Ambassador Jeffrey Davidow, principal deputy assistant secretary of state for African affairs, was in charge of furnishing assistance to the negotiations, as well as protecting US interests. Deputy Chief of Mission Cameron Hume of the US embassy to the Holy See in Rome provided day-to-day coverage of the talks. The negotiations began in July 1990 and terminated with the signing of a final agreement on October 4, 1992, in Rome.[8]

During the twenty-six months of negotiations, the usual difficulties of compromising on the wording of a new constitution or the disposition of fighting forces were not the main hurdle. Instead, it was Afonso Dhlakama's deep distrust. The ultra-secretive leader of RENAMO had lived through too much deception on the part of both the Portuguese colonialists and the FRELIMO regime to be willing to make the great leap from guerrilla fighter to politician with confidence.

To overcome Dhlakama's skepticism, the Bureau of African Affairs enlisted the help of people whom he trusted. President Daniel Arap Moi of Kenya was friendly with Dhlakama through their common evangelical Christian beliefs and activities. During a meeting with me at the Namibia independence celebrations in March 1990, President Moi expressed astonishment at our depiction of Dhlakama as a gross violator of human rights. Moi said: "How can you call him a human rights violator? Wherever he goes, Dhlakama distributes Bibles." Moi proved most helpful in persuading Dhlakama to meet with me and other US officials, who reassured him that an agreement with FRELIMO would be fully implemented.

Another African head of state who provided invaluable help was Robert Mugabe, the founding president of Zimbabwe. He and Dhlakama were from the same ethnic group, the Shona, who straddle the Mozambique-Zimbabwe border. Mugabe invited Dhlakama to visit him in Zimbabwe, where he encouraged him to trust the peace process. After Mugabe's pep talk, the negotiations moved quickly to their final success and signature.

Mugabe chaired the signing ceremony in Rome on October 4, 1992. That was the very day that Jonas Savimbi rejected the results of the election in Angola—toward which the US government had worked so hard—and decided to return to war.[9]

Liberia Descends into Tragedy

When army sergeant Samuel Kenyon Doe staged a violent mini coup that overthrew Liberian president William R. Tolbert Jr. on April 12, 1980, he killed not only President Tolbert but also quite a few of the political elite, including the president's son, A. P. Tolbert. The assassination of the young Tolbert was particularly significant because it made a neighboring head of state very angry. That person was Félix Houphouët-Boigny, president of Côte d'Ivoire.

Knowing he was a target of Doe's team of assassins, Tolbert and his wife, Daisy, took refuge in the home of the Côte d'Ivoire ambassador. The Ivoirian envoy decided to transfer the couple to the residence of the French ambassador, where they were likely to be more secure.

Doe's colleagues, army enlisted men, knew nothing about such things as diplomatic immunity and the sanctity of foreign embassies. They brazenly invaded the French ambassador's house, extracted A. P. Tolbert, and proceeded to kill him. In addition to President Houphouët-Boigny's reaction to this extreme violation of international law, he was deeply angered by the fact that A. P. Tolbert's wife, Daisy, was his own beloved adopted daughter.[10]

Houphouët-Boigny bided his time and waited almost a full decade before taking his revenge against President Doe. On Christmas Eve 1989, a band of 200 guerrilla fighters, under the command of Liberian Charles Taylor, crossed the border from Côte d'Ivoire into Liberia's Nimba County. President Doe's response was to send his troops into the region and totally destroy any village through which the rebels transited. It was a scorched earth policy. Doe had no problem doing this because his Krahn ethnic group was not located there.

Slowly, the rebels advanced toward the capital, Monrovia, with much destruction and killing on the way. Charles Taylor, who had trained in Libya along with his fighters, was being supplied from Libya through Burkina Faso and financed by Côte d'Ivoire.

The first US reaction was to offer good offices to the two sides in the hope of finding a compromise solution. President Doe sent a delegation to

Washington in January 1990 seeking assistance. To appease the invaders, who were calling for democracy, the Africa Bureau made suggestions, for example, to advance the elections to mid-1990 and allow the rebels to compete fairly. Unrealistically, Doe refused because it would "violate the constitution." He had no understanding of his government's plight. In essence, he wanted the United States to get rid of the rebels.

Unlike in the internal conflicts in Angola, Ethiopia, and Mozambique, the United States was not enthusiastic about becoming involved in Liberia's war. The Liberian people had always wanted to be a dependent of the United States, but the United States has never wanted them. For that reason, the United States encouraged the Economic Community of West African States (ECOWAS) to take the lead. Under the leadership of Nigeria and Ghana, ECOWAS stood up an intervention force, the ECOWAS Ceasefire Monitoring Group (ECOMOG), which they sent to Liberia with the objective of ending the fighting and beginning a democratic electoral process.

Needless to say, ECOWAS members Côte d'Ivoire and Burkina Faso objected vehemently to the intervention of ECOMOG against their surrogate, Charles Taylor, who called his guerrilla force the National Patriotic Front of Liberia (NPFL). ECOMOG was able to stop the NPFL from capturing Monrovia but was unable to defeat them. It was not until 1997, seven years later, that the Nigerians persuaded Charles Taylor to stop the war and accept an electoral process. Although most Liberians hated Taylor, they feared him so much that they elected him to the presidency. They could not stand the idea of his restarting the war.

The US role in the Liberian conflict during the George H. W. Bush administration was minimal, concentrating on protecting US citizens and US property. Nevertheless, there were some timely US actions. For example, when Senegalese president Abdou Diouf made an official visit to Washington in September 1991, President Bush recommended that he send a battalion to Liberia to join the ECOMOG force. This initiative was in response to Charles Taylor's complaint that he could not negotiate with any government involved in ECOMOG because he totally distrusted it. He wanted to work only with other West African governments that had no previous involvement with the war. President Diouf agreed to send a battalion to Liberia with US logistical assistance.

In June 1991, I had met in Abidjan with Burkina Faso president Blaise Compaoré, who was working closely with Charles Taylor by allowing Libyan arms to arrive at his international airport to be transported across Côte d'Ivoire to the Liberian border. I asked him why he was supporting a war in Liberia that was causing so much suffering. He responded that he had made a mistake in supporting Taylor. I asked if he would stop sending arms, and he said he would. But it was a lie. He continued the supply of arms.

I had also met with Côte d'Ivoire's president Houphouët-Boigny in August 1990 to encourage him to find a way to stop the war. His reaction was to deny his massive involvement, while also expressing a willingness to contribute to peace. In fact, Houphouët-Boigny was primarily interested in getting rid of Samuel Doe because of Doe's total incompetence and criminal thievery, and not so much to avenge his adopted son-in-law, A. P. Tolbert. Doe was a disgrace to the West African community.

Like so many others who have initiated surrogate wars in Africa, Houphouët had the naive belief that the war would be over in sixty days or less, with Samuel Doe being swept away with ease. What he did not understand was that ethnic feeling in Liberia was so intense that Doe's Krahn tribe in the army was sure they would be killed if captured. Thus they fought to the death, thereby prolonging the war.

Seven years of war destroyed most of the Liberian infrastructure, with much work remaining to be done by subsequent administrations. Would the outcome have been different if the United States had taken charge of the problem? The administration's decision to allow ECOWAS to take the lead was probably the right one, under the circumstances.[11]

Somalia Becomes a Humanitarian Tragedy

The Breakdown of Order

The independent nation of Somalia began as a merger between Italian and British colonies. Subsequently, the people of Somalia were able to unify when they faced external threats or enemies. This was true during Somalia's war with Ethiopia during 1977–1978. In the absence of external threats, however, the Somalis were hopelessly divided among extended families known as clans. Although they spoke the same Somali language and shared the same Muslim religion, the Somali clans were constantly at each other's throats. When any one clan held political power, all the others were excluded from resources.

In January 1991, Somali president Mohamed Siad Barre's government collapsed completely under insurgent pressure from other clans. President Siad Barre was forced to flee to neighboring Kenya. Because of extensive banditry in the capital city, Mogadishu, all of the US embassy's employees and their families were urgently evacuated. Those Americans were fortunate, because US naval ships headed toward Kuwait for Operation Desert Storm, designed to eject Iraq from its illegal invasion, were in the vicinity of Mogadishu when the embassy's call for support came in. Navy helicopters were sent to the embassy compound in Mogadishu and successfully evacuated all of the families, including those of some other friendly embassies.

The rest of 1991 was devoted mainly to mediation efforts among the clans designed to reestablish a central government. The United States, though on the sideline of these mediations, blessed several results designed to bring about a new government of national unity. All resulting governments collapsed soon after being established, leaving Somalia in a state of extreme instability.

In the absence of a central government, heavily armed warlords were providing security, while making money through their control of external and internal trade. Toward the end of 1991 and throughout 1992, drought caused a decrease in agriculture and a growing food deficit. The international community sent humanitarian relief, which was increasingly hijacked by warlords who controlled internal transportation routes. The warlords did not allow the humanitarian assistance to go to the intended destinations without payment. The peasantry, especially women with young children, were unable to pay. Relief agencies were starting to send reports of starvation during July 1992.

The Bureau of African Affairs recommended an emergency US military airlift of food to interior airports not controlled by warlords. The initial military response was to urge that civilian contracts be executed to send food aid through the private sector. But President Bush agreed with the State Department and ordered that a US military airlift be initiated.

By November, the situation had become quite grave. Andrew Natsios, director of the Office of Disaster Assistance in the US Agency for International Development, was giving press conferences daily to call attention to the unfolding tragedy.

President Bush Takes Charge

After the presidential election in which he was defeated, President Bush nevertheless continued to deal with crisis issues around the world. Immediately after the election, reacting to both classified and public information, President Bush asked the State Department for a recommendation on Somalia. The Bureau of African Affairs prepared a memorandum recommending that the United States ask for a UN military enforcement operation under Chapter VII of the UN Charter. The president sent the memorandum to the Joint Chiefs of Staff for comment.

The Joint Chiefs, headed by General Colin Powell, responded that a UN force normally takes six months to become operational. The Somali crisis required immediate action because mothers and babies were dying of starvation every day. CNN was calling the US public's attention to this crisis every day. Members of Congress were demanding action. The Joint Chiefs' response concluded that only the United States could project the necessary force rapidly.

President Bush made some quick decisions and directives:

- To the Joint Chiefs: Prepare to intervene in Somalia in order to make sure humanitarian aid is distributed to those in dire need.
- To Secretary of State Lawrence Eagleburger: Proceed to New York and negotiate an agreement with UN Secretary-General Boutros Boutros-Ghali, according to which the US military would take immediate action in Somalia, while the UN would begin to organize a UN peacekeeping force to take over from the US military at the end of six months. At that point, the US military would depart, leaving only a small contingency intervention force based on ships offshore.
- To the State Department's Bureau of African Affairs: Immediately start to recruit African governments to contribute their troops to the Somalia rescue operation, either as partners with the US operation or, six months later, as part of the UN force.

Retired US diplomat Robert Oakley, who had been the US ambassador to Somalia and to Pakistan, was named to head up the entire operation, covering both military and civilian activities. He wore two hats, representing both the US government and the United Nations.

When President Bush left office on January 20, 1993, the Somalia intervention was in full swing and was fulfilling its objective. Humanitarian supplies were flowing to the needy populations, and the armed militias were being kept in check.

The Bureau of African Affairs was proud of Botswana, which was in a high state of military readiness and thus able to participate in the initial intervention at the side of the US military. Later, during the evaluations, the US military had nothing but the highest praise for the Botswana military.[12]

The South African Bombshell:
"We Are Ending Apartheid Voluntarily"

During the last two years of the Reagan administration (1987–1988), a steady stream of nongovernmental visitors from South Africa came bearing optimistic news. They were mainly from the worlds of business and journalism. Their message was that change was coming in South Africa. The older generation of white political leadership was in the process of retiring or dying. A new generation in their fifties, with new ideas, was coming to power.

The predictions offered to the Reagan administration became realities with a lightning bolt during the first year of the Bush administration. In August 1989, I traveled to South Africa to meet with Ambassador William Swing and South African officials to take the temperature of the internal political and economic situations. The country was just beginning a presidential election exercise, exclusively within the white minority community.

After my arrival, I was informed that Minister of Education F. W. de Klerk wanted to see me. He was in the Indian Ocean coastal city of Durban, where he was beginning his campaign for the presidency. The US consul-general in Durban, F. Allen "Tex" Harris, took me to Minister de Klerk's seaside hotel, where de Klerk invited me for a one-on-one discussion.

As the candidate of the National Party, de Klerk was quite confident that he would win the presidential election in the whites-only election. Through me, he wanted to give President Bush an advance view of what he planned to do after taking office in January 1990.[13]

First, he explained that he had grown up in the apartheid system and believed in it fervently. For a long time, he had believed that the different races had to live in separate nations with separate governments. As of 1989, however, he had reached the conclusion that the apartheid system could not possibly work for the benefit of any of the races, above all not for the white race. For South Africa to grow its already substantial economy, it needed the full collaboration of the majority black people. They had to be full partners in the economic system. If the black people were to be full partners in the economic system, they had to be full partners in the political system. There could not be two levels of citizenship.

Having reached the conclusion that apartheid was becoming a total impediment to the nation's economic future, de Klerk planned to start dismantling the system, begun in 1948, as soon as he took office in January

1990. He would begin by legalizing all of the prohibited political parties, including the most important representative of the black population, the African National Congress, and the South African Communist Party. He also intended to release all persons incarcerated for political reasons, most notably Nelson Mandela, the hero of the black population and worldwide anti-apartheid icon. Mandela had been imprisoned on Robben Island with several dozen of his associates for twenty-seven years. After these initial acts, negotiations would begin for a "new political dispensation."

Needless to say, de Klerk's revelation was fantastically heartening. He swore me to secrecy, except for President Bush and Secretary of State Baker. I so promised.

Meanwhile, back in Washington President Bush and Secretary Baker were quite naturally delighted at the report of de Klerk's statement to me. President Bush said that he would order the lifting of sanctions against South Africa as soon as de Klerk took his first steps to abolish apartheid.

In October 1989, the Senate Foreign Relations Committee, under Democratic majority control, decided to mark the third anniversary of sanctions with a review of their impact on South Africa's government and the South African people. I was slated to be the chief US government witness.

About two weeks before the committee hearing, the State Department received an informal message from Senator David Boren of Oklahoma, chairman of the Senate Intelligence Committee. The Foreign Relations Committee, he said, would begin with a question about the impact of sanctions on South Africa. He recommended that the response not be totally negative. In other words, do not say that the sanctions only made matters worse for the South African people and had no impact on the determination of the government to maintain the apartheid regime. Boren explained that the entire Congress was proud of the Anti-Apartheid Act of 1986, because it demonstrated to the American people their abhorrence of that evil system. If the State Department, in a public hearing, were to denounce the sanctions as useless and counterproductive, it would constitute an insult to the Congress. He issued the warning because he knew of President Bush's total dislike of these particular sanctions.

Boren's message triggered a debate in the executive branch as to exactly how the department's witness would respond to the question about the impact of sanctions after three years of implementation. Clearly, the apartheid regime was still in place and had not shown much evidence of being hurt by sanctions. At the same time, the absence of new business investment, as well as a certain amount of disinvestment, had hurt the economy. With Boren's advisory in mind, the State Department and the White House found a workable compromise.

Sure enough, the first question at the hearing, from Democratic senator Paul Simon of Illinois, chairman of the Africa Subcommittee, was about the impact of sanctions. As agreed, I responded that the sanctions had had a somewhat negative impact on the black population because of increased unemployment caused by significant disinvestment on the part of the private sector. Conversely, the sanctions had not really hurt the underlying economic situation of the white community. Nevertheless, for the white minority population, the sanctions were having a psychological impact that made them feel increasingly isolated and worried about the future.

The follow-up question came from Democratic senator Paul Sarbanes of Maryland, who asked, in view of the increasing worry on the part of South African whites, would it not be timely to increase sanctions in order to put more pressure on them to think seriously about ending apartheid?

With F. W. de Klerk's statement still resonating in my mind, I said: "Senator Sarbanes, the South African white community is in the middle of a presidential election. It looks like there is a younger generation coming to power. Why don't we agree to meet again in March [1990] to determine if these rising stars develop some new policies that might ameliorate the harsh political system. If there are no changes, then we can discuss a possible increase in sanctions." Hearing a State Department witness utter the words "discuss a possible increase in sanctions," the Democrats on the committee appeared quite pleased. Sarbanes himself said: "That sounds reasonable. OK, let's meet again in March."

The next day, the South African press had a big headline quoting Foreign Minister Pik Botha as saying, "We do not accept ultimatums." The next day as well, I met Under Secretary of State for Political Affairs Robert Kimmitt in passing. He said, "You bought us some time, Hank."

Undoing the Sanctions Regime and Assisting the Negotiations

Immediately after taking office in January 1990, de Klerk took the actions that he had promised, resulting in tumultuous celebrations surrounding

Nelson Mandela's release from prison. Immediately thereafter, President Bush ordered that all necessary steps be taken to lift sanctions.

The Anti-Apartheid Act of 1986 set down precise conditions that had to be met before sanctions could be lifted. It was more easily said than done. For example, the act said that all political prisoners had to be released. To be able to certify that, State Department lawyers had to travel to South Africa to look into all ambiguous cases. The whole process of dismantling sanctions took a lot of time and a lot of personnel, but the outcome was inevitable. Sanctions were lifted by the end of summer 1990.

After the euphoria of President de Klerk's actions in January 1990, the difficult work remained to be accomplished. Negotiations for a new political system would not be simple. Everyone wanted a one-person, one-vote democracy. But the whites needed to be sure they would not lose everything under a black majority government. Some of the leaders in the African National Congress were believers in Marxism and communism. Their views had to be taken seriously.

President Bush demonstrated on several occasions that he was truly interested in a successful outcome in South Africa. In June 1990, he suggested to Secretary of State Baker that the United States offer to mediate in the negotiations between the white minority government and the various political parties and organizations within the nonwhite communities. The State Department made the offer to both the white government and the African National Congress. Both came back with the identical response: "Thank you very much, but we are all South Africans together, and we will do the negotiations without any outside assistance."

The official negotiations began in December 1991 within a forum designated as the Convention for a Democratic South Africa (CODESA). Not unexpectedly, the negotiations were quite tough. Ironically, after having refused US mediation, the protagonists tended to call on US ambassador Princeton Lyman for assistance whenever they reached an impasse. On one occasion in 1992, I had to go to South Africa to help negotiations resume after a nasty interruption. Extremist whites had started setting off explosions in black residential areas in an effort to sabotage the negotiations. They felt they had succeeded when Nelson Mandela said that the negotiations would be stopped because of the white violence. I gave a press conference in Pretoria delivering the message that the halting of the talks constituted a victory for the extremists. This resulted in a resumption of negotiations. A South African daily newspaper, *Business Day,* commented: "Why is it necessary for American Assistant Secretary Cohen to come here to tell us what should be basic common sense?"[14]

The CODESA negotiations continued to 1994, with the writing of a new democratic constitution and the installation of the nation's first majority-rule government, under President Nelson Mandela.

From Assistant Secretary Chester Crocker's marathon negotiations begun in 1981 to the independence of Namibia, followed by the ending of the apartheid system in 1994, it can be said that US policy, over three administrations, constituted a major contribution to peace and democracy in southern Africa.

Africa Also Played an Important Role in Bush's Middle East Policy

As indicated earlier, US relations with the Soviet Union and Portugal were instrumental in the deep involvement of the United States in conflict resolution in Ethiopia, Angola, and Mozambique. In the same vein, it is important to note that President Bush's most important initiative in the Middle East, war against Iraq, had both diplomatic and military African involvement.

Africa and the Iraq War

Iraq's invasion and occupation of Kuwait began on August 2, 1990. Secretary of State Baker met with Iraq's foreign minister and demanded that Iraq must withdraw from Kuwait. When Iraq refused to comply, President Bush decided that force must be used.

President Bush did not want the use of force against Iraq in Kuwait to be a unilateral US action. He wanted authorization from the United Nations Security Council, and he wanted other governments to participate in the military action against Iraq.

In late August 1990, Secretary Baker asked me to come to his office. The subject was Iraq. He told me that President Bush wanted a unanimous vote in the Security Council authorizing the use of force against Iraq. He looked at the list of the fifteen members of the Security Council and "discovered" that there were three African nonpermanent members: Côte d'Ivoire, Zaire (now DRC), and Ethiopia. Assuming a serious demeanor, Baker said: "Hank, you will make sure we get all three African votes in favor of the use of force." My response was: "Welcome to Africa, Mr. Secretary."

In early September 1990, we decided that the best approach to the three African governments would be for Secretary Baker and myself to meet their foreign ministers in Geneva. All three agreed to meet us, and we saw them, individually, on the same day during the second week of September.

Zaire's minister was Jean-Nguza Karl-i-Bond, former ambassador to the United States. After Baker made his argument, Minister Nguza indicated that he expected his head of state to give his approval.

The Ethiopian minister was Tesfaye Dinka. I had gotten to know him through our ongoing mediation efforts to end the war of Eritrean secession described earlier. At this point, Ethiopia had every reason to cooperate with the United States, especially on an issue that was of relatively low interest to them. Minister Dinka indicated that he had already had his president's approval to support the US position and that he would look into the possibility of lobbying the other nonpermanent members of the Security Council.

Côte d'Ivoire's minister was Amara Essy, an old friend of mine. Unlike his two predecessors, however, Essy was unenthusiastic about voting for the UN to declare war on Iraq. He said that his president, Félix Houphouët-Boigny, did not like war. He was a man of peace. For that reason, he could not reply to Baker's request immediately. He had to return home to consult with his president.

Essy then expressed a grievance he had to Secretary Baker. He explained that during his periodic visits to Washington he was unable to meet with anyone higher than Assistant Secretary Cohen. He had ministerial rank, after all. Secretary Baker sympathized with his complaint and told Essy to let him know the next time he would be in New York for UN business. Baker promised to send a US government aircraft to New York to transport him to Washington. Essy thanked him and left, apparently satisfied. Within a few days, Essy sent a message through his ambassador in Washington that President Houphouët-Boigny had authorized a yes vote on the UN resolution to declare war on Iraq.

The UN Security Council debate on the proposal to use force against Iraq, under Chapter VII of the UN Charter, took place on November 29, 1990. The debate was at the ministerial level, with Secretary Baker representing the United States. Baker asked all of the regional assistant secretaries to be in New York at the UN in case of need. We watched the debate on television. The Security Council approved the resolution to authorize the use of force against Iraq. The vote was not unanimous. Ecuador voted no. But the three African members, as promised, all voted yes.[15]

After the session, Baker joined the assistant secretaries in the holding room. He gave me a hug because the Africans had voted yes as promised.

African Participation in Combat

During the Carter administration, the United States had negotiated military base rights and military transit rights in several East African countries, in anticipation of a possible Soviet military penetration south from Afghanistan. The United States needed these African facilities because Saudi Arabia and the other Gulf nations did not want to host US military contingents. They wanted the US military to be close by but "over the horizon" (see Chapter 9).

The attitude of the Saudis and their neighbors changed quickly as soon as the Iraqi army invaded Kuwait. At that point, the United States was invited to station forces at the front line within the Arab countries near Kuwait. Consequently, the African facilities negotiated by the Carter administration played only a minimal role in Operation Desert Storm.

President Bush knew that the US military would play the major role in Desert Storm, but he wanted other governments to participate as well. Several NATO governments sent military units to fight in the operation, and one African country, Senegal, sent troops. Senegal's contingent suffered a major tragedy on March 22, 1991, when a transport aircraft crashed in Saudi Arabia, killing ninety-two of their soldiers. The incident occurred after the fighting had stopped. When I expressed condolences to Senegalese president Abdou Diouf, he said that the Senegalese people knew that the deceased soldiers, all Muslims, had gone to heaven because they had perished in Saudi Arabia immediately after having visited the holy city of Mecca.[16]

President Bush served only one term, but regarding Africa, his administration had been very, very busy.

12

William J. Clinton: 1993–2001

The Clinton administration conducted US relations with Africa with the best of intentions. Unfortunately, the outcomes were mostly unhappy. US policy demonstrated less than good judgment much of the time. The administration's major challenges during eight years in power included the Black Hawk Down incident in Somalia in 1993, the Rwandan genocide of 1994, and Africa's first continent-wide war, from 1998 to 2002.

Somalia: The Failed State That Resists Repair

When President Clinton took office in January 1993, President Bush's Operation Restore Hope was ongoing. The 28,000 US troops and several thousand others from twenty-six nations had stabilized most of Somalia. Humanitarian supplies were moving to places where families had been close to starvation six weeks earlier. In addition, fighting among the different clans and warlords, especially in the capital, Mogadishu, had been greatly reduced. The UN Security Council named this the United Nations Operation in Somalia (UNOSOM), which would later come to have a second phase.

After six weeks on the ground, the military requested permission to deploy tanks and other armored vehicles in Somalia. Clinton's secretary of defense, Les Aspin, refused the request. This decision was to become significant a few months later, in October 1993.

As agreed between the Bush administration and the UN Secretary-General, the US-led phase of UNOSOM I ended after six months, on May 4, 1993. The US military contingent was reduced to fewer than 5,000 personnel, and Ambassador Robert Oakley departed. Operation UNOSOM II began under full UN control. The new overall commander was retired US admiral Jonathan Howe. His last position before retiring had been as assistant national security adviser during the final two years of the Bush administration. During Bush's first two years, Howe had served as the assistant secretary of state for political-military affairs.

For UNOSOM I, under US control, Ambassador Oakley had a policy of not attempting to disarm any of the independent armed Somali militias. The objective was to eliminate barriers to the distribution of humanitarian relief to save people from starvation. Force was to be used, if necessary, only to open transportation routes.

After six months, the UN began to think about the future of Somalia. "Nation building" became part of the conversation among the UN project managers. Somalia had not had a functioning central government since January 1991. Warlords and clan leaders controlled the various regions and subregions. The Somali people were living under a form of anarchy. Because of the clan system of extended families, a growing consensus held that a highly decentralized cantonal system, similar to Switzerland's, would be the most likely solution for Somalia.

Attempts to reconstitute a central government were ongoing. Negotiations among warlords took place, but they were unable to agree on a new president. The main problem centered on one warlord, Mohamed Farah Aideed, leader of the Habr Gidr clan, who insisted that only he merited the presidency. He based his claim on the leading role that he played in the overthrow of the hated Siad Barre dictatorship in January 1991. He refused to join in any consensus. He alone could be acceptable as head of state. His fighters were well armed. Ironically, at the time, his son was in the United States serving as a sergeant in the US Marines.

Thinking about a post-humanitarian transition to nation building, Admiral Howe directed his Pakistani contingent to aggressively patrol in the center of Mogadishu, within Aideed's area of control. The mission was to survey Aideed's inventory of arms and munitions. The Pakistanis executed the order on June 5, 1993. That deployment of Pakistani troops to the heart of Aideed's territory turned out to be a significant mistake. The Pakistanis were ambushed and severely decimated, with twenty-four killed in action.

The UN Security Council met immediately and authorized "all necessary means" to punish the perpetrators. Admiral Howe, too, wanted to punish the killers of his troops. As a four-star US admiral, Howe naturally looked to the remaining US forces to apply the necessary means. He arranged for US Special Forces and Rangers, who were positioned on ships offshore, to carry out the necessary operation.[1]

Operation Gothic took place on October 3, 1993, with the US Special Forces and Rangers attacking in Black Hawk helicopters. The mission was to kill or capture Aideed and his top lieutenants. Although the US attackers unleashed tremendous force, killing several thousand of Aideed's troops, the Somalis resisted with their own abundant firepower. Using rifle-projected grenades, the Somali fighters shot down two of the helicopters and killed eighteen US fighters. Several dead Americans were dragged through the streets, their bodies mutilated. All of this was photographed and sent around the world.

President Clinton claimed to be totally unaware of this operation and appeared totally shocked when the news came through. His first reaction was to order that reinforcements be sent to bolster the strength of the remaining US forces. He also addressed the nation, pointing out that the United States had saved many Somali lives in Operation Restore Hope, an action in the highest tradition of America's humanitarian response to suffering worldwide. He then decided that all US military personnel would depart from Somalia no later than March 1994. He also ordered that US military personnel in Somalia would no longer engage in combat operations unless attacked. Clearly embarrassed by the tragedy, Clinton was soundly criticized by the press and the public, as was Admiral Howe.[2]

As part of the political fallout from the tragedy, Defense Secretary Les Aspin resigned because of his earlier decision to refuse the deployment of tanks and other armored vehicles to Somalia. If available to Operation Gothic, such equipment might have made a significant difference in achieving the mission to neutralize Aideed.[3]

President Clinton's decision to withdraw US troops caused the UN to give up on the idea of engaging in nation building in Somalia. The remaining UN forces were therefore withdrawn by March 1995.

In addition to the embarrassment caused to President Clinton, still in his first year in office, the Black Hawk Down tragedy also tarnished the reputation of the UN in the eyes of the American public and made the UN increasingly vulnerable to anti-UN propaganda within the United States. The irony is that the operation was planned exclusively between Admiral Howe and the US military. The UN Office of Peace-keeping, in New York, was not involved. In addition, President Clinton did nothing to defend the UN against unfair accusations of responsibility for the disastrous outcome.[4]

Warlord Aideed, a former army general and Somali ambassador to India, escaped capture by US Special Forces but suffered a heart attack and died one year later. Even with him gone, the Somali political elites continued to find it impossible to unite to form a consensus government until well into the middle of the Obama administration in 2012. And even then, Somalia remained fragile and internally violent and was eventually penetrated by Islamic terrorists linked to al-Qaeda and Osama bin Laden. Nevertheless, seen from the point of view of the original humanitarian objective, Operation Restore Hope was a huge success.[5]

Perhaps the most significant fallout of the Black Hawk downings was their impact on the Clinton administration's response to the Rwandan genocide of April–June 1994.[6]

Hutus Murdering Tutsis in Rwanda

In 1972, the Nixon administration was confronted with genocide in the tiny nation of Burundi, situated on Lake Tanganyika due east of giant Zaire (now Democratic Republic of the Congo). At that time, the minority Tutsi ethnic group, with about 15 percent of the population, controlled political power. When educated members of the majority Hutu population challenged that power, the ruling Tutsis engaged in the murder of any Hutu with more than a fifth-grade education. Neighboring Tanzania brought the genocide to an end, but only after 100,000 Hutus had been killed. The US government's response was essentially passive (as recounted in Chapter 7).

In neighboring Rwanda, with exactly the same Hutu-Tutsi mix as Burundi, the majority Hutu ethnic group was able to take power at independence from Belgium on July 1, 1962. The political situation in Rwanda was exactly the opposite of the one in Burundi.

Because of historical grievances and Tutsi efforts to sabotage the majority Hutus' coming to power in Rwanda, the Hutu regime, with much civilian assistance, engaged in pogroms against ordinary Tutsis throughout the Rwandan territory. This resulted during 1962–1963 in an outflow of approximately 300,000 Tutsi refugees into neighboring Uganda and Burundi, with the vast majority settling in southwestern Uganda.

Rwanda had a civilian government until 1973, when a military coup assumed power, with General Juvénal Habyarimana taking over as head of state. The general took a very hard line concerning the Rwandan Tutsi refugees living in neighboring countries. He declared that they would never be allowed to return, because tiny Rwanda was overpopulated.

During the second half of the Carter administration and continuing into the George H. W. Bush administration, the Habyarimana regime began to accept political and economic reforms, with the international donor community providing significant economic development assistance. In early 1990, during his conversations with US ambassador Bruce Flatin and with visitors from the UN High Commission for Refugees (UNHCR), President Habyarimana began to change his mind about allowing the Tutsi refugees the right of return. He also abolished the single-party system and opened Rwanda to multiparty politics. Significantly, new political parties were established with mixed Hutu and Tutsi membership. The outlook was promising.[7]

Ugandan President Museveni's Surrogate War

On October 1, 1990, about 5,000 armed Ugandan soldiers invaded neighboring Rwanda. All of these soldiers were from Rwandan Tutsi refugee families, having grown up and been educated in Uganda. Ugandan Tutsi officers were especially strong in the Ugandan military intelligence service. The invaders called themselves the Rwandan Patriotic Front (RPF). Their mission was to "liberate" Rwanda.

In reality, the invasion had two purposes. President Museveni of Uganda wanted to get rid of the Tutsi refugees. The general Ugandan population resented what they considered Tutsi arrogance and sense of superiority. Museveni saw his Tutsi military officers as a threat to his own power. The Tutsi officers wanted to overthrow the Hutu regime in Rwanda, restore traditional Tutsi minority power, and bring all of the Tutsi refugees back to their ancestral homeland. The fact that the Habyarimana regime was liberalizing and democratizing made the military action all the more urgent for the Tutsi invaders.[8]

The invading force did not enjoy an instant military success. The Tutsis were stalemated not far from the Ugandan border for the first several months. French and Belgian troops were helping the Rwandan army.[9] The Bush administration's initial reaction was to go into conflict resolution mode and urge negotiations. The protagonists were all Rwandans, after all. The Rwandan Patriotic Front initially refused negotiations, because they considered the Habyarimana regime illegitimate. They also saw that the Rwandan government was spending enormous amounts of money on buying arms and recruiting thousands of men into the army. They thought they could wait until the regime ran out of money and thus would be easily overthrown.[10]

The military stalemate continued through all of 1991, thus providing time for the newly invigorated Organization of African Unity to offer its good offices in search of conflict resolution. The newly elected and energetic OAU secretary-general, Tanzanian diplomat Ahmed Salim Salim, was particularly interested in taking charge of the problem.

In the spring of 1992, the French foreign ministry asked the US Bureau of African Affairs to join in applying pressure on the Rwandan Patriotic Front to accept mediated negotiations. My French counterpart, Henri Dijoud, invited me to come to Paris for joint discussions with the Ugandan foreign minister, Paul Ssemmogere. Since the government of Uganda was supplying the Rwandan Patriotic Front with all of its arms, food, and medical support, we believed that the application of pressure on Uganda constituted the best strategy. The French, who were the main arms donors to the Rwandan army, were particularly anxious to see the beginning of negotiations, preceded by a ceasefire.

The discussion with the Ugandan foreign minister was short and effective. I told him that the United States was one of Uganda's most important foreign aid donors and that we would have to reconsider our good relations if the Rwandan Patriotic Front continued to refuse to enter into negotiations with the Rwandan government. It was useful that the minister was accompanied by military officers clearly identifiable as members of the Tutsi ethnic group.

The Rwandan Patriotic Front quickly agreed to negotiations, which began in July 1992 in the Tanzanian conference center in the Kilimanjaro town of Arusha. The United States was invited to have an observer present throughout the negotiations. The State Department assigned as the observer David Rawson, a career Foreign Service officer. He had spent his childhood in a missionary family in Burundi and was fluent in the Kinyarwanda language of neighboring Rwanda. Rawson reported that during his informal conversations at meals and coffee breaks, the Tutsi Rwandan Patriotic Front delegates continually expressed disdain and disgust toward the Hutu Rwandan negotiators. They considered the Hutu tribe inferior to themselves.

In contrast to its aggressive involvement in conflict resolution in Ethiopia, Angola, and Mozambique, the Bush administration's posture toward the Rwanda conflict was essentially passive, on the margins of the OAU mediation effort. In retrospect, the Bush administration could have taken a much tougher line with President Museveni when the RPF invasion began in October 1990. It could have blatantly accused him of surrogate war and applied pressure to bring the RPF back to Uganda, while at the same time increasing pressure on Habyarimana to allow the refugees to return. It was definitely a missed opportunity.[11]

Enter the Clinton Administration

When the Clinton administration came into office in January 1993, the Arusha negotiations were still in progress, with no early end in sight. Official US observer David Rawson was appointed ambassador to Rwanda. His hosts did not necessarily appreciate his fluency in the Kinyarwanda language. At one point, President Habyarimana, only half joking, told me that Ambassador Rawson was causing embarrassment, because the Rwandans could not say anything confidential in his presence.

The Clinton policy continued the Bush policy of watchful waiting for the results of the Arusha negotiations. Meanwhile, a ceasefire was in effect. It was fascinating that the Tanzanian diplomat leading the mediation was addressed as "Ambassador Washington," his real name.

On August 4, 1993, the Arusha talks finally reached an agreement, which provided for a transition to an eventual democratic election. To allow the Rwandan Patriotic Front to transition from an armed insurgent group to a political party, the Arusha agreement authorized the RPF to send political party officials to reside in the capital city of Kigali, along with their armed security. This part of the agreement was successfully implemented. The Arusha Accords also gave the RPF 40 percent of the army and half of the future cabinet, even though the Tutsi ethnic group represented only 15 percent of the population.[12]

The agreement also called for a small UN peacekeeping force of 5,000 troops, stationed near the capital city under the command of a Canadian officer, General Roméo Dallaire. The force was called the United Nations Assistance Mission for Rwanda (UNAMIR).

In January 1994, most observers had reached the conclusion that the Arusha Accords were not viable. In a hypothetical free and fair election, neither the Rwandan Patriotic Front nor the majority party of President Habyarimana could possibly hope to win. The Ugandan Tutsi invaders could not win elections in a majority-Hutu voting population. Nor could the ruling party of government win, because it had become a family fiefdom of the president. The majority Hutus no longer had confidence in the regime. The main conclusion was that both the government and the RPF had an incentive to look for a nondemocratic solution to the conflict and were essentially in a period of regrouping prior to the war starting up again.

In the Bureau of African Affairs, the reaction to the gloomy consensus was, above all, not to panic and to hope for the best.

The Rwandan Genocide Begins

On April 6, 1994, seven months into the implementation period of the Arusha Accords, President Habyarimana was killed in an airplane crash. It was not an accident. He was returning from an OAU meeting in Tanzania with Burundi's president Cyprien Ntaryamira in an aircraft with a French crew. Ground-to-air missiles of unknown origin shot down the aircraft.

The deliberate assassination of the two presidents effectively ended the Arusha peace process. Within a day, ethnic extremists in the Rwandan regime launched a previously planned campaign of genocide to kill as many ethnic Tutsis as possible. Bands of party youth and military thugs roamed the countryside murdering Tutsis, while radio propaganda urged ordinary Hutus to find their machetes and go out and kill Tutsis on their own. In short, "You are authorized and encouraged to kill your neighbor."

For their part, the Rwandan Patriotic Front resumed their full battle mode and started advancing toward the capital city of Kigali. The civil war had expanded into total ethnic conflict.

After the Hutu extremists murdered some Belgian troops, the Belgian government removed all of their troops, who were members of the UNAMIR contingent. In New York, the Security Council's first reaction was to demand that the blue helmets in UNAMIR be removed from harm's way. UNAMIR commander Dallaire, however, sought reinforcements so that he could try to prevent the spread of genocide. Instead, his force was reduced from 4,500 to 250 troops. One company of UNAMIR troops, from Ghana, refused to leave and managed to protect several thousand Tutsis in a soccer stadium.

Determined to do something about the genocide, UN Secretary-General Boutros Boutros-Ghali communicated with African governments, requesting any available troops for a peace enforcement mission. He received commitments for 5,500 troops. During the third week of April, the Secretary-General requested the Security Council to authorize sending this force under Chapter VII of the UN Charter. It was during the debate over this request that the impact on US policy of the Black Hawk Down disaster in Somalia a year earlier became evident.

The United States Stonewalls the UN Security Council

During the Security Council debate, the statements made by the US permanent representative, Ambassador Madeleine Albright, were clearly designed to discourage and delay intervention in Rwanda. Her first statement was to claim that there were "insufficient funds" to support the recommended military intervention. Ambassador Albright and all other US government spokespersons were under instructions not to speak of "genocide" in public statements. The only term they could use was "acts of genocide."[13]

The same evening as Ambassador Albright's statement, I was invited to join a panel on the *PBS NewsHour* television program. In the discussion about unfolding events in Rwanda, I said I could not believe that Ambassador Albright was serious in her claim that there were insufficient funds available for the purpose of stopping a genocide. At that point I was six months into my retirement from the Foreign Service.

After it became obvious that the United States was embarrassing itself by remaining negative toward any effort to save the Tutsis who were still alive, the United States agreed to vote for a resolution authorizing a force of 5,500 to go to Rwanda to try to stop the fighting.[14] But even then, the United States managed to drag its feet. Because only the United States had the necessary airlift to move troops rapidly to Rwanda from different countries in Africa, it effectively controlled the timing of the entire operation.

First, the United States insisted that the UN Secretary-General provide an operational plan. To assist him, the Pentagon sent a team to work with the UN military planners. This took a precious two weeks. Then the question of payment for the transportation was raised. The United States insisted that the UN finance the transport, but the necessary funds were not immediately available. By mid-June, arrangements had still not been made.

The US delay on transporting the UN troops so exasperated the French government that President François Mitterrand decided to send 2,500 of his own troops as an interim force prior to the eventual arrival of the UN force. France sought and received UN Security Council approval on June 22, 1994, and immediately sent its force. The French objective was to establish a safe zone in southwestern Rwanda within which Tutsis could escape the genocide.[15] The French called their move Operation Turquoise and managed to save many thousands of Tutsi lives between their arrival and the final victory of the RPF in Kigali on July 17, 1994.

Because of that RPF victory, approximately one million Hutus decided to leave Rwanda for fear of Tutsi revenge. Many of them departed Rwanda for neighboring Zaire through the French safe zone. In the aftermath of Operation Turquoise, the Hutu refugees ended up in camps just across the border in Zaire.

The French government was accused of complicity in the escape of many Hutu extremist *génocidaires* through their safe zone, and certainly a good number did escape that way. But the intent was clearly to save Tutsi lives. The French forces could not stop all refugees and question them as to their political affiliations. In any event, most of the extremists escaped directly across the border into Zaire before the arrival of the Rwandan Patriotic Front forces.

The RPF's final victory came before the United States could get its act together and transport the authorized UN rescue force. The gigantic Hutu refugee population sitting perilously close to the Rwanda border in Zaire created a new security problem for the Central African subregion. As for Washington, the US failure to even attempt to stop the genocide instantly tarnished the Clinton administration's image, especially in Africa. To the American public, especially within the academic and humanitarian communities, Clinton's decision to prevent an intervention in Rwanda left a sour taste. The number of Tutsis presumed killed in the genocide varies. My own estimate is about 350,000. Other estimates go as high as 800,000.

Afterward, a lingering question persisted. The UN Secretary-General had not asked the United States to send troops to Rwanda. He had recruited 5,500 African troops. All he wanted from the United States was urgent transportation. Why was the Clinton administration so reticent? The US military convincingly used the "slippery slope" argument. African troops would have considerable difficulty dealing with the complex situation in Rwanda. Underlying the actual genocide was a continuing civil war between the Rwandan Patriotic Front, supported by Uganda, and the Rwandan regime that was continuing to receive arms and training from the French. The African force under UN auspices would run into considerable trouble, according to this argument, requiring the United States to send backup forces to their rescue. After the debacle of the downing of the Black Hawks in Somalia a year earlier,

President Clinton could not take the political risk of having to send US military units back to Africa after such a brief interval.

According to my sources in the State Department at the time, two key persons on the National Security Council staff, Ambassador Don Steinberg and NSC Human Rights Director Susan Rice, argued forcefully that the United States should stop blocking the dispatch of a UN force to Rwanda and actually assist it. The total blockage apparently came from Anthony Lake, President Clinton's national security adviser.

On the positive side, US policy toward the Rwandan genocide stimulated considerable debate as to the correct approach to genocide. The entire concept of the "responsibility to protect" began to mature as a result of this debate. In his final year in office, President Clinton said: "If the world community has the power to stop it, we ought to stop genocide and ethnic cleansing."[16]

On March 28, 1998, Clinton made a brief stop in Rwanda during a tour of Africa. In his remarks at the airport, Clinton issued an apology for his decision in 1994 not to intervene to stop the genocide.[17]

Fallout from the Rwandan Genocide Destabilizes Zaire

The RPF victory on July 17, 1994, settled the question of control of power in Rwanda. The Tutsi minority was back in charge for an indefinite period. The million Hutu refugees who had departed for asylum across the border in Zaire were grouped into five separate camps, with the help of the UN High Commission for Refugees. The Hutu extremists of the fallen Rwandan government quickly controlled these camps and wasted no time in organizing guerrilla raids into Rwanda. Zaire government troops did not hesitate to sell arms to the extremists. Zaire's President Mobutu had been a close friend and ally of the late Rwandan president Habyarimana and was not opposed to undercover assistance to the Hutu fighters.[18]

The UN High Commission for Refugees had difficulty coping with the refugee situation. Normally, refugee camps are supposed to be situated no closer than fifty miles from the border of their countries of origin, but there was no way the UNHCR could enforce this in Zaire against the will of the Mobutu regime.

At the time of the RPF invasion of Rwanda from Uganda on October 1, 1990, Lieutenant-Colonel Paul Kagame, the RPF commander, was a student at the US Military Command and General Staff College in Fort Leavenworth, Kansas, where he had been enrolled as a Ugandan military officer since July 1990. Within days of the invasion, Kagame requested early release so that he could return to Uganda to participate in the liberation of Rwanda, his ancestral home.[19]

The original commander of the RPF was General Fred Rwigyema, a son of Rwandan Tutsi refugees, who had risen to the position of deputy commander of the army of Uganda. There could be no greater proof that President Museveni was totally in support of this operation than Rwigyema's position in the Ugandan army. Shortly after the start of the invasion, Rwigyema was mysteriously killed by a "sniper." Kagame had requested early release from the US military school in order to take command after Rwigyema's death. After the RPF took power in Kigali, Kagame demonstrated his keen political instincts by installing Pasteur Bizimungu, a Hutu, as president. Kagame became vice president but continued to hold the real power behind the scene.

Not long after the RPF government was installed, President Bizimungu complained to the international community about the constant attacks from the refugee camps in Zaire. By early 1996, the Rwandan government was really fed up. That spring, Vice President Kagame told US secretary of defense William Perry: "If the international community does not get a handle on it, Rwanda will have to."[20]

The Rwandan Army Destroys the Camps and Moves Against Mobutu

On October 27, 1996, elements of the Seventh Battalion of the Rwandan army crossed into Zaire and attacked one of the five refugee camps. This was the beginning of the end of the refugee camps. The Rwandan government's approach to the refugees was to urge them to return home. Most of the refugees, about 800,000, just crossed the border and walked back to their villages. The remainder, about 200,000, led by the Hutu extremists, went westward, deep into the Zaire rainforest, headed toward the provincial capital, Kisangani, at the beginning of the navigable section of the long Congo River. It was this latter group that considerably complicated the security situation in the eastern Zaire subregion.

The US government's view of the Rwandan action to destroy the refugee camps can be summed up as "a wink and a nod." With the Zaire government cooperating with the extremists in the refugee camps, there was no way the international community could solve the problem. The Rwandan army action provided the only solution possible.

At the same time that the Rwandan army attacked and destroyed the refugee camps, a longtime anti-Mobutu rebel fighter based in Tanzania, Laurent Desiré Kabila, invaded Zaire with several thousand armed troops. Kabila called his movement the Alliance of Democratic Forces for the Liberation of Congo (AFDL). His troops were anti-Mobutu Congolese, mostly from the Tutsi ethnic group, along with volunteers from Rwanda, Burundi, and Uganda. Initially, the Rwandan and Ugandan governments denied any knowledge of the AFDL, but they later acknowledged that the movement had their full support.[21]

While the Rwandan military invasion was designed to destroy the refugee camps, the AFDL invasion was designed to overthrow the Mobutu regime in Kinshasa. The US reaction to this was silence. Anti-Mobutu guerrilla operations based in Tanzania, Uganda, and Angola had occurred with regularity throughout the mid-1980s. The US response to all of these had been to help Mobutu repel them. This time, though, the United States said nothing, thereby signaling, "No objection."

The beginning of the end of the United States–Mobutu special relationship actually started in the final year of the Bush administration. After the 1992 election in Angola, the United States had stopped supporting the UNITA insurgency in Angola and thus no longer needed access to Zaire's airbases.

The difference between the Bush and Clinton administrations was that Bush remained friendly toward his old friend Mobutu until the end of his administration, while the Clinton people had nothing but total disdain for the corrupt dictator and were hoping for, and looking forward to, his departure.

The Kabila Insurgency Advances Toward Kinshasa

The Kabila insurgency had the overthrow of Mobutu as president of Zaire as its first objective. But on the way to Kinshasa, their secondary objective, as required by their Rwandan sponsors, was to catch up to the Hutu refugees who refused to return to Rwanda when their camps were destroyed in October 1996. Among those refugees were the Hutu extremists who had organized and conducted the 1994 genocide. The Rwandan government wanted them caught and eliminated. Just by the simple act of refusing to return to Rwanda, any Hutu refugee who sought refuge in the Zaire rainforest was under suspicion of having engaged in genocide.

The United States did not have a strong position on the fighting in eastern Zaire that resulted from Kabila's AFDL invasion and subsequent insurgency. On November 15, 1996, the United States voted for UN Security Council Resolution 1080, calling for a ceasefire and the arrival of a temporary multinational force. Next came UN Security Council Resolution 1097 of February 1997, calling for a ceasefire, the withdrawal of external forces and mercenaries, and the opening of a national sovereignty dialogue. On this basis, South African president Nelson Mandela, aided by his vice president, Thabo Mbeki, offered to mediate between Kabila and Mobutu. But Kabila was reluctant. He wanted total victory and the departure of Mobutu.

In February 1997, approximately 60,000 Hutu refugees were temporarily settled in the town of Tingi Tingi, located approximately 140 miles southeast of the provincial capital, Kisangani. On March 2, 1977, Kabila's army, along with a Rwandan troop contingent, engaged in a full assault on Tingi Tingi. From that point on, accounts differ as to exactly what happened, but it appears certain that wholesale massacres took place.

According to my own sources in the Congolese army at the time, the Rwandan military separated the inhabitants of Tingi Tingi into two groups, Rwandan Hutu refugees and regular Congolese inhabitants of the town and surrounding region. The Congolese citizens were not bothered. But the Hutu refugees were massacred. The local Congolese witnessed the massacre, thereby ensuring that the true story would come out. The nature of the action, the mass killing of Rwandan Hutu because of their ethnicity, constituted genocide in my view.

The accounts of genocide triggered an investigation by the UN Commission on Human Rights, whose report concluded, "There is little doubt that Mr. Kabila's forces committed atrocities as they marched across the Congo." But there was no formal accusation of genocide.[22] An American named Reed Brody, who was one of the UN inspectors, corroborated the UN report. In an interview on Radio France International on March 14, 1997, Brody accused Kabila's army of mass killing at Tingi Tingi.[23]

Ironically, the Hutu extremists, who had been with the refugees moving west into the interior of the Congo, escaped capture at Tingi Tingi. Most of them were able to cross into the neighboring Central African Republic or Republic of the Congo.

After Kabila's army passed Kisangani on their way toward Kinshasa, the government of Angola decided to furnish assistance. Angola had every reason to want to see Mobutu leave power. He had been assisting the internal insurgent movement UNITA, which was still at war with the Angolan government five years after renouncing the results of the 1992 election.

As a result of the combined assistance of the governments of Uganda, Rwanda, and Angola, Laurent Kabila and his AFDL army were able to force Mobutu to leave the Congo for exile on May 17, 1997, departing from his tribal residence in Gbadolite in the north. Earlier in May, President Clinton's special envoy for Zaire/Congo, former governor Bill Richardson, had visited Mobutu with a special message from Clinton urging Mobutu to depart. The message told Mobutu what he had already surmised. No help was available from his old friend, the United States.[24]

Immediately after Mobutu's departure, Kabila traveled from his home base in Lubumbashi, the copper mining capital in southeastern Zaire/Congo, to Kinshasa, where he proclaimed himself president of the Congo. He declared that the name "Zaire" was henceforth abolished, and the nation returned to its original name at independence, the Democratic Republic of the Congo.

In terms of international law, the Rwandan government was in a state of blatant violation. It had invaded the Congo to destroy the refugee camps and supported and accompanied a Congolese rebel group in an insurgency that overthrew the recognized government of Zaire, making Rwanda clearly guilty of illegitimate cross-border aggression. In this particular case, US policy viewed the Rwandan action as essentially an act of mercy that relieved the people of the Congo from the yoke of the corrupt Mobutu regime. There was absolutely no US objection to this action, neither public nor private. Unfortunately, Washington's general satisfaction with Rwanda's action tended to fade into cynicism after only a short time.

A Bad Start for Kabila's Relations with the United States

The State Department was fully inclined to have good relations with the Kabila government from the very start in May 1997. The Clinton administration had demonstrated a determination to see Mobutu leave power, so their credentials with Kabila should have been positive. The UN investigation into the massacres at Tingi Tingi was still ongoing, so the United States tended to downplay that event in an effort to establish good relations with Kabila.

But Kabila had lived through three decades of observing the United States provide support to Mobutu against various Congolese insurgent groups. US support to Mobutu had been bipartisan. Both Democratic and Republican administrations had provided him with military support when Congolese rebels threatened his regime.

President Laurent Kabila could not find it in his heart to trust the Clinton administration, despite all the goodwill it demonstrated. He could not trust any US government. President Clinton sent his special representative, Reverend Jesse Jackson, to Kinshasa, but Kabila refused to meet with him. During a visit to Kinshasa by Secretary of State Madeleine Albright, Kabila showed obvious disdain during their joint press conference. He was also reportedly rude to Assistant Secretary of State Susan Rice and National Security Council senior Africa adviser Gayle Smith when they visited. Nevertheless, Kabila was invited to President Clinton's meeting with "new African leaders" during his tour of Africa in March 1998. The United States gave him the benefit of the doubt.[25]

Kabila's Internal Political Image Becomes Tarnished

When Kabila declared himself president of the Congo on March 17, 1997, Rwandan "advisers" immediately surrounded him. Most of Mobutu's military officers had gone into exile, and the Rwandan military filled the vacuum. The chief of staff of the Congolese army was James Kabarebe, one of Rwanda's highest-ranking generals. Rwandan intelligence also took over that function from Mobutu's former colleagues.

The Rwandan Tutsi advisers were not discreet. They were visibly arrogant. They confiscated apartments and vehicles. It was not long before the Congolese population branded Kabila as a tool of the Rwandans. His position was becoming increasingly embarrassing.

As the Rwandans were tightening their control over Kinshasa, their military in the eastern regions never really left after destroying the refugee camps in October 1996. Those who did not accompany Kabila to Kinshasa remained to take control of artisanal mining operations in the provinces of South Kivu, North Kivu, and Ituri. This enabled Rwandan businesspeople to engage in the profitable export through Rwanda of Congolese gold, columbium-tantalum (coltan), and tin ore. The net result was the diversion of significant mining revenue from the Congo to Rwanda.

While the United States was making a less than successful effort to befriend Kabila, it had become quite friendly with the new Rwandan regime, especially with Vice President Paul Kagame. Consequently, Washington did not view the Rwandan chokehold over the Congo's security and economy as a source of concern. But it increasingly became a matter of concern for Kabila.

Kabila Expels the Rwandans

By July 1998, Kabila's political situation had become untenable. He had to do something dramatic. He decided to expel all of his Rwandan "advisers." Army Chief of Staff James Kabarebe was the first to be fired, on July 14. By July 28, all of the Rwandan and Ugandan military and intelligence people had returned to their respective countries.

Needless to say, the Rwandans were not happy. In addition to their total loss of influence and control in Kinshasa, the Congolese people had begun to hurt Congolese Tutsi communities in acts of revenge.

Knowing the sorry state of the Congolese military, James Kabarebe decided on a plan to rapidly retake power in Kinshasa. This was to be done in two phases. First, anti-Kabila Congolese dissidents were recruited to form an insurgency similar to the one that Kabila himself had formed to invade his country in 1996. This new group called itself the Rally for Congolese Democracy (RCD) and included a number of well-known intellectuals. Second, Kabarebe decided on a bold effort to capture the capital city, Kinshasa, through a quick strike, destroy the Kabila regime, and install the RCD.

In early August 1998, the chief of the military office of the president of Angola, General Manuel Hélder Vieira Dias, popularly known as Kopelipa, was informed about the Rwandan effort to recruit Congolese politicians to oppose Kabila. He was wondering why the Rwandans, who were allies of Angola in the military action to overthrow Mobutu in 1996, had not kept him informed. So, he called General Kabarebe to ask what was happening. The response was that nothing was happening. There were no plans to do anything in the Congo.

On August 10, 1998, Kabarebe and 500 Rwandan and Ugandan soldiers commandeered three civilian aircraft and flew to Kitona airbase in the extreme western region of the Congo, about 120 miles from Kinshasa. About a hundred Congolese troops there had earlier been undergoing training by the Rwandans and were easily persuaded to join the rebellion.[26]

At that point, Washington was totally distracted by the horrendous terrorist bombings of the US embassies in Nairobi, Kenya, and Dar es Salaam, Tanzania, and thus not focusing on the military action in the Congo.

After taking over Kitona airbase, the Rwandan-Ugandan column moved eastward toward Kinshasa, with little opposition. Within a week, they had captured the INGA electric power station that controlled power in the capital city. Toward the end of August, they were on the verge of capturing Ndjili Airport on the outskirts of the capital city. At that point, the Angolan air force and army intervened and drove the rebels back toward the Atlantic Ocean in the port city of Matadi. Rwanda sent aircraft to the Matadi airport to pick up the troops and fly them to airfields in northern Angola controlled by the UNITA insurgent movement. From there, they were exfiltrated back to Rwanda.

Africa's "World War" Starts and Expands

That the Rwandans had not kept the Angolans informed and were working with the UNITA insurgents in Angola caused great suspicion on the part of the Angolans, who decided to intervene on the side of President Kabila. However, the defeat of the Rwandan-Ugandan invaders on the outskirts of Kinshasa did not constitute the end of the war. On the contrary, Rwanda and Uganda were occupying three mineral-producing provinces in the east—Ituri, North Kivu, and South Kivu—and their combined armies were threatening to enter the important copper-mining province of Katanga. This was the beginning of a major conflict that came to be known as Africa's "world war" or "continental war."[27]

The Congo was a member of the Southern African Development Community (SADC). Kabila asked for a summit meeting of SADC to address the conflict in the eastern regions of his country. He asked for military assistance to push out the invaders. Three southern African governments—Angola, Namibia, and Zimbabwe—decided to send troops, because they considered the Rwandan-Ugandan action, correctly, to be an illegal act of aggression against a SADC member state. Other friends of the Congo, Sudan and Chad, also agreed to help Kabila fight the invaders.

The war was not a conflict among massed armies but rather one of much movement of hit-and-run mobile units. Nevertheless, the result was catastrophic. Ordinary Africans in the eastern Congo could not plant their crops, nor did they have access to basic medical care. Military units on both sides were exceptionally destructive of indigenous populations. The extraordinary death toll during the course of the war between 1998 and the final ceasefire in 2002 was estimated to be 5 million. The toll in Congolese human life was six times higher than that of the Rwandan genocide.

UN Ambassador Holbrooke Takes Charge of US Africa Policy

During the final two years of the Clinton administration, the State Department's Bureau of African Affairs was not active in the search for peace in the Congo. But Ambassador Richard Holbrooke, US permanent representative to the United Nations, decided to do something about this crisis in Central Africa. Holbrooke had earlier achieved a major diplomatic victory in mediating a solution to the war in Bosnia in 1995 through the famous Dayton Accords.

In January 2000, the United States held the presidency of the UN Security Council. Ambassador Holbrooke, without reference to the Department of State, decided to initiate a multilateral peace effort to end the war in the Congo. He started by sending out invitations to a summit meeting of the nations involved in the Congo war to engage in negotiations at the Security Council, under his mediation.

A major impediment to Holbrooke's project was the refusal of Congolese president Laurent Kabila to come to New York for the discussions. About six months earlier, a mutual Congolese friend had invited me to come to Kinshasa to meet with Kabila. After becoming acquainted, Kabila said that he wanted to hire my consulting firm to help establish his new diplomatic mission in Washington. He wanted a totally clean slate and had appointed as his ambassador to the United States Professor Faida Mitifu, who was then on the faculty of Georgia State University. Mitifu had been one of the leaders of the anti-Mobutu movement within the Congolese diaspora in the United States. Totally inexperienced in both government and diplomacy, she needed experienced advice for a year or two to establish her embassy. I accepted President Kabila's assignment.

When Kabila initially refused to come to New York at Ambassador Holbrooke's invitation, Ambassador Mitifu asked me to intervene. I spent several hours on the phone with Kabila in an effort to persuade him to participate. I emphasized that his presence would be good for his image and might actually help end the war. Finally, he said, "OK, I will come to New York; but if those American friends of Mobutu manage to kill me, it will be your fault."

Holbrooke's summit meeting did not end the war, but he succeeded in arranging a substantive meeting between Kagame and Kabila, who both promised to continue the dialogue. What was striking in terms of diplomatic practice was that the US permanent representative to the United Nations took charge of the Congo crisis issue on behalf of the United States without any reference to the State Department's Bureau of African Affairs.

On January 16, 2001, President Laurent Kabila was assassinated by one of his security guards. The wartime allies got together and decided that Kabila's son Joseph would succeed him as interim head of state. The war continued into the George W. Bush administration, which made a significant contribution to a ceasefire and eventual peace arrangement.

The Islamic Government of Sudan Introduces Terrorism to Africa

The National Islamic Front Takes Power in Sudan

From the time of Sudan's independence from England on January 1, 1956, its Arab-speaking minority has ruled the country. The majority of Sudanese are Muslim. (Since the secession of mostly Christian South Sudan in 2011, the percentage of Muslims in Sudan has increased significantly.)

At the same time, the majority of Sudanese speak African languages, not Arabic. Until August 1989, the Arab-speaking minority practiced a form of democracy within their own ruling community. There were regular elections. Various political parties competed. There was a free press. There were free labor unions.

In August 1989, there was a military coup in Sudan, planned and organized by one of the Arab political parties, the National Islamic Front (NIF), which had consistently won only about 15 percent of the vote in periodic elections. As of August 1989, although the military was in power, political elites within the NIF were deciding policy. In particular, Islamic ideologue and NIF chairperson Hassan al-Turabi, a graduate of a French university with a doctorate in law, was the chief policymaker.[28]

Hassan al-Turabi aspired to be a leader of revolutionary Islam worldwide. Internally, he turned Sudan into a police state, abolishing the free press, political parties, and civil society. Externally, he used

Sudanese diplomatic facilities to send assistance to Islamist extremist groups in Algeria and Egypt. He also encouraged Middle Eastern extremist groups to establish branch offices in Khartoum. As of November 1992, almost every Middle Eastern extremist group had an office in Khartoum. The George H. W. Bush administration maintained normal relations with the NIF regime, despite its support for extremist activities in the Arab world. The administration's main interest in Sudan was the civil war in the southern region, where the African population, mostly Christians and animists, suffered from malnutrition, disease, and warfare against civilians. The administration's efforts to mediate in that war never came to fruition.[29]

Sudan-Based Terrorism Hits the United States

On February 26, 1993, terrorists exploded a bomb in the underground garage of the World Trade Center in New York City, killing six persons, injuring several more, and causing considerable damage. The act was traced to Sudan, where a Saudi citizen named Osama bin Laden had his headquarters. His organization was called al-Qaeda, meaning "The Base." His purpose was to kill as many Americans as possible in order to punish the United States for sending military units to profane the holy land of Saudi Arabia during the 1990–1991 Gulf War.[30]

Bin Laden started his war against "infidels" in 1989 in Afghanistan, where he received a warm welcome from the radical Islamist Taliban regime. He had gone there to join the fight against the Soviet invaders, who retreated in 1988. He returned to his home in Saudi Arabia in 1990, where he remained until the government decided that his activities were too detrimental. He was expelled in 1991 to Sudan, where he found a permissive atmosphere under the patronage of Hassan al-Turabi. With lots of money from his rich father's construction business in Saudi Arabia, bin Laden established a training camp there for guerrilla fighters. He also looked for opportunities to hurt the United States.

His first act was to finance the World Trade Center bombing in New York City in February 1993. The extensive negative publicity about this action caused the Sudanese government in June 1996 to expel bin Laden, who then returned to his original base in Afghanistan.

In August 1998, terrorists bombed the US embassies in Nairobi and Dar es Salaam, with great loss of life and considerable material damage. These acts were traced to bin Laden in Afghanistan and his cell in Nairobi.

Shortly after the embassy bombings, President Clinton ordered cruise missile strikes on two targets: a pharmaceutical plant in Khartoum where it was believed poison gas was being manufactured, and a terrorist training camp in Afghanistan financed by Osama bin Laden. The plant in Khartoum turned out to be clean, but President Clinton's attack sent a signal to the Sudanese that they needed to get rid of the various extremist offices. The Sudanese government shut down the terrorist offices and stopped supporting terrorist operations in Africa. The Clinton administration had applied economic sanctions against Sudan while bin Laden was still there. After his departure, the administration decided not to lift the sanctions, and they remained on the books until 2017.[31]

The Sudanese government's repressive warfare against the Sudanese Christians living in the southern part of the country continued unabated, with much criticism from human rights groups around the world. It was the George W. Bush administration that was later able to make an important contribution to the resolution of that conflict in 2006.

Clinton's Africa Policy Ends on a High Note: Free Trade

In 1994, early in the Clinton administration, Congressman Jim McDermott, a Washington state Democrat, organized an unofficial nonpartisan brainstorming session about Africa's sluggish economic growth. Though not a member of the Foreign Relations Committee, he had been a Foreign Service doctor who served at the US embassy in the Congo and maintained a keen interest in Africa.

McDermott said that Africa was still lagging behind the rest of the developing world despite four decades of considerable foreign aid from the United States, Europe, Japan, and the World Bank group. The brainstorming group's mandate was to come up with new ideas.

After several sessions, the group reached consensus on the importance of attracting private investment, both African and foreign, as the motor of economic growth. One way to accomplish that was to provide incentives to Africa to sell manufactured products internationally. The group rallied around the slogan "Trade not Aid."

The final recommendation was to offer Africa a nonreciprocal free trade arrangement. In other words, anything that Africa could produce would be allowed to enter the United States duty-free. With such an arrangement, investors would find it profitable to establish manufacturing facilities in Africa to make products that they could sell in the United States competitively.

Congressman McDermott liked the proposal and took it to the chairman of the House Ways and Means Committee, Charles Rangel, Democrat of New York. That committee is responsible for the entire taxation sector, including customs duties. Rangel liked the concept of giving duty-free entry to African products, but balked at the slogan "Trade not Aid." At his insistence, the slogan was changed to "Trade and Aid." Rangel consulted Republican members of the committee and found general enthusiasm for the concept.

Legislative language was completed and approved in 1995. The entire process was delayed, because the Clinton administration was sensitive to American organized labor's fear of any proposals that would facilitate the entry to the United States of goods produced by foreign cheap labor. For that reason, final enactment of the legislation was delayed until 2000, the administration's last year in office.

On May 18, 2000, President Clinton signed into law the African Growth and Opportunity Act (AGOA).[32] This legislation constituted the first "new idea" in United States–Africa economic relations since the early 1960s. It was enacted initially for fifteen years and subsequently renewed until 2025. Any discussion of United States–Africa relations since Clinton highlights AGOA as one of the US government's key achievements.[33]

In terms of the practice of foreign policy, AGOA serves as an excellent example of the major role that members of Congress and congressional committees frequently play.

Overall, the Clinton administration could not look back at its Africa policy with much satisfaction. The clouds of the Rwandan genocide and Africa's "continental war" were sources of major policy distress that remained in memory decades later.

13

George W. Bush:
2001–2009

When President George W. Bush addressed a joint session of the US Congress on September 20, 2001, he talked about his three priorities in foreign and national security policy:

- The United States will engage in preventive war as a way of deterring potential attacks.
- The United States will take unilateral action, if necessary, to protect the American people.
- The United States will spread democracy and freedom around the world, emphasizing free markets, free trade, and individual liberty.[1]

On the basis of this doctrine, President Bush's policy toward Africa turned out to be one of the most creative of any presidency, both before and after his two-term mandate.

Fighting the HIV/AIDS Pandemic and Malaria in Africa

At the beginning of the Bush administration, Africa suffered from a massive epidemic of HIV/AIDS. In some countries, such as Botswana and South Africa, one in four adults were infected.

In May 2001, the Bush administration allocated $200 million to the UN Global Fund to Fight AIDS, Tuberculosis, and Malaria. This was just the beginning. In 2003, President Bush and Congress established the President's Emergency Plan for AIDS Relief (PEPFAR), funded at $15 billion and destined mostly for sub-Saharan Africa.

By the time of the 2008 presidential election, 3 million Africans were receiving lifetime treatment with AIDS medicine. In addition, 57 million Africans had been tested for HIV. Significant amounts of money were also allocated to the prevention of HIV, with an emphasis on the distribution of condoms. The PEPFAR program continued well beyond the end of the Bush administration into the Obama and Trump administrations.[2]

The biggest killer of children in sub-Saharan Africa has been, and continues to be, malaria. There is no cure for malaria. The main antimalarial activity must be prevention. In June 2005, the Bush administration introduced the President's Malaria Initiative. This program had an initial budget of $1.2 billion over five years, with an emphasis on insecticide-treated bed nets and indoor spraying. Subsequently, the administration continued its support to the UN Global Fund to Fight AIDS, Tuberculosis, and Malaria.[3]

The Millennium Challenge Corporation

The most innovative program derived from the Bush Doctrine has been the Millennium Challenge Corporation (MCC). The Millennium Challenge Act of 2003 established a new US government agency designed to revolutionize US policy toward the promotion of economic development in the developing world. The MCC operates worldwide. It is not exclusive to Africa, but many countries in Africa participate in the program.

The concept behind the MCC is that the good performers are the ones most likely to benefit from development assistance. Therefore, devise a set of criteria designed to determine who the good performers are. In addition, allow nongovernmental expert organizations to rate each government against these criteria.

Under a criterion of economic freedom, governments are rated on their investment in people, their protection of private property, their promotion of market forces, and their respect for workers' rights. For sociopolitical issues, the governments are rated on political pluralism, transparency and accountability, and investment in people through education and health programs. Other criteria include control of corruption, human rights, and just and democratic governance.

Ratings are calculated according to scores assigned by different institutions. For example, the World Bank publishes an annual volume titled *Doing Business*. Every government in the world is rated as to the ease or difficulty of establishing and running a business. Freedom House, a nongovernmental organization (NGO), provides ratings on political pluralism, degree of democratization, and such things as freedom of the press. The NGO Transparency International provides annual ratings on corruption, as reported by companies trying to do business in different nations.

Eligible countries are low- or lower-middle-income. Once selected as to eligibility, the MCC negotiates a compact that promises a certain amount of funding, usually between $200 million and $500 million, in return for a feasible plan for the development of such economic sectors as power, transportation, or vital infrastructure.

The MCC program has been an enormous success in Africa. As a result, African leaders and intellectuals often cite George W. Bush as "Africa's best American president." Some examples of successful MCC program recipients include Benin, which now has a modern port that serves as a trade hub for several countries in West Africa; Senegal, which has a new international airport that serves as the main airline hub for West Africa; and Cape Verde, which is now on its way to becoming a totally renewable-energy country.

Debt Relief

The World Bank Group began major lending to sub-Saharan Africa through its International Development Association (IDA) soft-loan window during the second half of the 1970s. The soft-loan terms were truly soft. Repayment terms began with a ten-year grace period, followed by a rate of 1 percent for servicing the loan. To qualify for such lending, recipient countries were required to sign on to major economic reforms. Nevertheless, by the beginning of the twenty-first century, African debt to the World Bank had become unsustainable. Among the Group of Eight (G8) donor nations, the United States under the Bush administration became a champion of debt relief. Thus was born the debt relief program under the Heavily Indebted Poor Countries (HIPC) Initiative. As in predecessor programs, eligibility for HIPC status depended on evidence of increasingly sound economic policies. The Bush administration was an enthusiastic supporter of the HIPC designation from its very inception.[4] One of President Bush's last acts was to persuade the donor community to finance IDA lending to the point of being interest-free.

Saving the Forests of the Congo Basin

The second largest tropical forest in the world, after the Amazon rain-forest in Latin America, is the one in the Congo Basin, covering the Democratic Republic of the Congo, Gabon, Cameroon, and the Republic of the Congo (Brazzaville). Safeguarding the Congo Basin's forest is vital for the battle against climate change.

The Bush administration was one of the pioneers in the formation in September 2002 of the Congo Basin Forest Partnership (CBFP). Under the leadership of US secretary of state Colin Powell, the CBFP was launched that month at the Johannesburg World Summit on Sustainable Development. The objective of the initiative, which groups together forty nations, was to promote conservation and responsible management of the Congo Basin's tropical forests. The United States allocated $53 million to help finance the initiative and has contributed annually ever since. The US Congress wrote US participation into law through the Congo Basin Forest Partnership Act on February 12, 2004.[5]

Three Lingering, Devastating Conflicts

Congo's "Continental War"

The terrorist attacks of September 11, the Middle East, and weapons of mass destruction in Iraq were the Bush administration's most significant national security issues. But there were African issues that were also considered important and worthy of attention at high levels. When George W. Bush came into office in January 2001, three African conflicts were continuing to cause tremendous suffering among civilian populations.

The "continental war" in the Congo, which began in August 1998, showed no sign of abating. The Clinton administration had done virtually nothing to encourage a solution. On January 16, 2001, shortly before President Bush's inauguration, President Laurent Kabila was assassinated by one of his own security guards.

Early on in the Bush administration, Secretary of State Colin Powell took advantage of a visit to Washington by Rwandan president Paul Kagame to suggest that he remove his troops from the Congo, pursuant to an earlier agreement. As the entire Rwandan operation in the Congo had no basis in legitimacy, Kagame complied with Secretary Powell's recommendation. This led to a lengthy peace negotiation hosted by the government of South Africa in the resort town of Sun City.[6]

In 2002, a new constitution for the Congo was written and a new transitional government formed under the late Laurent Kabila's son Joseph. With a coalition of the major political parties, the transition lasted until 2006, when Joseph Kabila won the first postwar presidential election. US diplomats were observers during the Sun City negotiations and provided constructive suggestions, including the unamendable two-term presidential limit.

Colin Powell's initiative was a key catalytic factor in bringing the Congo's "continental war" to an end. It was unfortunate that the Clinton administration did not initiate its own process earlier, in view of the vast loss of lives that the conflict caused. Indeed, it is only fair to ask why the Clinton administration did not pressure the Rwandans to withdraw immediately after their illegal military invasion began in August 1998.

The Sudanese Civil War

Of particular interest was the civil war in the Sudan. George W. Bush won his first election by a narrow margin. Highly significant in his base of support were the votes of the evangelical Christian community. Since early in the George H. W. Bush administration, representatives of this community had been calling attention to the suffering of the African peoples of southern Sudan, adherents of Christian and animist faiths who accounted for approximately one-third of the Sudanese nation.

The people of southern Sudan had been engaged in a war for independence against the Arab-controlled government in Khartoum since 1983. Their political movement was called the Sudan People's Liberation Movement. Their grievances were many and valid. The government in Khartoum had never provided resources for the south in support of infrastructure, health services, or education. The south was truly a neglected, poverty-stricken region.

The George H. W. Bush administration had been concerned mainly with humanitarian relief for the south, because the Khartoum government periodically interrupted the movement of food supplies as part of their war strategy. Bush offered to mediate between the Khartoum government and the SPLM between 1989 and 1991. During that period, the Khartoum government, under the military rule of President Omar al-Bashir, was inclined to negotiate independence for the south, but the leader of the SPLM, Colonel John Garang de Mabior, was more interested in his vision of a united Sudan under the control of the African majority, comprising both Muslims and Christians. He rejected control of Sudan by the elites of the Arab minority. Garang missed an opportunity to win independence for his people, because at that time al-Bashir and his advisers felt that the south was not worth fighting for. This view prevailed before the prospect of major crude oil production in the south during the 1990s changed the political calculus.[7]

The Clinton administration was concerned mainly with the presence in Sudan of Middle Eastern terrorist and extremist groups, as noted in Chapter 12. In addition, the situation in the south was complicated by internal ethnic conflict within the SPLM, which the Khartoum regime encouraged and financed. SPLM leader John Garang of the Dinka ethnic group was opposed by Riek Machar, the leader of the Nuer ethnic group. Various nongovernmental groups, as well as interested congressional committees in the United States, made attempts to reconcile the two leaders. But this scenario effectively prevented the Clinton administration from attempting to mediate an end to the north-south conflict during its time in office.

George W. Bush and the evangelical Christians. When George W. Bush came into office, Republican political leaders from the evangelical Christian community immediately approached him to promote US intervention on behalf of the Christian population of southern Sudan. The most prominent of these advocates for southern Sudan was Senator James Inhofe, Republican of Oklahoma, who testified actively before the Senate Foreign Relations Committee. He also cosponsored the Sudan Peace Act, signed into law on October 21, 2002. This legislation accused the Sudan government of committing genocide that reportedly resulted in the deaths of 2 million Christian southerners since the beginning of the war in 1983.[8]

President Bush reacted to the pressure from Senator Inhofe in September 2001 by appointing former Republican senator John Danforth, an Episcopal minister, as his special presidential envoy for peace in Sudan. In cooperation with Britain and Norway, Ambassador Danforth arranged for peace talks between the government of Sudan and the

SPLM to be held under the auspices of the Intergovernmental Authority on Development (IGAD), an East African institution.

A decade earlier, the George H. W. Bush administration was concerned mainly with humanitarian relief for the south, because the Khartoum government periodically interrupted the movement of food supplies as part of its war strategy. In keeping with his emphasis on conflict resolution in Africa during his time in office between 1989 and 1993, George H. W. Bush offered to mediate between the Khartoum government and the SPLM. Negotiations began in Kenya in May 2002 and continued until December 2004. During this period, the conferees reached agreement on a number of protocols on various issues covering north-south relations during a six-year postwar transition period. These protocols addressed security arrangements, wealth sharing, power sharing, resolution of ongoing subregional conflicts, and implementation issues. The entire package was adopted as the Comprehensive Peace Agreement (CPA) on January 9, 2005, at the United Nations in New York.

Secretary of State Colin Powell signed as the witness for the United States.[9] Observers agreed that the George W. Bush administration played a key role, first in launching the negotiations, and second in achieving the agreement.

The core of the agreement consisted of a six-year transition period during which the people of southern Sudan would exercise self-government under nominal Sudanese sovereignty. The government of Sudan in Khartoum was reconstituted as a coalition government with ministers from the south as well as the north. SPLM chairman John Garang was named vice president of the coalition government. The United Nations Security Council voted to deploy a combined peacekeeping force of 10,000 military, police, and civilian experts. At the end of six years, the people of the south would hold a referendum to decide between independence or remaining in Sudan.[10]

For President Bush, the CPA fulfilled his promise to his evangelical Christian supporters to free southern Sudan's Christian population from decades of discrimination and repression on the part of the Arab government in Khartoum.

The Darfur Conflict in Parallel with CPA Negotiations

While the CPA negotiations were taking place in Kenya, another civil conflict raged in Darfur province in northwestern Sudan that was particularly horrendous in terms of human suffering. It was a conflict caused in part by climate change. Pastoral Arabic-speaking tribes in the drought-stricken northern segment of Darfur were driving south in search of food for their livestock. There they encountered sedentary, agricultural tribes of African-language speakers who violently resisted the invasion. This struggle became a major conflict, with the Arab Sudanese government supporting the pastoralists.

The Khartoum government helped organize an elite group of camel-riding Arab fighters called Janjaweed, who killed men, women, and children indiscriminately. Hundreds of thousands of civilians were killed, and millions were displaced. Because of the Sudanese government's support for the Janjaweed, the international community applied sanctions against Khartoum, while looking for ways to end the fighting. Eventually, the International Criminal Court (ICC) indicted Sudanese president Omar al-Bashir for crimes against humanity because of his government's support for acts of genocide in Darfur.[11]

The George W. Bush administration encouraged negotiations to end the Darfur conflict, although it was not involved directly. President Bush received some of the African agricultural resistance leaders in an effort to promote peace talks.

The Sudanese government's support for the killing of civilians in Darfur was only one of its many offenses. When Iraq invaded Kuwait in 1990, President al-Bashir came out in support of President Saddam Hussein's aggression. As a result, Saudi Arabia expelled 200,000 resident Sudanese guest workers.

In general, the Khartoum government badly needed peace in the south to begin to come out from under international pressure and sanctions. In addition, the start of major crude oil production in an area that straddled the north-south border required the increasingly expensive deployment of major Sudanese military protective forces. Southern rebel operations were making life difficult for the oil companies, thereby inhibiting full production. The CPA allowed a major expansion of oil production at a time of high prices, which benefited both the northern and southern governments.

Despite Khartoum's cooperation in the negotiations for southern self-determination, the Bush administration continued sanctions against the regime, begun under President Clinton, because of the atrocities being committed in Darfur.

CPA implementation. Implementing the CPA required international support. The United States was active in enacting resolutions at the UN

Security Council in 2005 that provided for a multidimensional UN peace support group, comprising 10,000 troops, 750 police, and 600 civilians. The government of Norway, one of the supporting troika members, along with the United States and the United Kingdom, agreed to hold a meeting of donor governments in Oslo to recruit support for the UN operation in the south. In addition, the United States opened an office in Juba, the principal city of the south.

The first four years of South Sudan's self-government evolved while the Bush administration was still in office. The euphoria generated by the CPA was such that the Bush foreign policy team failed to see the great tragedy unfolding before their very eyes. The UN security force saw what was happening, but the administration and governance of the new nation was not part of their mandate. South Sudan was destined to become a violent, ethnic-conflicted failed state even as it was being born. But it was the next US administration, under Barack Obama, that reaped the whirlwind.

Islamist Extremism Takes Root in Somalia

After the Clinton administration suffered the Black Hawk Down tragedy in Somalia during its first year in office, no one paid much attention to that nation. When the George W. Bush administration took office in January 2001, Somalia had been without a central government for ten years. Despite governmental anarchy, the Somali population was somehow surviving.

Various geographically divided clan warlords provided protection, but protection was not the same as governance. There were no schools, hospitals, or transportation facilities. The main airport and seaport in Mogadishu were closed. Life was nasty and dangerous.

In 1993, a new type of organization came into existence. In one of the neighborhoods of Mogadishu, a local leader named Sheikh Ali Dheere formed a civic-security-benevolent society that he called the Islamic Court. The role of the Islamic Court was to provide protection against the predatory warlords, who demanded a percentage of every transaction. In addition, the justice, education, and health services that the Islamic Court provided were dictated by sharia law. In its small enclave, the Islamic Court represented the return of a form of decent governance.

Following this example, other Mogadishu neighborhoods organized Islamic courts. After the year 2000, the courts expanded to villages outside the capital city. By 2005 there were a total of eleven Islamic courts, which confederated to form the Islamic Courts Union (ICU) and reopened the Mogadishu airport and seaport. After September 11, 2001, any entity bearing the word "Islamic" in its name was under suspicion in the United States. Nevertheless, the benefits to the people living within the jurisdiction of the Islamic courts were important enough to attract the support of many outsiders. In the United States, the debate within the Somali diaspora was lively, with the consensus concluding that the Islamic courts deserved the benefit of the doubt.[12]

In 2004, militants affiliated with al-Qaeda, Osama bin Laden's terrorist group, began to infiltrate the armed protective units of the Islamic courts. These militants came from a missionary group that infiltrated Somalia from Sudan, al-Ittihad al-Islamia (AIAI), under the leadership of Hassan Dahir Aweys. As the Islamic courts began to concentrate more on jihad, as opposed to local governance, they caught the attention of the Bush administration.

In early 2006, at the request of the State Department's Bureau of African Affairs, the CIA organized an alliance of warlords, the Alliance for the Restoration of Peace and Counter-Terrorism (ARPCT), and began a military operation against the ICU. The operation went badly for the US clients. The ICU defeated the ARPCT and thereby gained total control of the capital city of Mogadishu.

As the militants in the ICU continued to gain strength, the ICU was transformed into al-Shabaab (The Youth), the terrorist organization that since 2006 has terrorized Somalia, southern Kenya, and southern Ethiopia. At that point, the United States, having designated Somalia an Islamic terrorist–concentration country, promoted a resolution at the UN Security Council, on December 6, 2006, authorizing Ethiopia and other governments in the Horn to intervene militarily in Somalia against al-Shabaab. The rise of al-Shabaab provided a new priority focus for the US joint military base in Djibouti, Camp Lemonnier, established in 2002 to support the US invasion of Iraq. For the remainder of the Bush administration, continuing throughout the Obama administration and into the early Trump administration, al-Shabaab continued to keep Somalia in a state of dangerous instability.[13]

Would the situation have turned out differently if the Bush administration had provided encouragement and support to the Islamic Courts Union during their early growth period, 2001–2002? The use of the word "Islamic" in the name rendered US cooperation virtually out of the question politically.

Overall, the Bush administration's national security policy was almost totally preoccupied with Iraq and the Middle East. Nevertheless, Africa gained more than its expected share of attention.

Creation of the Africa Command

In the realm of United States–Africa military relations, the Bush administration initiated a major administrative change within the US military's chain of command. After the end of World War II, the US military had organized itself into geographic combat commands to fulfill its worldwide responsibilities. These commands conducted relations with foreign military counterparts and planned for potential operations in their regions of responsibility, pursuant to presidential decisions.

Prior to the Bush administration, military responsibility for potential operations in Africa had been divided among three combat commands. European Command (EUCOM) had responsibility for the largest number of African countries in northern, western, central, and southern Africa. Several eastern African countries were linked to US Central Command (CENTCOM), which focused mainly on the Middle East and southern Asia. The African nations CENTCOM covered were Egypt, Sudan, Kenya, Ethiopia, Eritrea, Djibouti, and Somalia. And Pacific Command (PACOM) covered the African island nations in the Indian Ocean: Madagascar, Mauritius, the Comoros, and the Seychelles.

Because of the growing security challenges in Africa arising from the collapse of regimes in northern Africa and the rise of terrorism in western and eastern Africa, President Bush decided to consolidate military responsibility for United States–Africa relations within a single Africa Command (AFRICOM), with headquarters in Stuttgart, Germany.

Since its creation, AFRICOM was involved in the NATO operation to depose Libyan leader Muammar Qaddafi. It has continued through the Obama and Trump administrations to support African nations in their war against jihadist terrorists in the Sahel region and Somalia.

Of particular interest to US diplomats in Africa is the existence in AFRICOM of a deputy to the commander for civil-military relations. This position is always occupied by a senior Foreign Service officer who has previously served in Africa as an ambassador. The position exists in recognition of the high priority that the US government assigns to economic development in all of its relations with Africa, including the military.[14]

14

Barack H. Obama: 2009–2017

The fact that President Barack Obama's late father was an African citizen of Kenya is well known. What is less well known is that his father came to the United States in 1960 as a result of the famous "Kenyan Airlift," jointly sponsored by the Department of State and the Kennedy Family Foundation.

Senator John F. Kennedy was in the midst of his presidential campaign in 1960 when he was approached by a charismatic young Kenyan trade union leader named Tom Mboya, a protégé of the American Federation of Labor–Congress of Industrial Organizations (AFL-CIO). Mboya persuaded Kennedy that young Africans would benefit from higher education in the United States. Kennedy found money in his family foundation, which the State Department matched at the request of Vice President Richard Nixon, Kennedy's opponent in the presidential race.

Obama's father was among the first 300 Kenyan students to come to the United States as a result of the Kennedy–State Department effort. He was the first ever African to study at the University of Hawaii, where he met and married Obama's mother, Ann Dunham. President Obama was born in Hawaii on August 4, 1961. Thus it is fair to say that President Obama was connected to US policy toward Africa from the very beginning.[1]

Obama's Realism Tempers Africa's Euphoria

Obama's election in November 2008 stimulated a great feeling of pride throughout sub-Saharan Africa. With the election of a "son of the soil" as the US president, a wave of "Obamamania" swept across the continent. Many Africans believed that Africa would gain importance in overall US foreign policy.[2]

Under Obama, US foreign policy paid significant attention to Africa but not necessarily in the way that Africans expected. Obama was determined to persuade them that African economic development is essentially a challenge and responsibility for the Africans themselves, and not primarily that of the international community.

Obama's initial message to the African people was not what they expected to hear from one of their own. Above all, they anticipated a major expansion of US development assistance. Instead, Obama gave them a sermon. During his first visit to Africa as president, in 2009, he addressed Ghana's parliament, saying, "We must start from the simple premise that Africa's future is up to the Africans."[3] No matter how much development assistance Africa receives from the international community, the outcome will be determined by the policies and practices that African governments themselves establish. In other words: "Development is your problem, Africa. We can only assist."

During his two terms, President Obama went to Africa four times, visiting seven countries. He was the first US president to visit Kenya and Ethiopia. All of his public speeches and statements reiterated his basic premise, that Africa's own policies and actions are the determining factors in development. Unlike any of his predecessors, he consistently uttered the word "corruption" in public settings.

Trade and Investment:
The Way to Go for Africa

Obama's second message to Africa focused on the importance of trade and investment as the key to the kind of rapid economic growth needed to lift the African masses out of poverty. In this regard, Obama's policy was not a new one, but his focus on trade and investment was much more intense and focused than that of his predecessors.

During the George H. W. Bush administration, the State Department's Bureau of African Affairs was pleasantly surprised to see a senior USAID Foreign Service officer, Warren Weinstein, traveling around Africa talking to governments about eliminating bureaucratic and political impediments to private investments. Weinstein's initiative stimulated similar action by the World Bank, which established its annual worldwide scorecard report *Doing Business*. This annual report informs individual governments how well they are doing in terms of creating an enabling environment for indigenous private investors.[4]

As noted earlier, President Clinton signed the African Growth and Opportunity Act (AGOA) into law in 2000. The law was designed to encourage private investments in production facilities in Africa that would take advantage of duty-free entry into US markets, as authorized by the act. And President George W. Bush made the creation of private sector incentives an important element of his signature Millennium Challenge Corporation initiative.

President Obama elevated the African private sector to an even higher-level policy priority. In this respect, Obama established two signature programs: Power Africa and Feed the Future.

Electric Power: Africa's Most Significant Economic Deficit

When President Obama came into office in 2009, the deficit of affordable electric power in sub-Saharan Africa was enormous. The colonial administrations had established power grids in all of their African colonies, but these were limited to the main cities and towns. Even in these urban locations, individual homes of working-class Africans often lacked connections, while power lines did not extend into the villages in between.

In countries with rich natural resources and strong export revenues, the limitations of the colonial electric grids were often overcome through the purchase and use of expensive-to-run diesel generators. Toward the mid-1980s, Nigeria was producing three million barrels of crude oil per day at prices near $100 a barrel. With all of this revenue, Nigeria became the biggest importer of diesel generators in the world. This expedient was good for government and multinational business but provided no benefits for the ordinary African. The high cost of diesel power also crowded out other possible investments.

Neglect of the maintenance of the power grids colonial administrations left was probably the biggest cause of the power deficit. Newly independent African governments neglected maintenance when they should have been upgrading and expanding their power grids to meet the needs of the growing populations in their major cities.

The Obama administration correctly reached the conclusion that without electric power in the twenty-first century, development was effectively impossible. When Obama came into office, less than 35 percent of the people in sub-Saharan Africa had access to electric power.

The Obama administration's response to Africa's power deficit was to launch a comprehensive interagency project called Power Africa. As stated in the administration's own literature, the goal was to add 10,000 megawatts of new power generation and expand access to power to 20 million households and businesses by 2030. USAID was designated as the coordinating agency for Power Africa.[5]

The key element of the program was envisaged as a public-private partnership. The main players were to be private companies willing to invest in power generation, with electric utilities signing contracts to purchase the power under long-term contracts called independent power purchase agreements.

A USAID Power Africa office under the direction of senior Foreign Service officer Andrew Herscowitz was initially established in Nairobi, Kenya, then relocated to Pretoria, South Africa. Herscowitz had twenty-five advisers whose missions were to help African governments identify the potential for new power generation and establish the necessary conditions to attract private investors.[6]

The overall plan for Power Africa involved multiple agencies with dedicated budget allocations. Beyond USAID, the most important were US International Development Finance Corporation (DFC), formerly the Overseas Private Investment Corporation (OPIC), the Millennium Challenge Corporation (MCC), and the US Trade and Development Agency (USTDA). DFC's role is to provide competitive financing to the private companies. The MCC gives priority to electric power in its project agreements with African governments. The USTDA provides the studies necessary for the private sector to determine profitability and feasibility.

In a project completed in Senegal in 2016, to cite just one example, the Contour Global Corporation of New York installed an eighty-six-megawatt, dual-fuel power plant, with eighteen-year financing from OPIC and the World Bank Group's International Finance Corporation (IFC). This addition to Senegal's power grid eliminated power outages in the capital city, Dakar, and is earning the US company a 15 percent rate of return. The government of Senegal invested nothing but signed a contract to purchase the power at a fixed rate.[7] At a signing ceremony in

Washington in 2015, the director-general of the Senegalese electric utility said that the power from the Contour Global facility would be available at the lowest cost from any source.[8]

As of the end of Obama's tenure in the White House, Power Africa had facilitated the financial close of eighty power transactions valued at more than $14.5 billion and expected to generate more than 7,200 megawatts of power in sub-Saharan Africa. In addition, Power Africa had begun to explore the expansion of "beyond the grid" power to locations where small solar installations can fill the electricity gap for households and small businesses until transmission lines can expand subconnections to the main grids.[9]

While the financing for 7,200 megawatts had been arranged by the end of the Obama administration, only 2,500 megawatts had actually been installed by the time Obama left office. Nevertheless, the Power Africa program is considered one of the most innovative, significant, and relevant of any US development projects in Africa. Its private sector profit-making aspect makes it especially important.

Food Imports Divert African Resources from Development Investments

During the same post-independence period when African governments were neglecting their electric power requirements, diminishing food production also became a major impediment to development.

After independence, major population movements from the African rural areas to the cities in search of employment required increased food production in the rural areas. Unfortunately, the neglect of infrastructure presented serious obstacles to farmers' access to regional markets and other distribution centers. The only alternative was to increase food imports. Thus, in a growing number of African countries, increased production of minerals and commercial agricultural crops such as cocoa, coffee, and cotton brought more and more workers to the cities and to the agricultural plantations. Revenue earned from these exported commodities had to be used to import food to feed the urban workers rather than serve as investments for more production facilities. It was a vicious cycle that the Obama administration recognized as a major roadblock to sustainable development, equal to that of the electric power deficit.

In June 2009, at the annual G8 summit in L'Aquila, Italy, President Obama announced a $3.5 billion three-year program designed to enhance food security, thereby attacking the root causes of hunger and poverty. A year later, in 2010, he launched the Feed the Future (FTF) initiative as an official US program, targeting twelve countries, eight of them in Africa. To manage this program, USAID created a new Bureau for Food Security in November of that year.[10]

What made the Feed the Future program particularly interesting was its emphasis on the farmer as a businessperson, not as a simple peasant who needed supplementary food. One year after the program began, the Congressional Research Service said the following about the early results: "Launched in 2009, the 'Feed the Future' initiative has to date helped nine million farmers gain access to new tools and technologies, and improved the diets of eighteen million children."[11]

Increasingly, as the FTF program took hold, there were more and more reports of agriculture becoming a new source of revenue and food self-sufficiency for individual African countries. For example, as of the end of 2016, Nigeria's production of cassava (manioc) had reached 34 million tons a year, the largest in the world. In addition to being a staple food for people in West Africa, manioc is important for livestock feed and industrial starches. The UN Food and Agriculture Organization called the Nigerian expansion of cassava production "an industrial revolution."[12]

The more that African nations can produce their own food, the more resources will be available for investments in infrastructure, education, and health facilities. Obama's Feed the Future initiative, essentially a transfer-of-technology program, is certainly worth preserving by future administrations.

The United States–Africa Leaders' Summit

Obama's last major African event was the United States–Africa Leaders' Summit in Washington on August 4–6, 2014. The event constituted the wrapping up of his four trips to Africa with a last appeal to the African heads of state to do what is necessary to attract investors, both foreign and domestic. In the words of the White House statement afterward: "The August 4–6 Summit advanced the Administration's focus on trade and investment in Africa and highlighted America's commitment to Africa's security, its democratic development, and its people."[13]

In addition to Obama's constant reiteration of his "trade and investment" theme, the summit included over a hundred leading US business leaders who were already involved with Africa or exploring various possibilities. During three days, there was plenty of time for individual and collective meetings. The US business leaders were avid for opportunities to make money in Africa, given the right conditions. For the first time, many of the African leaders were hearing directly from investors about the impediments to investing.

The official theme of the August 2014 summit was "Investing in the Next Generation," with an emphasis on stimulating growth and unlocking opportunities for young people coming out of schools and universities. A related program President Obama initiated was the Young African Leaders Initiative (YALI), designed to identify those in the rising generation of African leadership who might benefit from exposure to US culture and entrepreneurship. During his Africa Week, on August 3, 2014, Obama met with 500 YALI participants who were midway through their programs. They had begun with six weeks of introduction to US culture and politics at the University of Virginia. They then went to assigned enterprises throughout the United States to learn about US business practices. Individual participants are known as Mandela Fellows.

To facilitate the YALI participants' networking after their return to Africa, USAID established four regional leadership centers, in Ghana, Kenya, Senegal, and South Africa. According to the White House announcement, the centers provide "courses on leadership and multiple subjects across a variety of sectors, support entrepreneurship through mentoring, technology and access to capital, and facilitate enhanced professional networking." The regional leadership centers are designed to partner with local business to provide opportunities for the YALI returnees to begin their own businesses with small financial grants.[14]

As of the end of the Obama administration, the YALI program was continuing with full enthusiasm. An announcement dated January 18, 2017, two days before Obama left office, said: "USAID invests $38 million in new YALI centers to support young emerging leaders in Africa."[15]

Dealing with Terrorism, Wars, and State Disintegration

Continuing Bad News from Somalia

When the Obama administration came into office in January 2009, the main focus of Islamic-based terrorism continued to be in Somalia. After the failure of the George W. Bush administration's effort to destroy the Islamic Courts Union in 2006, the radical armed wing of the movement al-Shabaab (The Youth) became dominant and expanded its operations beyond the original area of operations in the capital city of Mogadishu.

As al-Shabaab expanded, Somali clan leaders tried to organize an interim federal regime to replace the Siad Barre government, which had collapsed in 1991. In view of the dangerous security situation, transitional government negotiating sessions were taking place in Nairobi, Kenya. Somali transitional federal governments rose and fell in fits and starts, with the first interim president to set up shop in Mogadishu, Adbullahi Yusuf Ahmed, arriving on January 8, 2009.[16]

The Obama approach to Somalia changed nothing from the Bush approach. The United States had an ambassador based in Nairobi, Foreign Service officer John Yates, accredited to the Somali transitional federal government. The Obama policy was designed to assist the transitional federal government to gain strength and to achieve national reconciliation.

In February 2009 the Obama administration supported a UN Security Council resolution that authorized the African Union (AU) to deploy a peacekeeping mission to Somalia. The thrust of the resolution focused on supporting dialogue and reconciliation by protecting all Somalis involved in discussions aimed at the peaceful resolution of all disputes. Because al-Shabaab was intent on imposing Islamic rule on all of Somalia by force of arms, the African Union Mission in Somalia (AMISOM) had no choice but to become a fighting force.[17] The Obama administration provided advice and training to the transitional federal government and supported AMISOM with targeted attacks on al-Shabaab leadership from US military units stationed in Camp Lemonnier in Djibouti.

Throughout Obama's two terms, AMISOM managed to drive al-Shabaab out of Mogadishu as well as the southern port city of Kismayo, but the movement continued to operate in the countryside, with occasional suicide bombings in Mogadishu causing havoc. On August 20, 2012, the transitional federal government of Somalia came to an end, and was replaced by a federal government replete with a federal parliament. Because of enhanced security in Mogadishu, the US embassy moved there from Nairobi.[18]

Somali Jihad Raises Its Ugly Head in Minnesota

The governance vacuum and overall chaos in Somalia between 1991 and 2012 caused hundreds of thousands of Somalis to become international refugees. Most went to neighboring countries, especially Kenya, that already had a significant population of well-integrated Somali

Kenyans. In the tradition of US refugee policy, about 200,000 Somali refugees were resettled in the United States during 1991–1999. The largest Somali diaspora community in the United States settled in the Minneapolis–St. Paul "Twin Cities" region of Minnesota. There was virtually no interest in al-Shabaab in this community until February 2012, when the movement pledged allegiance to al-Qaeda, the perpetrators of the September 11, 2001, attacks in New York and Washington.

After being expelled from Afghanistan by US forces in 2002, al-Qaeda was based in Pakistan. Al-Shabaab's adherence to al-Qaeda gave the movement access to al-Qaeda's worldwide propaganda machine. This resulted in a small number of Somali youth living in Minnesota becoming interested in possibly going to Somalia to join in Islamic jihad.[19]

In June 2016, nine Somali youth pleaded guilty or were convicted in federal court in Minneapolis of conspiracy to support terrorism. These individuals were intercepted before they could go to Somalia to participate in al-Shabaab's terrorism. The lure of jihad became even stronger after the Islamic State in the Levant (ISIL) emerged as a major terrorist organization in January 2014.[20]

In 2009, about two dozen Somali youth from Minnesota had managed to make their way to Somalia to join al-Shabaab. A few of them were killed in action, including one who became a suicide bomber. Between 2009 and 2016, the Federal Bureau of Investigation (FBI) identified and dismantled the network within the Minneapolis–St. Paul area that was responsible for recruiting and sending Somali youth to join al-Shabaab.[21]

Overall, among the different Somali communities in the United States, it was only Minneapolis that produced a few jihadists. The overall majority of Somalis in the United States have been loyal citizens and permanent residents, with a significant number joining the US military.

Boko Haram Adopts Terrorism in Nigeria

The population of the northern half of Nigeria is over 90 percent Muslim. Since Nigeria's transition from military to civilian rule in 1999, several of the individual states in the northern region established Muslim sharia law to govern family, inheritance, marriage, and related issues. Individual state governments varied in their transparency and commitment to the welfare of their populations.

One of the most corrupt state governments has been that of Borno State in Nigeria's far northeast, on the edge of Lake Chad. The successive governors of Borno have been Western-educated. By contrast, the education system of Borno has been essentially quranic, with very little effort at bringing modern education to the masses.

To protest the unbalanced state of education in Borno, in 2002 a spiritual leader named Mohammed Yusuf founded an organization that he called Boko Haram, a short version of the local language name, which is translated as "Western education is sin." The name was inspired by the fact that the governors were all educated at universities in Britain or the United States, while so many of their young male citizens had only quranic education and were therefore unemployable.

During election years 1999, 2004, and 2009, the governor of Borno hired several thousand young men to campaign for his reelection, as was customary in most of Nigeria's thirty-six states. Each time he was reelected, he refused to pay them. It was this arrogant contempt for the uneducated youth that triggered the establishment of Boko Haram. This Borno governor was educated at a UK university. The young men who were cheated and treated with disrespect associated the governor's attitude with his Western education.

Between its founding in 2002 and the 2009 election, Boko Haram became increasingly popular within the Muslim population, especially among the young men who had only a quranic education. The organization began to become a threat to the establishment. On July 30, 2009, the Nigerian army arrested Boko Haram's spiritual leader, Mohammed Yusuf, and turned him over to the police. While being transported to the police station, Yusuf was summarily executed.

Replacing Yusuf as head of Boko Haram was Abubakar Shekau, a militant Salafist Islamist, who decided that the organization had to go terrorist. He wanted it to pressure the federal government of Nigeria to place the entire nation under total sharia law as the only way to eliminate Nigeria's notorious corruption.

From that point, Boko Haram went on a rampage in northeastern Nigeria, killing and bombing at random, with a large number of suicide bombings perpetrated by male and female children. The Nigerian security forces were unable to contain them. The international community, including the United States, criticized the Nigerian army for punishing villages where Boko Haram operated. The United States was required by congressional criticism to suspend sales of military equipment to the Nigerian military.

In 2014, Boko Haram started attacking villages in neighboring Cameroon, Chad, and Niger. That same year, the terrorist group captured 276 female students from the boarding school Chibok. This brought the movement to the attention of the US public because of the distressing nature of the act. First Lady Michelle Obama was seen on television with a sign that read "Free our girls."

Boko Haram was exceedingly destructive. In 2014 the movement was responsible for more deaths than the Islamic State in Iraq and Syria (ISIS). According to the Global Terrorism Index, published by the Institute for Economics and Peace, Boko Haram was responsible for 6,144 deaths that year, while ISIS was responsible for 6,073. Of particular significance was that over 95 percent of the people killed were Muslim.[22]

Because the Nigerian army had a reputation for competence, the United States did not do much to furnish assistance to help defeat Boko Haram. In view of the wide publicity given to the kidnapping of the Chibok girls in 2014, the United States provided some military advisers to help locate the young women, with modest success. The State Department had designated Boko Haram as a foreign terrorist organization in 2013. During the Obama period, Boko Haram pledged allegiance to ISIS, amid growing evidence that the movement was receiving arms and money from al-Qaeda in the Maghreb (AQIM), an Islamic terrorist group operating in northern Niger and Mali.[23]

As of the end of the Obama administration, the Nigerian government was claiming that Boko Haram had been driven out of every village or road that it had controlled; but it was clearly still carrying out bombings and killing raids on police, church, and market facilities. While the Obama administration was concerned about the impact on Nigeria, Niger, and Chad, there were no indications that the US mainland was being targeted.

At the same time, in view of the Boko Haram connection to AQIM, a movement considered to constitute a major threat to Western interests, the Obama administration deployed advisers to Niger and Chad, both of whose militaries were heavily involved in the fight against terrorism. US drone bases were established in Niger's capital city of Niamey and in the northern mining city of Agadez. At the end of the Obama administration, there were 800 US military personnel in Niger alone.

Arab Spring Fallout in Northern and Sub-Saharan Africa

Probably the most significant foreign policy and national security event during the Obama administration was the so-called Arab Spring. Between

2010 and 2012, popular uprisings against corrupt, repressive, and authoritarian regimes in several Arab countries resulted in the overthrow of dictators, with a variety of end results, including chronic instability in some cases.[24]

In December 2010, Tunisia was the first Arab nation to experience a popular uprising against its authoritarian regime. In less than a month, in mid-January 2011, Tunisian president Ben Ali went into exile, and the Tunisian people entered a relatively peaceful transition period leading to a democratic outcome. The Tunisians called it the Jasmine Revolution.[25]

The Tunisian revolution stimulated popular uprisings in other Arab countries, including Egypt, Syria, Bahrain, Algeria, and Yemen. The Obama administration's role in these crisis situations varied from interested observation to active diplomacy. In Egypt, for example, twelve days of massive protests in February 2011 led to President Hosni Mubarak's resignation. The United States actively encouraged Mubarak to resign, against his inclination to use lethal force against the demonstrators. The post-Mubarak transition led to a democratic election, followed a year later by a military takeover. As of the end of the Obama administration, the military continued to govern Egypt. The Egyptian experience contrasted sharply with Tunisia's. The Obama administration was comfortable with both outcomes.[26]

Obama's Intervention in Libya's Arab Spring: Triumph and Deception

Protests began throughout Libya on February 14, 2011, three days after Mubarak's resignation in Egypt. Rebels controlled the principal eastern city of Benghazi by February 18. By February 20, protests had spread to the capital city, Tripoli. Instead of considering resignation or negotiations, Muammar Qaddafi, Libya's leader and head of state, opted for total war. In his army's unsuccessful effort to recapture control of Benghazi, unarmed civilians were killed along with rebel combatants. In addition, Qaddafi's rhetoric on television and radio was extremely menacing.

The special circumstances of the popular uprising in Libya and the dictator's reaction generated great interest in the international community. On February 26, the UN Security Council enacted a resolution demanding a halt to the use of lethal force against Libyan civilians. The resolution also expressed the view that Libya's violence against civilians might constitute a crime against humanity and asked all member nations to refrain from the sale of military items to Libya. At that point, there was, as yet, no request for member governments to intervene directly.[27]

One month later, the UN Security Council enacted an even stronger resolution that reflected a "deteriorating" situation in Libya. The resolution used language that effectively invited member states to intervene: "The Security Council authorizes member states to take all necessary measures to protect civilians and civilian populated areas under threat of attack in the Libyan Arab Jamahiriya, including Benghazi." The UN language authorizing member states to "take all necessary measures" constituted an open invitation for governments to intervene militarily.[28]

The NATO Intervention

On March 19, 2011, in response to the UN Security Council resolution, the US, British, and French militaries began Operation Odyssey Dawn with the firing of 110 Tomahawk missiles from ships, hitting twenty Libyan air and missile defense targets. This was the first Arab Spring uprising in which the United States decided to intervene directly in order to protect civilians from government atrocities.

After the US, British, and French attacks, it was clear that the intervention would be going beyond the protection of civilians to an effort to accomplish regime change and that no other outcome could stop the carnage against civilians. Hence, on March 24, 2011, NATO took over the UN-authorized intervention. Thus began Operation Unified Protector, designed to achieve regime change. This operation continued until October 20, 2011, when Muammar Qaddafi was killed in his home city of Sirte after rebels captured him in a state of lonely abandon. His elite military guards had all disappeared.

Why did President Obama decide to intervene in Libya, when he refrained from intervening in Syria, where the repression of the popular uprising was just as horrible or even worse than in Libya? It is also difficult to say that the United States had strategic or national interests in Libya.

Indications also suggested that Qaddafi's inflammatory rhetoric did not actually match the facts on the ground. It also appeared that far fewer civilians had been killed than had been reported and that it might have been possible to negotiate an exit for Qaddafi.

Interestingly, senior US policy advisers, including Secretary of State Hillary Clinton, National Security Adviser Susan Rice, and Policy

Planning Director Samantha Power, all had painful memories of the US failure to intervene in the Rwandan genocide of 1994, as well as in the Bosnian massacres of 1995, when they were involved in the Clinton administration. They were apparently determined not to abdicate the US "responsibility to protect" yet one more time.[29]

Unfortunately, the failure to follow up the intervention with efforts to stabilize Libya after Qaddafi's death and prevent it from becoming a failed state had a devastating impact on several countries in sub-Saharan Africa. Thus it was not the intervention in Libya per se that caused trouble for sub-Saharan Africa, but its poorly managed aftermath.

A Perfect Storm for Regional Destabilization

When Qaddafi's military failed to recapture Benghazi after rebels had taken control, he turned his wrath to the demonstrators in Tripoli, threatening mass killings and causing NATO to intervene. Even before NATO began its action, a variety of factions had already established regional and subregional regimes.

The NATO onslaught caused the Qaddafi system to fall apart. On March 30, Foreign Minister Moussa Koussa resigned and debarked to the United Kingdom. On April 30, a missile killed one of Qaddafi's sons, Seif al-Arab.

The most important development was the disintegration of Qaddafi's military, which was composed largely of mercenary fighters from Libya's southern African neighbors, Mali and Niger. These fighters were comfortable beating up on Libyan civilians, but they were not about to take on NATO. So the mercenaries stopped fighting and returned to their own countries, with all of their vehicles and weapons and a lot more confiscated from the arsenals.

This development caused massive destabilization in Mali and minor destabilization in Niger. Some units in northern Mali joined up with al-Qaeda in the Islamic Maghreb and began attacking northern Malian towns. Tuareg fighters formed a Mali Islamic movement, called Ansar el Dine, that began destroying ancient Muslim temples and shrines in historic towns, such as Timbuktu and Atar. The government of Mali and its military were in such distress that a military coup ousted the regime for a brief period before the French could intervene.

In addition to the destabilization of northern Mali, the disintegration of the Qaddafi regime opened the doors to the movement of arms throughout the Sahel region, including to Boko Haram in Nigeria.[30]

Internally, Libya had several centers of power, including Benghazi, Tripoli, and Misrata. Misrata became a center of Islamic terrorism, with fighters from the Islamic State in the Levant infiltrating by sea.

As of the end of the Obama administration, Libya continued to be unstable politically, with the economy subject to decline every time oil shipments were interrupted by independent militia attacks. Obama's mistake in Libya was his administration's failure to use expert analysis to prepare for the aftermath of regime change in Libya. President George W. Bush's similar experience with regime change in Iraq, together with President Obama's experience in Libya, gave rise to a new basic rule in US national security policy: "Do not get rid of a foreign regime until we know for sure what will be replacing it."

President Obama recognized his administration's judgment lapse when he said, "Our failure to deal with the aftermath of our intervention in Libya was my biggest foreign policy regret."[31] The unfortunate aftermath of the Libyan intervention notwithstanding, it is fair to say that the original intent of saving civilian lives from wanton Libyan government violence was largely accomplished. But Libya's collapse, with the opening of its arms depots to terrorists, drug traffickers, and other criminal elements, had a profound impact on the African countries to the south of Libya that lasted well beyond Obama's departure from office in 2017.

The Great Tragedy of South Sudan (Continued)

As previously described, the Comprehensive Peace Agreement between the government of Sudan in Khartoum and the Sudan People's Liberation Movement was signed in 2005 with the strong support of the George W. Bush administration. The agreement provided for the SPLM to govern South Sudan autonomously during a six-year transition period, while still under Khartoum's token sovereignty.

When the Obama administration came in, the transition in South Sudan had already completed almost four of its six years. During those four years, there were signs of disaster ahead. The South Sudanese transitional government was made up, essentially, of guerrilla fighters from the civil war. There was a total absence of individuals with political experience, except for Colonel John Garang, the head of both the Sudanese People's Liberation Army (SPLA) and its political arm, the SPLM. The flow of oil money was shared equally between North and South Sudan.

The combination of oil money and ex-guerrilla fighters' hunger for reward, after so many years of fighting in the bush, resulted in a totally wasted transition. The oil money was blatantly stolen, and the fighters who constituted the South Sudanese army decided that everyone should be an officer and nobody should be an enlisted man. At the end of the Bush administration, the South Sudanese army had 400 generals in a total contingent of 10,000 men. Scant attention was paid to the building of institutions, the training of administrators, or the upgrading of the basically nonexistent infrastructure. Unfortunately, John Garang, the charismatic leader of the SPLM, was killed in a helicopter crash while returning from Uganda only one month after the transition began.[32]

Two years after the start of the Obama administration, the independence of South Sudan occurred on July 9, 2011, following a popular referendum that voted for separation from Khartoum with 98.8 percent of the vote. Two years later, in 2013, civil war broke out among various ethnic groups, the main battle being between President Salva Kir's Dinka tribe and Vice President Riek Machar's Nuer tribe.

During two years of war, 2.2 million civilians became displaced, with several hundred thousand becoming refugees in neighboring Uganda. The fighting was particularly horrible. Women and children were not spared, and rape was used as a weapon of war. A ceasefire was negotiated by the African Union in 2015, but fighting never really stopped, continuing right through to the end of the Obama administration.[33]

Like the Bush administration before it, the Obama administration could deal with the South Sudan tragedy only through support to UN and African Union peacekeeping, as well as to humanitarian relief operations. Basically, both administrations failed to learn from the history of previous similar transitions of unstable nations from repressive dependency to total independence in a relatively short period of time.

Namibia, East Timor, and Cambodia constituted useful examples. All three were coming out of civil conflict. All three had UN-supervised transitions within which UN career officials controlled key functions, while they trained locals to take over. All three were successful to the extent that the transitions were relatively stable and the incoming indigenous governments had the capabilities to govern.

Sudan was treated differently because the international community, including, above all, the United States, romanticized about the long-suffering "gentle" people of South Sudan, so much so that they were in a state of denial about the possibility of highly destructive civil conflict.[34]

15

Donald J. Trump: 2017–2019

When Donald Trump came into office in January 2017, he had a list of international treaties and several multilateral economic agreements, entered into by several of his predecessors, that he considered inimical to US interests. These included the nuclear limitation agreement with Iran, the Joint Plan of Comprehensive Action (JCPA); the Trans-Pacific Partnership (TPP); the Paris Agreement on climate change; and the North American Free Trade Agreement (NAFTA). By executive order, he announced the withdrawal of the United States from the JCPA, TPP, and Paris Agreement and demanded renegotiation of NAFTA.[1]

Canada, Mexico, and the United States renegotiated NAFTA in 2017–2018 and agreed to a revised accord on September 30, 2018. President Trump, Mexican president Enrique Peña Nieto, and Canadian prime minister Justin Trudeau signed the accord on November 30, 2018, under the new name, the United States–Mexico–Canada Agreement (USMCA).[2]

In President Trump's expressed views, a number of international trade agreements were unfair to the American worker, because they allowed foreign products to be sold in the United States at considerably cheaper prices than those for the same merchandise manufactured in the United States. It was therefore somewhat surprising that President Trump and his team did not focus on the African Growth and Opportunity Act, signed into law by President Clinton in 2000 (see Chapter 12). This law, which was designed not to be subject to review prior to 2025, stipulates that virtually all products made in sub-Saharan Africa can enter the

United States duty-free. The law gives African nations a major advantage over other exporting countries. As a result, some investors, who were already exporting to the United States from their own countries, established new production facilities in Africa. This was especially true for investors from Taiwan (apparel) and Germany (automobile parts).[3]

The only comment about AGOA from a Trump administration official came in 2018 from Commerce Secretary Wilbur Ross, who expressed an interest in negotiating a total two-way free trade agreement with a single African country, by way of upholding the principle of reciprocity. As of mid-2019, such a bilateral negotiation had not yet begun.[4]

For the first two years of the Trump administration, 2017–2018, US policy toward Africa was one of continuity. The major programs put in place by Presidents Clinton, George W. Bush, and Obama remained in place, and were fully funded.

The Administration's Initial Concentration on Crisis Management

Where the Trump administration distinguished itself in Africa during the first two years was in crisis management. In June 2018, after a meeting with African leaders in New York, President Trump asked the US permanent representative to the United Nations, Ambassador Nikki Haley, to travel to South Sudan and the Democratic Republic of the Congo to determine how the United States might be helpful in ending violence and instability in those countries.

In South Sudan, where the civil conflict appeared totally intractable five years after independence, Ambassador Haley recommended that the United States continue to support African regional mediation. In the DRC, however, Haley determined that the United States could play a significant direct role.

In 2014 and 2015, the DRC's neighboring countries Rwanda and the Republic of the Congo changed their constitutions to eliminate two-term limits for heads of state. In both countries, the heads of state then ran for third terms and were reelected. The Obama administration was critical of these actions in both countries and instructed the US ambassadors to express this criticism in public.

In the DRC, the constitution also limits the president to two elected terms and stipulates that the two-term limitation cannot be abolished by parliamentary amendment. Changing this particular constitutional clause would require approval by a popular referendum. When DRC president Joseph Kabila announced in 2015 that the DRC would hold a referendum to abolish the two-term limitation, the popular reaction was so loud and so negative that he abandoned the idea. What he did instead was fail to hold the presidential election scheduled for November 2016. By mid-2017, with no presidential election in sight, the internal political situation in the DRC had become quite tense. It was to address this particular political crisis that Ambassador Haley went to the DRC in June 2018.

Her visit succeeded in establishing a democratic outcome.[5] After a three-hour meeting with President Kabila, Haley announced that Kabila had promised to hold a presidential election no later than December 2018 and had made a commitment not to be a candidate to succeed himself. Kabila had not previously spoken in those terms to the Congolese public. As of January 2019, the DRC had completed a presidential election, and a new president, Felix Tshisekedi, had been sworn in to replace Joseph Kabila. Much of the credit for this positive outcome belonged to Ambassador Nikki Haley and the Trump administration. Of particular significance was the fact that this election marked the first peaceful transition of power in the Congo since it gained its independence from Belgium in 1960.[6]

A Trump Policy Toward Africa Begins to Emerge in December 2018

Ambassador John Bolton was sworn in as President Trump's third national security adviser in April 2018. In December 2018, for his first formal public foreign policy statement, Bolton chose to talk about Africa. His overarching point was that African prosperity would be good for the United States in a number of ways. US export markets would be expanded, and the need for US economic assistance would be reduced. Hence, official US government policy would emphasize support for investments by the US private sector.

True to his ideological reputation, Bolton characterized China's massive engagement in Africa as predatory, designed to control the continent's natural resources through the offer of loans that may never be repaid, and declared that the US private sector would effectively compete with China. He gave a name to the Trump administration's program to encourage private investments: "Prosper Africa."

Bolton also had a solemn message for the Africans. The United States will do whatever is in its own best interest. Aid will not be wasted in African countries in which corruption is diverting the nations' own resources to private bank accounts. In addition, the United States will begin to keep score with respect to how African governments support US policies. This will be especially important in the United Nations, where African delegations frequently vote against the United States. This happens most often during votes on Israeli-Palestinian issues.[7]

As of mid-2019, the government's development assistance arm, the US Agency for International Development, had begun gearing up for a "Prosper Africa" project. The emphasis would be on advising African governments on creating an enabling environment for the private sector, especially with respect to the rule of law, the enforcement of contracts, the maintenance of vital utilities, and the proper management of ports and transportation.[8]

Tibor Nagy Takes Office as US Assistant Secretary of State for Africa

President Trump selected Ambassador Tibor Nagy as his assistant secretary of state for Africa in July 2018. Nagy had retired from the career Foreign Service in 2003 to become a faculty member at Texas Tech University. In addition to his teaching duties, Nagy was active in support of Republican politicians and policies. He was thus qualified as both an expert in US-African relations and a Republican Party militant. During his career, Nagy had served mainly in Africa, including ambassadorships to Guinea and Ethiopia.

In his public policy statements, Nagy has echoed John Bolton's emphasis on increasing Africa's prosperity through investment and trade. In addition, he has called attention to Africa's "youth bulge," with 40 percent of Africa's population being under the age of twenty-five. Nagy was encouraging the expansion of educational and employment opportunities for these young people as an important motor of economic growth.

With respect to US-African political relations, during his first twelve months in office, Nagy played significant roles in consolidating the Congo's democratic transition and in Sudan's transfer of power from military to civilian rule, during the first half of 2019.[9]

The Trump Administration's Foreign Assistance Budget-Cutting Attempts

The Trump administration's rhetoric promoting African prosperity was not matched by its budget requests, which sought major reductions in foreign assistance. In his foreign assistance budget requests for both fiscal years 2019 and 2020, President Trump recommended reductions of 30 percent. On a bipartisan basis, the US Congress restored the full amounts, reflecting long-standing support for assistance to the developing world.

Where the Congress expressed full agreement with the Trump administration was in the belief that economic development needs less charity and more private investment. Consequently, the Congress enacted legislation establishing a new agency, the US International Development Finance Corporation (USIDFC), known as the Build Act, which states: "This bill establishes the United States International Development Finance Corporation to facilitate the participation of private sector capital and skills in the economic development of countries with low- or lower-middle-income economies and countries transitioning from nonmarket to market economies in order to complement U.S. assistance and foreign policy objectives."[10]

The language of the legislation conforms fully to the public statements about US-African relations made by National Security Adviser Bolton and Assistant Secretary for Africa Nagy. Effective October 1, 2019, the USIDFC replaced the Overseas Private Investment Corporation (OPIC), which provided private sector guarantees against political risks abroad, as well as financing for high-priority sectors such as energy. With an initial budget of $60 billion, the USIDFC totally dwarfed the newly defunct OPIC. It was expected that the bulk of the new agency's efforts would be directed at Africa.[11]

Terrorist Expansion in Africa

While the Islamic State and its various terrorist franchises were retreating in the Middle East, as of 2018–2019 they were expanding their operations in Africa's Sahel region. The Sahel is a west-to-east belt of countries immediately south of the Sahara Desert. It extends from Senegal and Mauritania on the Atlantic Ocean in the west to Sudan and Somalia on the Red Sea in the east.

Building on local armed Islamic groups, Islamic State franchises began to grow in the Sahel after the fall of Libyan leader Muammar Qaddafi in 2011. Southern Libya, in a state of anarchy, became a major source of arms for Islamic militant groups operating in the Sahel. In addition to terrorism, these groups were active in drug trafficking, kidnapping for ransom, gold smuggling, and trafficking in persons.

The Obama administration had deployed US military advisers to Niger and organized the construction of a drone base in the Nigerien city of Agadez. Also, during the Obama administration, US Africa Command established a full military base in Djibouti on the strategic strait of Bab-el-Mandeb, between the Red Sea and the Indian Ocean.

The objective of the US military deployments in the Sahel region was, and remains, to assist African governments to combat the depredations of Islamic terrorist militias. All deployments are advisory, except in Djibouti, where US military units engage in targeted actions against Islamic groups. In Djibouti, most actions involve air-to-ground operations.[12]

The Trump administration inherited, and continued, these deployments, with some reductions of deployed personnel in keeping with the president's determination to reduce the US military presence abroad. Together with the French army, which also has a significant troop presence in Mali, the major challenge for the administration in the Sahel region is the growing inability of the African governments to cope with the terrorist attacks. The underlying socioeconomic issues that push unemployed youth to join the Islamic militias are an additional challenge for the indigenous regimes.

As of mid-2019, the Trump administration continued to rely on the local African governments to deal with the Islamist threat, with US advisory and logistical support. Apparently, no obvious contingency planning existed for a possible deterioration in the security situation as of that time.

Bipartisan Support for Overall US-African Relations

Since the 1960s, US policy toward Africa has received bipartisan support for economic development among US political groups. The Trump administration's first two years of Africa policy could be described as a period of continuity. The major Africa-oriented projects introduced by several of President Trump's predecessors have remained intact during his administration. These have included the Millennium Challenge Corporation under President George H. W. Bush, AGOA under President Clinton, the HIV/AIDS program known as PEPFAR under President George W. Bush, and President Obama's Power Africa and Feed the Future. With Prosper Africa, President Trump expressed his intention to add to the overall US effort to help Africa catch up to Southeast Asia and Latin America in reducing poverty.[13]

As usual, it was, and is, up to the Africans to take advantage of the availability of US support.

16

Reflections on Successes and Failures

Building on President Eisenhower's policy decision to emphasize economic development in the newly independent African nations, President Kennedy and the Congress enacted the Foreign Assistance Act of 1961. This legislation created the US Agency for International Development, which consolidated the administration of all existing programs, including the Marshall Plan for European recovery, the special program for Greece and Turkey, and the Alliance for Progress in Latin America. The 1961 act also created a special fund for Security Supporting Assistance, which allocated money to friendly governments facing security challenges. The fund's name was changed to the Economic Support Fund in 1971 to emphasize its economic development purpose.[1]

"Foreign Aid" to Emerging Africa

As individual African colonies gained their independence, introducing substantial US development assistance became the US government's highest priority for the continent. For example, in early 1962, the US consulate-general in Kampala, Uganda, received an instruction to prepare for the arrival of thirty USAID personnel following the country's expected independence from the United Kingdom in the coming October. An expansion of the US Information Service facility was also anticipated for the creation of an American cultural center.[2]

The Kampala experience was replicated in every other US consular facility in Africa between 1960 and 1965. The policy imperative was to begin investing in visible programs as early as possible. The initial pattern could be described as scattershot—identify the problem and find the US experts who could solve it rapidly.

In Southern Rhodesia (now Zimbabwe) in 1963, for example, livestock herds were declining from sleeping sickness caused by the bite of the tsetse fly. USAID called upon the US Centers for Disease Control in Atlanta, Georgia, to propose a solution. The result was an experimental project that involved the sterilization of billions of male tsetse flies and releasing them into nature to destroy the tsetse fly population through nonreproduction. This particular project was canceled because of technical problems in collecting the male flies.[3]

In francophone Senegal in West Africa, the rainy season lasts only three months, supplying only enough pasture and water to take care of the livestock herds for six months. During the dry season, the herds were moved south into agricultural lands, where they met hostility from the farmers. USAID's solution was to send in earth-moving machinery to carve out large depressions that could hold enough rainwater to cover the needs of the six months of water scarcity. This project succeeded.[4]

Although these and similar projects throughout sub-Saharan Africa were worthwhile, there was an overall absence of planning to achieve sustainable economic development within a foreseeable period of time, causing criticism of USAID's program in Africa, chiefly among the budget appropriators in Congress. As this criticism grew, President Johnson called for a review of USAID's activities in Africa and asked Ambassador Edward Korry to take time off from his duties in Ethiopia to head up the Task Force to Review African Development Policies and Programs. After several months of study, on July 22, 1966, the task force issued what became widely known as the Korry Report. The report had a substantial impact on how the United States dispensed its aid to Africa for a full decade thereafter.[5]

The report began with a complaint about USAID involvement in too many small projects "dealing with almost every conceivable activity related to development, and at many levels." Furthermore, the amount of money available, $220 million per year, was too small "to conduct development programs in 33 countries." Therefore, the emphasis should be on finding "solutions to the complex and obdurate socioeconomic problems of rural development."

The report called for greater coordination and exchanges of data among donor nations. It also called for recognition of the fact that many small African states were not created with economic development in mind. The report called them "micro-states."

The report proposed that USAID concentrate on a limited number of sectors and designated infrastructure as the highest priority, because "infrastructure creates the regional groupings which will tie countries together." Beyond infrastructure, the report identified four important sectors that merited USAID attention: rural development, selected areas of education and health, and the promotion of private enterprise.[6]

Among other findings, the report noted the importance of agricultural development, not only for Africa but also for the eventual food needs of growing populations around the world. Regarding education, the report emphasized the importance of skills training to introduce African youth to the world of employment. Hence, technical education should receive priority. Health received priority status for two reasons: the inability of an unhealthy population to contribute to development, and the clear need for population control.

The report also recognized the significance of large fluctuations in the prices Africans were receiving for their exported commodities and demanded studies that could prevent "catastrophic declines in commodity prices."

Finally, the report recommended "the careful selection of specific African countries for a major development effort" by identifying "concentration countries" that have the size and population conducive to sustainable development. In this recommendation, political considerations were not to be excluded. And recognizing that the United States would not have Marshall Plan–size resources for African development, the report called for a coordination mechanism to bring together the efforts of various public and private donors, with the World Bank as the logical coordinator.[7]

President Johnson adopted the Korry Report and ordered that it become the guiding policy for US assistance to Africa. For US Foreign Service diplomats working on Africa policy, either in the State Department or in US embassies in Africa, the Korry Report could be boiled down to two new rules:

- Bilateral assistance would be limited to selected African countries that had the size and populations capable of using foreign assistance to realize real development. These countries would be designated as "concentration countries."

• Projects favoring regional cooperation that could reach large populations and large markets would be given priority. This policy came to be known as "regional priorities."

One of the first manifestations of the "concentration country" designation was the scramble among African governments to be considered eligible for the category. For example, what about middle-sized countries like Cameroon or Uganda? There was much bureaucratic debate about this issue. Of particular significance was the first ever designation of the private sector as an important factor in sustainable development.

The Nixon Administration's Concentration on Basic Human Needs

In the debate on foreign aid to Africa, the Nixon administration found Congress much more aggressive about policymaking than in the past. The Foreign Assistance Act enacted on December 17, 1973, established several new principles for the administration of foreign aid to Africa:

• Pay attention to human rights. Do not provide development aid to chronic human rights abusers.
• Encourage African "ownership" of Africa's development. African governments, not the donors, should be setting their priorities.
• Increase the amount of assistance moving through the private sector.
• Institute "new directions" that concentrate on the "basic human needs" of the rural poor.
• Make food production, population planning, health, education, and human resources the priority sectors.
• Improve the productivity and welfare of the rural poor.[8]

The introduction of human rights into the foreign assistance legislation was the work of Representative Donald Fraser of Minnesota. After the 1972 genocide in Burundi, Congressman Fraser chaired hearings about that event. His initiative of including human rights considerations in the 1973 foreign aid legislation led to the establishment in 1976 of the annual *State Department Human Rights Report,* which has had a profound influence on US foreign policy ever since.[9]

In the field in Africa, the "basic human needs" doctrine was taken very seriously. For most of the Nixon and Ford administrations, continuing through the Carter administration, USAID concentrated on Africa's rural areas. Maternal health and childcare, literacy for rural women, and basic health for village dwellers dominated the agendas.

In Senegal, for example, USAID had a project to dig 500 water wells with the objective of providing villagers with the water needed to grow vegetables for sale in local markets. US Peace Corps volunteers in the villages provided the training. In addition, USAID established "health huts" throughout the rural regions. Each health hut had a paramedic, a trained sanitation specialist, and a bookkeeper. The paramedic was trained to treat infant diarrhea, a major cause of childhood fatalities, and malaria. The sanitation specialist went from house to house to make sure there were no breeding pools for mosquitoes. The bookkeeper collected the local currency equivalent of half a dollar from each village resident seeking help to pay for new supplies. For every fifteen health huts, there was a central health facility with a trained nurse, a midwife, and a means of transportation. Village women were transported to the central health facility to give birth.

George H. W. Bush and Beyond

The George H. W. Bush administration established the first USAID office specializing in promoting an enabling environment for private investors. At the same time, USAID started participating in the newly organized Global Coalition for Africa, an intergovernmental grouping of donor and African governments designed to promote good governance, transparency, and the rule of law to give African businessmen and businesswomen confidence and a sense of security for their investments.

It was during the Bush administration as well that the World Bank took the lead in establishing the Highly Indebted Poor Countries Initiative, designed to forgive African development debts in return for good economic performance. In addition, the US and European aid agencies also gave the HIPC beneficiaries budgetary support.

From decade to decade, from the earliest programs of development assistance to Africa during the Kennedy administration to the final days of the Obama administration, US policy underwent dramatic change. What started out as "We know what you Africans need, and we will provide it" ended as "You Africans know what you have to do by way of reforms, and we, the donors, will help to the extent that you are serious about development. In any event, nothing positive can happen without a free and successful African private sector."

As of the end of the Obama administration, the population of the African continent was about one billion. A commodities' boom between 2000 and 2016 brought in a great deal of money, not all of which was diverted to corruption. This influx resulted in the development of a new African middle class, comprising about 15 percent of the African people. The African middle class started to attract private sector operators focused on retail consumption, including Walmart supermarkets and the Ford Motor Company, based in the United States. Unfortunately, most of the income from commodity exports continued to be used to import food. If President Obama's Feed the Future program succeeds, African entrepreneurs will have capital available for investments in production facilities. Encouraging self-sufficiency in food production and private entrepreneurship have to be among the high priorities for post-Obama US economic development policy in Africa going forward.

In addition to bilateral development projects in Africa organized through the US Agency for International Development, other channels of support exist. For African nations suffering from food shortages, mainly because of drought, Public Law 480 provides for the US Department of Agriculture to distribute surplus farm products to famine-stricken areas. The US government also provides funding to the UN Food and Agriculture Organization, which distributes food relief to countries suffering from food deficits.

Funds are also available for refugee relief administered by the State Department's Refugee Bureau. A separate independent agency, the African Development Fund, finances small, village-level projects. The US Congress created the fund to make sure that there was at least one program that could be completely isolated from foreign policy considerations.[10]

The Peace Corps

On March 1, 1961, President Kennedy issued an executive order establishing the Peace Corps, a program that was part cultural exchange, part economic development, and above all a design to win the hearts and minds of populations in the developing world. Congress formalized the new US government agency by enacting the Peace Corps Act on September 21, 1961. The program was particularly popular in Africa, where approximately 45 percent of the volunteers have been deployed over the more than half century of its existence. Speaking local languages, Peace Corps volunteers in Africa have transmitted knowledge and skills to the village level. Its many projects have included fish farming, vegetable growing and marketing, elementary school instruction, maternal and child health, and village sanitation.[11]

During the spring of 1987, President Reagan invited the president of Gabon, Omar Bongo, to make an official visit to Washington. A lunch with advisers followed a private discussion and a meeting in the cabinet room with advisers. The lunch was mostly social because the main bilateral business had been completed earlier. In the middle of the lunch, Bongo suddenly told President Reagan that he wanted to express a serious grievance. He said that he visited his home village in central Gabon about once every four months to see his family and chat with local leaders. On his last visit he saw a young white male living in the village who spoke the tribal language better than he did. With obvious tongue in cheek, Bongo said that he found the experience humiliating. Reagan laughed and said, "Mr. President, you have just given me evidence that the Peace Corps is a success."

Foreign Aid Includes Military Support

As noted earlier, a single unified US military combat command, AFRICOM, was established during the George W. Bush administration. However, AFRICOM did not constitute the beginning of United States–Africa military relations, which dated to the beginning of the wave of newly independent African states. In 1960, in the first year of independence for the Democratic Republic of the Congo, US Air Force transport aircraft played a major role in the movement of UN peacekeeping units to and from their respective countries.

Until the establishment of the US military base in Djibouti in November 2002, there were no US military facilities in Africa. The US base in Djibouti at Camp Lemonnier is designated the Combined Joint Task Force–Horn of Africa. As of mid-2019, 2,000 US military personnel were based there. The main military mission is counterterrorism, with the al-Shabaab terrorist group in Somalia the major target. In addition to counterterrorism in the Horn of Africa, the military personnel in the task force also focused on Yemen and other countries in the Gulf.[12]

Before the task force, the US Air Force had satellite tracking stations in Madagascar and South Africa. Otherwise, there were no other permanent US military facilities in Africa.

Education:
The Key in United States–Africa Military Relations

The US defense establishment has always opened the doors of its military schools to foreign military officers. African national military units have taken full advantage of these opportunities. Two major educational programs continue to incorporate foreign military students, one in the United States, the other in Africa.

International Military Education and Training (IMET) is a program financed through the State Department that brings foreign military officers to the United States for training in the many Defense Department schools around the United States. Africans are full participants in IMET.

Many African officers who have attended US military schools have gone on to become top commanders in their respective military establishments, an advantage at times of joint operations designed to end civil conflict in African countries. Under the presidency of one such participant, Paul Kagame, Rwandan troops have participated in joint peacekeeping operations in other African countries.

Kagame began his military career in Uganda, where his parents had come as political refugees in 1962–1963. Having risen to high rank in the Ugandan army, he had enrolled as a senior Ugandan army officer at the Command and General Staff College at Fort Riley, Kansas, in 1990. As soon as the Rwandan Patriotic Front invaded Rwanda from Uganda in October 1990, he departed the school early so that he could return to Uganda to join the RPF, which was engaged in combat in Rwanda. Toward the end of the 1980s he had begun plotting with his fellow officers of Rwandan origin to overthrow the government of Rwanda, a result they accomplished in 1994, but at the terrible cost of genocide against Rwanda's Tutsi population.

Graduates of US military schools are in the armed forces of virtually every African country. Probably the most prestigious academic course is the one at the National Defense University exclusively for African military officers at the rank of colonel.[13]

Military Training in Africa

US training of African militaries in Africa began in 1996, when the Clinton administration started the Africa Contingency Operations Training and Assistance (ACOTA) program. Previous training had been ad hoc, in support of specific operations, without any follow-up. The Clinton program involved setting up a full-time permanent training program in Africa to improve professional levels without reference to any particular problem or operation. It is still in operation. The motivation for the program's design was largely the failure of the international community to respond to the Rwandan genocide two years earlier, in 1994. The objective was to help African militaries develop the capacity to intervene in crisis situations such as the Rwandan genocide.

The funding for ACOTA and the selection of recipients are controlled by the State Department, and the program is administered by AFRICOM. Since the Clinton administration, well over 50,000 African military personnel have received ACOTA training. Many of these personnel have participated in UN peacekeeping operations in Darfur, South Sudan, the Central African Republic, and Somalia.[14]

In addition to training for rapid reaction, ACOTA support contains a significant component emphasizing "professionalism," including an emphasis on civil-military relations.

Expansion of Counterterrorism Support

After the death of Libya's Muammar Qaddafi in 2011, terrorist operations expanded in the Sahel region of Africa. This resulted in an expansion of the presence of US advisers and trainers from AFRICOM in Niger, Nigeria, Mali, Mauritania, and Burkina Faso. As of the end of the Obama administration, the presence of US military advisers was accompanied, in several situations, by advanced equipment that required special security arrangements. For example, the Combined Joint Task Force–Horn of Africa in Camp Lemonnier in Djibouti had eight predator drones and four fighter jets. In Niger, in both the capital city of Niamey and the central mining city of Agadez, there were US predator drone stations. As of mid-2019 there were 800 US military personnel in Niger. In Burkina Faso, in the main city of Ouagadougou, 120 US Air Force personnel operated surveillance aircraft that searched for terrorist fighting units in the surrounding Sahel subregion.

Overall, at the end of the Obama administration, there were about 3,500 US military personnel performing adviser and training duty in Africa. This raised the question of the overall impact on United States–Africa relations of this relatively large US military presence. Was the US military presence taking the oxygen out of the US-African diplomatic relationship? Was US policy toward Africa being militarized? To the extent that the Africans viewed the terrorist threat as authentic, they welcomed the US military presence. In addition, AFRICOM believed deeply in good civil-military relations. Accordingly, AFRICOM personnel visited many African countries from time to time in order to contribute to educational, environmental, and recreational projects. In the opinion of most observers, as of mid-2019, the US military presence was having an overall positive impact on United States–Africa relations.

US Military Assistance and Human Rights

Military units in the developing world, including Africa, sometimes lack the training, discipline, or leadership to behave properly toward civilian populations. Especially when terrorist groups reside within populations, military units will sometimes target enemies and innocent civilians alike. In recognition of this problem, Senator Patrick Leahy of Vermont in 2007 introduced legislation in the form of an amendment to the Foreign Assistance Act of 1962 that prohibits the provision of military assistance to foreign military units that "violate human rights with impunity."[15]

The key US government entity with responsibility for implementing the Leahy Amendment is the State Department's Bureau of Democracy, Human Rights, and Labor. During the final year of the Obama administration, under the Leahy Amendment, certain units of the Nigerian army that were pursuing the Boko Haram terrorists in the northeastern Borno State were cut off from US military assistance for a short period of time.

In general, the US foreign affairs and defense communities, including both civilian and military officials, are the first to emphasize the importance of good governance and economic development in the fight against extremism. In a hearing of the House of Representatives' Foreign Affairs Committee on the subject of counterterrorism in Africa on December 5, 2017, Deputy Secretary of State John Sullivan said: "Counterterrorism alone is not enough. What is needed are good governance, respect for human rights, political pluralism, economic development, democracy, free and fair elections, rule of law, security, water sanitation and medical services. These are the changes needed to improve the lives of people and prevent the extremists from recruiting them."[16]

The United States and Conflict Resolution in Africa

Until 1992, with the signing of the peace accord in Mozambique, conflict resolution in Africa was largely undertaken by the international community, especially the United States. During the period 1990–1993, the Organization of African Unity (now the African Union), under the leadership of its secretary-general, Salim Ahmed Salim, decided to establish its own mechanism for conflict prevention, management, and resolution.[17] Until that time, African governments were reluctant to become involved in civil conflicts because of their strict adherence to the principle of noninterference in the internal affairs of OAU member states. This principle turned out to be unworkable, because violent civil conflicts invariably have an impact on neighboring countries in the form of refugees, interrupted commerce, arms trafficking, and transportation disruptions.

The OAU's first important conflict intervention occurred in Rwanda in 1991, when it attempted to resolve the conflict between the Rwandan Patriotic Front, the Tutsi military that had invaded from Uganda, and the Rwandan government, led by President Habyarimana. The OAU recruited the mediating team from among senior African diplomats, and the government of Tanzania provided the venue at the conference center in the town of Arusha. The United States and other governments sent observers. This process resulted in the 1993 Arusha Accords, which thereby created a precedent for future OAU/AU interventions. The fact that the Arusha agreement of 1993 broke down in 1994 did not discourage the AU from taking charge of conflict resolution efforts from that point.

As of the Clinton administration, the US role in African conflict resolution changed from principal mediator to active supporter of the African Union, either directly or through the UN Security Council. During the George W. Bush administration, the United States began to send diplomats at the ambassadorial level to chronic conflict zones with the status of special envoy.

At the end of the Obama administration there were two US special envoys in Africa: former congressman Thomas Pariello was special envoy to the Great Lakes, including the Democratic Republic of the Congo,

Rwanda, and Burundi; and Ambassador Donald Booth was special envoy to Sudan and South Sudan. Earlier in the Obama administration, Ambassador Princeton Lyman, as special envoy for Sudan, played an important role in the transition of South Sudan to independence in 2011.

The idea behind the creation of the special envoy positions was to give greater visibility to intractable humanitarian problems caused by political conflict and to apply increased pressure on the protagonists.[18] The Trump administration continued the practice of naming special envoys to Africa's trouble spots. Peter Pham, director of African studies at the Atlantic Council of Washington, was named President Trump's special envoy to the Great Lakes region in 2017, and retired ambassador James Swan was called back to duty in 2019 to be the UN special representative to Somalia.

As of the end of the Obama administration, there was growing sentiment in the State Department that the special envoy position was not doing much more than undermining the regular bureaucratic mechanisms in US embassies and in country offices within the State Department.[19]

During the George H. W. Bush administration, the African Union established its Peace and Security Council, designed to emulate, in the African context, the United Nations Security Council. This entity has decisionmaking power with regard to interventions in the internal conflicts of member states. One of the important activities of the Peace and Security Council has been the support of democracy, including the sending of observers to elections.

The overthrow of elected governments, either by military coup or popular uprising, has diminished in Africa since early 1990. But when such overthrows occur, the African Union mobilizes to restore democracy. Good examples of the AU's work in this respect took place after military takeovers in Guinea (Conakry) in 2007 and in Burkina Faso in 2011. In both cases, the AU condemned the illegal military coups but offered to work with the military regimes to implement transitions to multiparty elections, which were accomplished successfully within a matter of months.[20]

Starting with the Clinton administration, US policy toward conflict in Africa has given priority to the mediating work of the African Union, with maximum US diplomatic and material support as needed, pursuant to Chapter VIII of the UN Charter as it pertains to the role of regional organizations.[21]

Disappointing Results

Despite substantial US and other international donor efforts to promote economic development in Africa, the results have been disappointing. While the United States, the European Union, the World Bank Group, and Japan were devoting significant resources to the promotion of rapid economic growth in sub-Saharan Africa, the first three generations of African leaders, between 1955 and 2019, had other priorities.

The European colonial powers bequeathed democratic, multiparty, parliamentary political systems. Within a short period of time, the Africans replaced the European systems with the African one-party state. The ruling parties had come out of the pre-independence liberation movements. Their leaders determined that African cultural norms could not tolerate the kind of unfriendly debates that take place within Western democratic systems. The African one-party state, emphasizing consensus building, was considered more suitable. In reality, the African one-party state became authoritarian and dictatorial, with the co-optation of civil society and the abolition of free speech through government control of the media.

With respect to economic policy, during the period 1960–1970, African leaders decided to emulate the socialist/labor European governments by nationalizing private enterprises, including plantations, transportation, banking, insurance, and manufacturing. Unfortunately, instead of managing these enterprises to earn and reinvest profits to finance expansion, African governments gave priority to the creation of employment. All of the enterprises had far too many employees, thereby requiring government subsidies to stay alive. In turn, the need for government subsidies took money away from essential services, including infrastructure maintenance, healthcare, and education. Needless to say, this environment did not lend itself to investments by the private sector. The overall result was an economic downward spiral through negative growth.

It was only after 1990 that the majority of African governments transitioned back to multiparty democracy and began to welcome investments by the private sector. Nevertheless, progress continued to be slow, with growth rates of 5 percent or less, when rates required for real growth should have been 10 percent or higher. Potential private investors continued to complain about the absence of the rule of law for the enforcement of contracts, as well as the deficits in electric power. While disappointed, the US government continued to preach and finance economic development for African nations, with the Trump administration naming its approach Prosper Africa.

China's Massive Presence in Africa: Good or Bad for the United States?

Since the early 1990s, during the George H. W. Bush administration, China has expanded its economy tremendously. This expansion required China to reach out to the rest of the world in search of energy and primary commodities. Africa, with its vast resources, became a natural target of China's outreach.

As a purchaser of African commodities, China approached African governments in several ways. With crude oil, for example, China negotiated what it called "win-win" deals. In return for a guaranteed quantity of crude oil, say 200,000 barrels per day, payable at prevailing world rates, China offered soft loans for infrastructure projects. These loans have come, and continue to come, from various Chinese institutions, including the Chinese Export-Import Bank, the China-Africa Development Fund, the China Development Bank, and the People's Bank of China. Between 2000 and 2014, Chinese institutions lent African governments and institutions $86 billion.

Chinese companies, both private and state-owned, have made large-scale investments in Africa, in manufacturing, agriculture, and infrastructure. In general, objective analyses have concluded that Chinese investments have been positive for African peoples in terms of increased employment, expanded infrastructure, and higher standards of living in the areas surrounding Chinese economic activity. However, not all Chinese companies are enlightened about African culture. They have created political problems regarding their treatment of workers and their indifference to environmental concerns in some countries, particularly Zambia. Overall, surveys of African opinion have given Chinese economic activity strong approval ratings. There is no doubt that Chinese investments in Africa have contributed to the growth of an African middle class, representing about 15 percent of the population.[22]

While China makes a point of noninterference in the internal affairs of African countries, it does need to protect its investments, and it does hope to be reimbursed for its massive loans. For this reason, China has slowly moved into African politico-military affairs in order to promote stability. In recognition of the stabilizing role of the African Union,

China has pledged $100 million in military assistance to the organization. China has also provided troops, police, and civilian personnel to six UN peacekeeping missions in Africa.[23] Since 2015, China's economic expansion has slowed, causing a significant decrease in its imports of African commodities and a commensurate slowdown in some African economies.

Another negative aspect of the Chinese-African relationship has been Africa's failure to defend itself against low-priced Chinese imports. Many of the Chinese workers who came to Africa with Chinese companies remained behind to establish retail businesses, which concentrated on importing Chinese goods and thereby inhibited the growth of indigenous manufacturing. The large apparel and textile manufacturing facilities in Kano, Nigeria, for example, went into steep decline as the result of Chinese imports.

There have also been reliable reports of shoddy work on some Chinese infrastructure projects. Hundreds of state-owned and private Chinese companies compete for contracts, and some do poor work, generating ill feeling. In general, however, the African people view the Chinese presence in Africa positively.[24]

Numerous observers have concluded that in Africa, China is in a state of ascendance, while the United States is in a state of comparative decline. China has replaced the United States as the biggest importer of commodities from Africa. But this is because the United States has become self-sufficient in crude oil and gas, which used to be major US import items from Africa.[25]

In general, it cannot be said that the Chinese presence in Africa is having a negative impact on United States–Africa relations. The United States retains its influence on major sociopolitical and foreign policy issues in Africa. The Chinese presence does not detract from the US presence. Indeed, it would not be a surprise to see US companies and Chinese companies collaborating on projects in Africa, each contributing their own special talents, a development that has already begun in several African countries.

The Chinese, like the colonial powers before them, and the Soviets, Cubans, Israelis, and Egyptians in between, have not diminished that indefinable special relationship between the United States and Africa.

Notes

Chapter 1: History

1. Peter Duignan and L. H. Gann, *The United States and Africa: A History* (Cambridge: Cambridge University Press, 1984).
2. http://www.u-s-history.com/pages/h357.html.
3. https://history.state.gov/milestones/1866–1898/spanish-american-war.
4. https://www.ourdocuments.gov/doc.php?flash=false&doc=62.
5. http://www.history.com/topics/world-war-ii/atlantic-charter.

Chapter 2: Franklin D. Roosevelt

1. US Department of State, *Foreign Relations of the United States* (hereafter *FRUS*), 1941, vol. 3, *Africa.*
2. http://www.history.com/topics/world-war-ii/battle-of-el-alamein.
3. https://en.wikipedia.org/wiki/Tunisian_Campaign.
4. http://www.jewishvirtuallibrary.org/the-french-vichy-regime.
5. https://www.britannica.com/event/Casablanca-Conference.
6. *FRUS,* 1942, vol. 2, *Europe: US-Vichy Relations,* Document 201.
7. Ibid., p. 557.
8. https://www.pinterest.com/pin/571323902703965288.
9. *FRUS,* 1942, vol. 1, *The United Nations,* pp. 37–42.
10. *FRUS,* 1941, vol. 3, *Africa,* p. 344.
11. *FRUS,* 1942, vol. 1, *The United Nations,* pp. 596–611.
12. *FRUS,* 1943, vol. 3, *Africa,* pp. 99–145.
13. Ibid., pp. 656–659.
14. http://www.presidency.ucsb.edu/ws/?pid=16591.
15. Ibid.
16. *FRUS,* 1942, vol. 4, *The Near East and Africa,* Document 27, Appointment of US representative resident in West Africa.
17. https://history.state.gov/milestones/1937-1945/yalta-conf.
18. http://www.presidency.ucsb.edu/ws/?pid=16591.

Chapter 3: Harry S. Truman

1. https://www.britannica.com/event/Dumbarton-Oaks-Conference.
2. https://www.senate.gov/artandhistory/history/common/generic/Featured
_Bio_Vandenberg.htm.
3. https://treaties.un.org/doc/publication/ctc/uncharter.pdf.
4. *FRUS*, 1945, vol. 1, *The United Nations*, pp. 789–790.
5. Ibid., p. 895.
6. Ibid., p. 1054.
7. *FRUS*, 1946, vol. 1, *The United Nations*, p. 599.
8. Ibid.
9. Ibid.
10. Ibid.
11. Ibid., p. 657.
12. Ibid., pp. 657, 704.
13. Ibid., p. 550.
14. *FRUS*, 1947, vol. 1, *The United Nations*, p. 281.
15. Ibid., p. 279.
16. Ibid., p. 289.
17. *FRUS*, 1947, vol. 5, *The Near East and Africa*, p. 727.
18. Ibid., p. 671.
19. Ibid., p. 674.
20. Ibid., p. 684.
21. Ibid., p. 698.
22. *FRUS*, 1950, vol. 1, *Foreign Economic Policy*, p. 160.
23. http://www.oxfordbibliographies.com/view/document/obo-9780199846733
/obo-.9780199846733-0058.xml.
24. *FRUS*, 1948, vol. 5, *Africa*, p. 524.
25. *FRUS*, 1950, vol. 5, *South Africa*, Document 972, US policy toward
Southwest Africa trusteeship.
26. Department of State, *Bulletin*, June 19, 1950, pp. 999–1003.
27. *FRUS*, 1948, vol. 5, *Africa*, p. 524.
28. *FRUS*, 1951, vol. 5, *Africa*, pp. 1269–1271.

Chapter 4: Dwight D. Eisenhower

1. *FRUS*, 1955–1957, vol. 18, *Africa*, p. 54.
2. Ibid.
3. Ibid.
4. Ibid., pp. 30–39.
5. Ibid., p. 40.
6. Ibid., pp. 57–66.
7. *FRUS*, 1952–1954, vol. 11, *The United Nations*, pp. 71–89.
8. Ibid.
9. *FRUS*, 1955–1957, vol. 18, *Africa*, p. 45.
10. Ibid., "National Security Council Report: NSC 5719/1."
11. *FRUS*, 1958–1960, vol. 14, *Africa*, pp. 1–11.
12. Ibid., pp. 19–20.

13. Ibid.

14. Ibid.

15. https://en.wikipedia.org/wiki/Force_Publique.

16. Lawrence Devlin, *Chief of Station Congo: Fighting the Cold War in a Hot Zone* (Washington, DC: PublicAffairs, 2007).

17. http://www.bbc.com/news/world-africa-22006446.

18. http://www.un.org/en/sc/documents/resolutions/1960.shtml.

19. Conor Cruise O'Brien, *To Katanga and Back: A UN Case History* (London: Hutchinson, 1962).

20. *FRUS,* 1958–1960, vol. 14, *Africa,* p. 160.

Chapter 5: John F. Kennedy

1. *FRUS,* 1961–1963, vol. 20, *The Congo Crisis,* p. 17.

2. Ibid., pp. 40–41.

3. Ibid., p. 1.

4. Ibid., p. 95.

5. Devlin, *Chief of Station Congo.*

6. http://www.globalsecurity.org/military/world/congo/adoula.htm.

7. *FRUS,* 1961–1963, vol. 20, *The Congo Crisis,* pp. 193–205.

8. https://www.youtube.com/watch?v=0KkjweVM-O4.

9. Frank Carlucci later went on to have a brilliant career in the Foreign Service as US ambassador to Portugal under President Nixon and national security adviser and secretary of defense under President Reagan.

10. *FRUS,* 1961–1963, vol. 20, *The Congo Crisis,* doc. 212.

11. Ibid., doc. 196.

12. Ibid., docs. 183–346.

13. *FRUS,* 1961–1963, vol. 21, *Kennedy in Africa,* docs. 187–188.

14. Ibid., doc. 189.

15. Ibid., doc. 202.

16. Ibid., doc. 209.

17. http://www.presidency.ucsb.edu/ws/?pid=8545.

18. *FRUS,* 1961–1963, vol. 21, *Kennedy in Africa,* doc. 217.

19. Ibid., doc. 200.

20. National Intelligence Estimate NIE 60/70-61, "Probable Developments in Colonial Africa," April 11, 1961. Available in *FRUS,* 1961–1963, vol. 21, *Kennedy in Africa,* doc. 190.

21. Williams memorandum to Secretary Rusk, February 25, 1963. Available in *FRUS,* 1961–1963, vol. 21, *Kennedy in Africa,* doc. 216.

22. *FRUS,* 1961–1963, vol. 21, *Kennedy in Africa,* doc. 311.

23. USUN telegram 831 to the State Department, September 20, 1961. Available in *FRUS,* 1961–1963, vol. 21, *Kennedy in Africa,* doc. 212.

24. State Department circular telegram to all US diplomatic posts in Africa, no. 2032, May 28, 1963. Available in *FRUS,* 1961–1963, vol. 21, *Kennedy in Africa,* doc. 219.

25. I was present at the dinner in question.

26. My observation as a member of the staff of the US embassy in Kampala in October 1962.

Chapter 6: Lyndon B. Johnson

1. *FRUS,* 1964–1968, vol. 24, *Africa,* doc. 187.
2. Ibid., doc. 188.
3. Ibid., doc. 412.
4. Ibid., doc. 405.
5. Ibid., doc. 200.
6. Ibid., doc. 457.
7. Briefings from the UK High Commission in Salisbury to US consulate-general, last week of October 1965. I was present for the briefings.
8. *FRUS,* 1964–1968, vol. 24, *Africa,* doc. 470.
9. Ibid., doc. 482.
10. Ibid., doc. 491.
11. Ibid., doc. 501.
12. Ibid., doc. 506.
13. I personally witnessed and participated in all of the measures taken to help Zambia overcome the problems associated with the economic boycott of Southern Rhodesia as described in these paragraphs. I was the economic-commercial officer at the US embassy Lusaka from November 1965 to October 1966.
14. *FRUS,* 1964–1968, vol. 22, *Congo,* docs. 313–366.
15. Ibid., doc. 452.
16. Ibid., doc. 454.
17. Ibid., doc. 459.
18. Ibid.
19. Ibid., doc. 484.
20. My personal observation.
21. *FRUS,* 1964–1968, vol. 23, *Congo,* doc. 488.
22. The Economic Section and the USAID mission were merged as a single office under the direction of the embassy counselor for economic affairs.
23. I participated fully in the McNamara visit.
24. *FRUS,* 1964–1968, vol. 23, *Congo,* doc. 498.
25. Ibid., doc. 504.
26. Ibid., doc. 505.
27. *FRUS,* 1964–1968, vol. 24, *Africa,* docs. 361, 363, 364.
28. Ibid., docs. 364, 367.
29. Ibid., docs. 367, 368.
30. Ibid., docs. 376, 377.
31. Ibid., doc. 385.
32. Ibid., doc. 386.
33. Ibid., doc. 396.
34. Ibid., doc. 402.

Chapter 7: Richard M. Nixon

1. I was at the US embassy in Kinshasa, Congo, at the time Nixon visited.
2. *FRUS,* 1969–1976, vol. E-5, pt. 1, *Sub-Saharan Africa,* doc. 7.
3. Ibid., doc. 58.
4. Ibid., doc. 60.
5. Judd Devermont, "The United States Intelligence Community's Biases During the Nigerian Civil War," *African Affairs* 116, no. 465 (2017): 1–12.

6. *FRUS*, 1969–1976, vol. E-5, pt. 1, *Sub-Saharan Africa*, docs. 25, 48.

7. *FRUS*, 1969–1976, vol. 28, *Southern Africa*, doc. 5.

8. Ibid., doc. 2.

9. Ibid., doc. 8.

10. National Security Decision Memorandum (NSDM) 38.

11. *FRUS*, 1969–1976, vol. 28, *Southern Africa*, docs. 16, 23, 27.

12. NSDM 75.

13. *FRUS*, 1969–1976, vol. 28, *Southern Africa*, docs. 39, 37, 54.

14. Ibid., doc. 15.

15. Ibid., doc. 17.

16. NSDM 38.

17. *FRUS*, 1969–1976, vol. 28, *Southern Africa*, doc. 23.

18. *FRUS*, 1969–1976, vol. 28, *Southern Africa*, doc. 32.

19. NSDM 81.

20. *FRUS*, 1969–1976, vol. 28, *Southern Africa*, doc. 40.

21. Ibid., doc. 70.

22. Ibid., doc. 45.

23. Ibid., doc. 72.

24. *FRUS*, 1969–1976, vol. E-5, pt. 1, *Sub-Saharan Africa, 1969–1972*, doc. 220.

25. Ibid., doc. 221.

26. This was an initiative of mine. I was director of Central African affairs in the State Department at the time. There are no documents released by the Office of the Historian describing this action.

27. *FRUS*, 1969–1976, vol. E-5, pt. 1, *Sub-Saharan Africa, 1969–1972*, doc. 223 (transcript of taped telephone call).

28. Michael Bowen, Gary Freeman, and Kay Miller, *Passing By: The United States and Genocide in Burundi—1972* (Washington, DC: Carnegie Endowment for International Peace, 1973).

29. James Peck, *Ideal Illusions: How the United States Government Co-opted Human Rights* (New York: Metropolitan, 2010), p. 55.

Chapter 8: Gerald Ford

1. *FRUS*, 1969–1976, vol. 28, *Southern Africa*, doc. 98.

2. Ibid.

3. Ibid., doc. 104.

4. Ibid., doc. 109.

5. https://www.cia.gov/search?q=The+CIA+station+chief+in+Leopoldville%2C+Larry+Devlin&site=CIA&output=xml_no_dtd&client=CIA&myAction=%2Fsearch&proxystylesheet=CIA&submitMethod=get.

6. *FRUS*, 1969–1976, vol. 28, *Southern Africa*, doc. 132.

7. Ibid.

8. Ibid., doc. 133.

9. Ibid., doc. 136.

10. Department of State, *Bulletin*, December 1, 1975, pp. 776–784.

11. *FRUS*, 1969–1976, vol. 28, *Southern Africa*, doc. 152.

12. Ibid., doc. 157.

13. Ibid., doc. 145.

14. Ibid., doc. 142.

15. Ibid., doc. 199.
16. Ibid., doc. 209.
17. Ibid., doc. 213.
18. Ibid., doc. 221.
19. Ibid., doc. 222.
20. Ibid., docs. 223–224.
21. *FRUS,* 1969–1976, vol. E-6, *Documents on Africa, 1973–1976,* doc. 130.
22. Ibid., doc. 140.
23. Ibid., doc. 139.
24. Ibid., doc. 147.
25. Ibid., docs. 148–149.
26. Ibid., docs. 152, 157.

Chapter 9: Jimmy Carter

1. Herman J. Cohen, *The Mind of the African Strongman: Conversations with Dictators, Statesmen, and Father Figures* (Washington, DC: New Academia, 2015).

2. In Herman J. Cohen's *Intervening in Africa: Superpower Peacemaking in a Troubled Continent* (New York: St. Martin's Press, 2000), chap. 2 provides background on the Eritrean insurgency.

3. Kenneth G. Weiss, *The Soviet Involvement in the Ogaden War* (Alexandria, VA: Center for Naval Analyses, Institute of Naval Studies, 1980).

4. *FRUS,* 1977–1980, vol. 17, pt. 1, *Horn of Africa,* doc. 27.

5. Ibid., doc. 32.

6. Ibid., doc. 38.

7. Ibid., doc. 47.

8. Ibid., docs. 57–58.

9. Ibid., docs. 61–62.

10. Ibid., doc. 64.

11. Ibid., doc. 66.

12. Ibid., doc. 85.

13. Ibid., docs. 70, 72, 74–75.

14. Ibid., doc. 79.

15. Cohen, *Intervening in Africa.*

16. *FRUS,* 1977–1980, vol. 17, pt. 1, *Horn of Africa,* doc. 84.

17. Ibid., doc. 108.

18. Department of State, *Bulletin,* October 10, 1980, p. 19.

19. I was US ambassador in Senegal then and participated in the operation.

20. Ibid.

21. *FRUS,* 1977–1980, vol. 16, *Southern Africa,* doc. 151.

22. Ibid., doc. 158.

23. Ibid., doc. 168.

24. Ibid., doc. 197.

25. Ibid., doc. 207.

26. Ibid., docs. 226, 230–231.

27. Ibid., doc. 235.

28. Ibid., doc. 236.

29. Ibid., doc. 242.

30. https://en.wikipedia.org/wiki/Lancaster_House_Agreement.

31. https://undocs.org/S/RES/435(1978).

32. https://en.wikipedia.org/wiki/Turnhalle_Constitutional_Conference.

33. *FRUS,* 1977–1980, vol. 16, *Southern Africa,* docs. 43, 46, 49.

34. Ibid., doc. 55.

35. Ibid., doc. 60.

36. Ibid., docs. 71, 74–75.

37. Ibid., doc. 73.

38. Ibid., doc. 78.

39. Ibid., docs. 92, 96.

40. Ibid., doc. 97.

41. Ibid., docs. 102, 120, 122.

42. *FRUS,* 1977–1980, vol. 6, *Soviet Union,* docs. 246–248.

43. Lannon Walker, "Travels with the Champion in Africa, 1980," *Foreign Service Journal,* October 2016.

44. Cohen, *The Mind of the African Strongman,* pp. 9–10.

45. I was deputy assistant secretary of state for intelligence and research at the time and had access to the intelligence in question.

46. Ibid.

Chapter 10: Ronald Reagan

1. Chester A. Crocker, speech in Honolulu about Southern Africa on August 29, 1981, reported in Bernard Gwertzman, "Official Says US Will Be Neutral on South Africa," *New York Times,* August 30, 1981.

2. http://www.sahistory.org.za/organisations/african-national-congress-anc.

3. https://undocs.org/S/RES/435(1978).

4. Crocker, speech in Honolulu.

5. *FRUS,* 1977–1980, vol. 16, *Southern Africa,* doc. 41.

6. https://www.globalsecurity.org/intell/ops/angola.htm.

7. Chester A. Crocker, *High Noon in Southern Africa: Making Peace in a Rough Neighborhood* (New York: Norton, 1992), p. 503.

8. Paul Lewis, "Angola and Namibia Accord Signed," *New York Times,* December 23, 1988, p. 6.

9. Cohen, *Intervening in Africa,* chap. 7.

10. Lewis, "Angola and Namibia Accord Signed."

11. Cohen, *Intervening in Africa,* chap. 7.

12. I was deputy assistant secretary of state for intelligence and research at that time and participated in the briefing described.

13. Cohen, *The Mind of the African Strongman,* chap. 10.

14. https://en.wikipedia.org/wiki/Toyota_War.

15. I was present at the luncheon in my capacity as senior director for African affairs on the National Security Council staff.

16. https://en.wikipedia.org/wiki/History_of_Liberia.

17. I was present at the meeting in my capacity as senior director for African affairs on the National Security Council staff.

Chapter 11: George H. W. Bush

1. I was present at a staff meeting chaired by Secretary of State James Baker in mid-June 1989 at which the directive was announced.

2. Assisting the Ethiopian Jews to emigrate to Israel was of particular interest to President Bush.

3. Tesfaye Dinka and I worked together for the Global Coalition for Africa, a World Bank–supported intergovernmental forum, from 1993 to 1998.

4. Cohen, *Intervening in Africa,* provides extensive details on the Ethiopian peace process, 1989–1991.

5. Cohen, *Intervening in Africa,* chap. 4, provides a more comprehensive account of US involvement in the Angolan peace process during the George H. W. Bush administration.

6. I was present during the conversation.

7. Crocker, *High Noon in Southern Africa,* pp. 244–248.

8. Cameron Hume, *Ending Mozambique's War: The Role of Mediation and Good Offices* (Washington, DC: US Institute of Peace, 1994).

9. Cohen, *Intervening in Africa,* chap. 7, provides a detailed description of the Mozambique peace process as seen from the State Department.

10. James Youboty, *Liberian Civil War: A Graphic Account* (Philadelphia: Parkside Impressions Enterprises, 1993).

11. Cohen, *Intervening in Africa,* chap. 5, provides full details of the war in Liberia and how policy unfolded during the George H. W. Bush administration.

12. Cohen, *Intervening in Africa,* chap. 6, provides full details of the US intervention in Somalia during the George H. W. Bush administration.

13. Cohen, *The Mind of the African Strongman,* chap. 14.

14. Princeton Lyman, *Partner to History: The US Role in South Africa's Transition to Democracy* (Washington, DC: US Institute of Peace, 2002).

15. UN Security Council Resolution 678, November 29, 1990.

16. Eric Schmitt, "After the War: 92 Senegalese Soldiers Die in Saudi Arabia Air Crash," *New York Times,* March 22, 1991.

Chapter 12: William J. Clinton

1. UN Security Council Resolution 857, June 6, 1993.

2. http://abcnews.go.com/blogs/politics/2014/04/bill-clinton-surprised-at-black-hawk-down-raid.

3. https://www.politico.com/story/2010/12/les-aspin-resigns-as-defense-secretary-dec-15-1993-046378.

4. "Somalia Was a United Nations Blunder," *New York Times,* March 26, 1994, editorial.

5. John L. Hirsch and Robert B. Oakley, *Somalia and Operation Restore Hope: Reflections on Peacemaking and Peacekeeping* (Washington, DC: US Institute of Peace, 1995). The authors evaluate the Somalia humanitarian operation as a major foreign policy success.

6. https://history.state.gov/milestones/1993-2000/somalia.

7. Cohen, *Intervening in Africa,* chap. 6.

8. "Don't Write Off Rwandan Violence as Ethnic: Uganda Shares the Blame," *New York Times,* April 20, 1994, letter to the editor.

9. Joyce E. Leader, interview by Charles Stuart Kennedy, October 29, 2003, Foreign Affairs Oral History Collection, Association for Diplomatic Studies and Training, https://www.adst.org/OH%20TOCs/Leader,%20Joyce%20E.toc.pdf?_ga=2.227450013.1658070092.1546642564-1884321325.1398958943, p. 58.

10. Herman J. Cohen, "Africa's Illegitimate Surrogate Wars," *American Foreign Policy Interests* (Journal of the American Committee on Foreign Policy Interests), September 4, 2014.

11. Cohen, *Intervening in Africa,* chap. 6.

12. https://peaceaccords.nd.edu/accord/arusha-accord-4-august-1993.

13. Leader interview.

14. UN Security Council Resolution 918, May 17, 1994.

15. UN Security Council Resolution 929, June 22, 1994.

16. Alan Kuperman, *The Limits of Humanitarian Intervention: Genocide in Rwanda* (Washington, DC: Brookings Institution, 2001), chap. 1.

17. Peter B. Levy, *Encyclopedia of the Clinton Presidency* (Westport: Greenwood, 2002), p. 308. See also Robert E. Gribbin, interview by Charles Stuart Kennedy, June 23, 2000, Foreign Affairs Oral History Collection, Association for Diplomatic Studies and Training, https://www.adst.org/OH%20TOCs/Gribbin,%20Robert%20E.toc.pdf?_ga=2.268350606.1658070092.1546642564-1884321325.1398958943, p. 100. Gribbin was the US ambassador in Rwanda.

18. Gribbin interview, p. 97.

19. Since the State Department financed Kagame's studies at the military school, I, as assistant secretary of state, had to give permission for his release.

20. Gribbin interview, p. 94.

21. https://en.wikipedia.org/wiki/Alliance_of_Democratic_Forces_for_the_Liberation_of_Congo.

22. Howard French and James C. McKinley Jr., "Hidden Horrors: A Special Report, Uncovering Guilty Footprints Along Zaire's Long Trail of Death," *New York Times,* November 14, 1997.

23. Radio France International, March 14, 1997.

24. Howard French, "Mobutu Leaves Capital of Zaire in What Many See as End to Rule," *New York Times,* May 8, 1997.

25. https://reliefweb.int/report/angola/how-kabila-lost-his-way-performance-laurent-d%C3%A9sir%C3%A9-kabilas-government.

26. Howard French, "Pilot's Account Seems to Confirm Rwanda Role in Congo Strife," *New York Times,* August 10, 1998.

27. Gérard Prunier, *Africa's World War: Congo, the Rwandan Genocide, and the Making of a Continental Catastrophe* (New York: Oxford University Press, 2008).

28. https://www.ft.com/content/cc008310-e47e-11e5-bc31-138df2ae9ee6.

29. Cohen, *Intervening in Africa,* chap. 3.

30. https://www.britannica.com/event/World-Trade-Center-bombing-of-1993.

31. https://en.wikipedia.org/wiki/Osama_bin_Laden.

32. PL 106, 200th Congress.

33. https://agoa.info/about-agoa.html.

Chapter 13: George W. Bush

1. Gary L. Gregg, "George W. Bush Foreign Affairs," University of Virginia Miller Center, https://millercenter.org/president/gwbush/foreign-affairs.

2. https://www.pepfar.gov.

3. https://unfoundation.org/how-to-help/donate/fight-aids-tuberculosis-malaria.html.

4. https://www.imf.org/en/Publications/Policy-Papers/Issues/2017/09/15/pp090117hipc-mdri-statistical-update.

5. https://pfbc-cbfporg/home.html.

6. "Powell to Urge Warring Parties to Exercise Restraint in Congo," *Chicago Tribune,* February 1, 2001. Powell was taking advantage of the presence of Kagame and Kabila in Washington to urge them to stop the fighting. Powell particularly urged Kagame to abide by accords calling for withdrawing foreign troops from the Congo.

7. Cohen, *Intervening in Africa,* chap. 3.

8. https://www.congress.gov/107/plaws/publ245/PLAW-07publ245.pdf.

9. https://www.usip.org/publications/2005/03/peace-agreements-sudan.

10. https://www.usip.org/publications/2005/03/peace-agreements-sudan.

11. https://foreignpolicy.com/2014/04/07/they-just-stood-watching-2.

12. http://web.stanford.edu/group/mappingmilitants/cgi-bin/groups/view/107#basic-info.

13. https://en.wikipedia.org/wiki/Camp_Lemonnier.

14. https://twitter.com/UnitedStatesAfricaCommand.

Chapter 14: Barack H. Obama

1. www.jfklibrary.org/JFK/JFK-in-History/JFK-and-the-Student-Airlift.aspx.

2. http://www.bbc.com/news/world-africa-38649362.

3. https://www.newsweek.com/president-obamas-legacy-africa-state-mind-493774.

4. https://data.worldbank.org/indicator/IC.BUnitedStates.EASE.XQ.

5. US Agency for International Development (USAID), *Power Africa Annual Report 2014,* https://www.usaid.gov/sites/default/files/documents/1860/United StatesAID_PowerAfrica_AR_July2014.pdf.

6. https://www.usaid.gov/powerafrica.

7. http://www.contourglobal.com.

8. I was present at the embassy of Senegal.

9. USAID, *Power Africa Annual Report 2016,* https://www.usaid.gov/news-information/videos/power-africa-2016-annual-report.

10. http://www.feedthefuture.gov.

11. Congressional Research Service, "The Obama Administration's Feed the Future Initiative," January 29, 2016, https://fas.org/sgp/crs/row/R44216.pdf.

12. http://www.fao.org/docrep/007/y5548e/y5548e07.htm.

13. https://obamawhitehouse.archives.gov/node/286081.

14. White House, "The President's Young African Leaders Initiative (YALI)," background and fact sheet, July 28, 2014.

15. USAID, "The Young African Leaders Initiative," January 18, 2017, press release, https://www.usaid.gov/yali.

16. https://www.cfr.org/backgrounder/somalias-transitional-government.

17. http://amisom-au.org/amisom-background.

18. https://en.wikipedia.org/wiki/History_of_the_transitional_federal_government,_Republic_of_Somalia.

19. http://www.bbc.com/news/world-africa-15336689.

20. http://www.washingtonexaminer.com/9-somali-men-in-minnesota... terrorism.../2607490.

21. www.npr.org/series/102787287/the-somali-minneapolis-terrorist-axis.

22. https://www.theatlantic.com/international/archive/2015/11/isis-boko-haram .../416673.

23. https://www.cfr.org/backgrounder/boko-haram.

24. https://www.dissidentblog.org/en/articles/arab-spring-timeline.

25. guides.library.cornell.edu/c.php?g=31688&p=200750.

26. https://rlphds.harvard.edu/faq/arab-spring-egypt.

27. UN Security Council Resolution 1970, February 26, 2011.

28. UN Security Council Resolution 1973, March 17, 2011.

29. http://www.rollingstone.com/politics/news/inside-obamas-war-room -20111013.

30. https://www.cfr.org/backgrounder/al-qaeda-islamic-maghreb.

31. https://www.theatlantic.com/international/archive/2016/04/obamas-worst -mistake-libya/478461.

32. Information provided by a UN officer assigned to South Sudan who was visiting the United States.

33. https://www.hrw.org/world-report/2017/country-chapters/south-sudan.

34. http://www.sahistory.org.za/dated-event/namibia-gains-independence (Namibia); http://www.mpil.de/files/pdf2/mpunyb_keller_9_127_178.pdf (Cambodia); http://www.tandfonline.com/doi/abs/10.1080/714002704 (East Timor).

Chapter 15: Donald J. Trump

1. https://foreignpolicy.com/gt-essay/understanding-trumps-trade-war-china -trans-pacific-nato.

2. https://ustr.gov/trade-agreements/free-trade-agreements/united-states -mexico-canada-agreement.

3. https://ustr.gov/issue-areas/trade-development/preference-programs/african -growth-and-opportunity-act-agoa.

4. https://agoa.info/news/article/15465-us-secretary-of-commerce-wilbur-ross -announces-1-billion-in-deals-during-africa-mission.html.

5. Statement by Acting Assistant Secretary of State for Africa Daniel Yamamoto, "Political Crisis in the Democratic Republic of the Congo," US House of Representatives, Foreign Affairs Subcommittee on Africa, Hearing, November 9, 2017.

6. https://usun.state.gov/highlights/8557.

7. https://www.whitehouse.gov/briefings-statements/remarks-national-security -advisor-ambassador-john-r-bolton-trump-administrations-new-africa-strategy.

8. https://www.washingtonpost.com/world/trump-administration-unveils-its -new-africa-strategy--with-wins-and-snags/2019/06/19/c751be4c-91f5-11e9 -956a-88c291ab5c38_story.html?utm_term=.46fcf3aaa334.

9. Remarks by Assistant Secretary of State Tibor Nagy, https://www.state .gov/baker-institute-for-public-policy-at-rice-university.

10. https://www.opic.gov/build-act/overview.

11. Ibid.

12. Deputy Secretary of State John J. Sullivan, "Counterterrorism Efforts in Africa," US House of Representatives, Committee on Foreign Affairs, Hearing, December 7, 2017.

13. Center for Strategic and International Studies, "U.S. Economic Engagement in Africa: Making Prosper Africa a Reality" (Washington, DC, April 2019).

Chapter 16: Successes and Failures

1. PL87-195.

2. I was the administrative officer at the US consulate-general in Kampala in 1962.

3. My personal observation while serving at the US consulate-general in Salisbury (now Harare).

4. My observation while stationed at the US embassy in Dakar, Senegal.

5. *FRUS,* 1964–1968, vol. 24, *Africa,* doc. 215.

6. Ibid.

7. Ibid.

8. http://ageconsearch.umn.edu/bitstream/7486/1/edc88-04.pdf.

9. https://www.state.gov/j/drl/hr.

10. Congressional Research Service, "Africa: U.S. Foreign Assistance, 1999," http://pdf.usaid.gov/pdf_docs/pcaaa813.pdf.

11. https://en.wikipedia.org/wiki/Peace_Corps.

12. https://en.wikipedia.org/wiki/Camp_Lemonnier#History.

13. https://www.britannica.com/topic/National-Defense-University.

14. http://www.africom.mil/what-we-do/security-cooperation/acota-africa-contingency-operations-training-and-assistance.

15. https://www.law.cornell.edu/uscode/text/22/2378d.

16. House of Representatives, Committee on Foreign Affairs, Hearing: December 7, 2017, "Counterterrorism Efforts in Africa," US Government Printing Office, Serial Number 115-103, Washington, DC, 2018.

17. John S. Moolakkattu, "The Role of the African Union in Continental Peace and Security Governance," *India Quarterly: A Journal of International Affairs,* October 6, 2010.

18. https://www.foreignaffairs.com/articles/1960-01-01/special-envoy.

19. https://www.politico.com/story/2017/08/28/tillerson-state-department-envoys-242118.

20. http://www.peaceau.org/en/page/38-peace-and-security-council.

21. Herman J. Cohen, "Africa and the Superpower," in Gunnar M. Sorbo and Peter Vale, *Out of Conflict: From War to Peace in Africa,* pt. 3 (Uppsala: Nordic Africa Institute, 1997).

22. https://www.cfr.org/backgrounder/china-africa.

23. Deborah Brautigam, "Five Myths About Chinese Investment in Africa," in *Foreign Policy Magazine,* December 4, 2015.

24. http://www.cnn.com/2016/11/03/africa/what-africans-really-think-of-china/index.html.

25. http://nationalinterest.org/feature/five-reasons-why-the-united-states-can%E2%80%99t-beat-china-africa-11094.7.

Bibliography

Bowen, Michael, Gary Freeman, and Kay Miller. *Passing By: The United States and Genocide in Burundi—1972.* Washington, DC: Carnegie Endowment for International Peace, 1973.

Center for Strategic and International Studies. "U.S. Economic Engagement in Africa: Making Prosper Africa a Reality." Washington, DC, April 2019.

Cohen, Herman J. *Intervening in Africa: Superpower Peacemaking in a Troubled Continent.* Basingstoke, UK: Macmillan, and New York: St. Martin's, 2000.

———. *The Mind of the African Strongman: Conversations with Dictators, Statesmen, and Father Figures.* Washington, DC: New Academia, 2015.

Congressional Research Service. "The Obama Administration's Feed the Future Initiative." January 29, 2016. https://fas.org/sgp/crs/row/R44216.pdf.

Crocker, Chester A. *High Noon in Southern Africa: Making Peace in a Rough Neighborhood.* New York: Norton, 1992.

Devermont, Judd. "The United States Intelligence Community's Biases During the Nigerian Civil War." *African Affairs* 116, no. 465 (2017): 1–12.

Devlin, Lawrence. *Chief of Station Congo: Fighting the Cold War in a Hot Zone.* Washington, DC: PublicAffairs, 2007.

Duignan, Peter, and L. H. Gann. *The United States and Africa: A History.* Cambridge: Cambridge University Press, 1984.

Harrison, Lawrence E., and Samuel P. Huntington. *Culture Matters: How Values Shape Human Progress.* New York: Basic, 2000.

Hirsch, John L., and Robert B. Oakley. *Somalia and Operation Restore Hope: Reflections on Peacemaking and Peacekeeping.* Washington, DC: US Institute of Peace, 1995.

Hume, Cameron. *Ending Mozambique's War: The Role of Mediation and Good Offices.* Washington, DC: US Institute of Peace, 1994.

Kenyon, Paul. *The Men Who Stole Africa.* London: Head of Zeus, 2018.

Kuperman, Alan. *The Limits of Humanitarian Intervention: Genocide in Rwanda.* Washington, DC: Brookings Institution, 2001.

Levy, Peter B. *Encyclopedia of the Clinton Presidency.* Westport: Greenwood, 2002.

Lyman, Princeton. *Partner to History: The U.S. Role in South Africa's Transition to Democracy.* Washington, DC: US Institute of Peace, 2002.

Mitchell, Nancy. *Jimmy Carter in Africa: Race and the Cold War.* Washington, DC: Woodrow Wilson Press, 2016.

O'Brien, Conor Cruise. *To Katanga and Back: A UN Case History.* London: Hutchinson, 1962.

Peck, James. *Ideal Illusions: How the United States Government Co-opted Human Rights.* New York: Metropolitan, 2010.

Prunier, Gérard. *Africa's World War: Congo, the Rwandan Genocide, and the Making of a Continental Catastrophe.* New York: Oxford University Press, 2008.

Rawson, David. *Prelude to Genocide: Arusha, Rwanda, and the Failure of Diplomacy.* Athens: Ohio University Press, 2018.

US Agency for International Development. *Power Africa Annual Report 2014.* https://www.usaid.gov/sites/default/files/documents/1860/United StatesAID _PowerAfrica_AR_July2014.pdf.

———. *Power Africa Annual Report 2017.* https://www.usaid.gov/news -information/videos/power-africa-2017-annual-report.

US Department of State, Office of the Historian. *Foreign Relations of the United States [FRUS].* https://history.state.gov/historicaldocuments/frus. Washington, DC.

———. 1941, vol. 3: *British Commonwealth, Near East, and Africa.*

———. 1942, vol. 1: *The United Nations.*

———. 1942, vol. 2: *Europe.*

———. 1942, vol. 4: *The Near East and Africa.*

———. 1943, vol. 4: *The Near East and Africa.*

———. 1945, vol. 1: *The United Nations.*

———. 1946, vol. 1: *The United Nations.*

———. 1947, vol. 1: *The United Nations.*

———. 1947, vol. 5: *The Near East and Africa.*

———. 1948, vol. 5: *Africa.*

———. 1950, vol. 5: *South Africa.*

———. 1951, vol. 5: *Africa.*

———. 1952–1954, vol. 11: *The United Nations.*

———. 1955–1957, vol. 18: *Africa.*

———. 1958–1960, vol. 14: *Africa.*

———. 1961–1963, vol. 20: *The Congo Crisis.*

———. 1961–1963, vol. 21: *Kennedy in Africa.*

———. 1964–1968, vol. 23: *Congo.*

———. 1964–1968, vol. 24: *Africa.*

———. 1969–1976, vol. E-5, pt. 1: *Sub-Saharan Africa.*

———. 1969–1976, vol. 28: *Southern Africa.*

———. 1977–1980, vol. 6: *Soviet Union.*

———. 1977–1980, vol. 16: *Southern Africa.*

———. 1977–1980, vol. 17, pt. 1: *Horn of Africa.*

Weiss, Kenneth G. *The Soviet Involvement in the Ogaden War.* Alexandria, VA: Center for Naval Analyses, Institute of Naval Studies, 1980.

Index

Aaron, David, 115–116
Acheson, Dean, 10–11, 27
ACOTA. *See* Africa Contingency
  Operations Training and Assistance
ACS. *See* American Colonization
  Society
Adamishin, Anatoli, 147–148
Addis Ababa, Ethiopia, 115–116, 150–
  151
Addou, Abdullahi Ahmed, 115
Adoula, Cyrille, 51–53
AFDL. *See* Alliance of Democratic
  Forces for the Liberation of Congo
Afghanistan, 129–131, 195–196
Africa, 2; African Asian Group in, 50;
  airports in, 11–12, 55; Ali in, 129–
  130; anticolonial wars in, 63–64;
  China in, 248–249; communist
  ideological threat in, 27–29, 32, 37;
  Cuban missile crisis and, 59–60; debt
  relief for, 201–202; decolonization in,
  36–38, 57; in Eisenhower's UN
  speech, 45; food imports, 215–216;
  Free France in, 7–8; HIV/AIDS in,
  199–200; instability of independent
  nations, 36–37; MCC in, 200–201,
  213; military defeats of Germany and
  Italy in, 5, 8; minerals exports, 63;
  Moscow Summer Olympics boycott,
  129–130; Nixon touring, 34–36, 40,
  85; OAU on, 59, 62–63; on Obama,
  212; in Operation Desert Storm
  combat, 173; Power Africa initiative
  in, 213–215; Sahel region of, 231–
  232, 243; self-government in, 29–30,
  32, 63 (*See also* African
  independence); Southern, liberation
  of, 63–65; Washington embassies of,
  61–62; white minority rule in, 57–59.
  See also specific countries
Africa, colonialism in, 1, 54–55; African
  nationalist movements against, 63–
  64; in Algeria, 22–23; Belgian
  Congo, 12–13, 41–44; British, 22, 57,
  65–67; in Eritrea, 23–24; French, 6–
  8, 21–23; German, 5, 95, 108;
  independence and, 22, 29–30, 32;
  Italian, 5, 108; in Namibia, 23–24;
  NATO and, 41; Portuguese, 25–26,
  57–58, 63–64, 90–91, 99–103, 158–
  162; in South Africa, 23–24; Soviet
  Union and, 26–29; US and, 1–2, 4,
  21, 23–30, 57–59
Africa, US and, 232–233; African
  independence, 38–39; aid, 54–57;
  Ali's tour, 130; bilateral relations
  between, 39–41; citizen involvement
  in policy, after Biafra, 89;

colonialism, 1–2, 4, 21, 23–30, 57–59; communism threat, 27–29; in conflict mediation and resolution, 142–143, 245–246; Dulles on, 32; economic development results, as disappointing, 247–248; foreign assistance budget, 231; free trade between, 196–197; "The Future of Africa" policy statement, 28–29; genocides, failure to act on, 97–98; instability, 36–37, 40–41; interests *versus* African liberation, 64–65; investment in, 212–217; Middle East policy, 171–173; military relations, 26–27, 55, 241–245, 243; nonalignment, 40; NSC 5719 on, 38; Prosper Africa program, 229–230; Rusk on, 54–55; Sears on, 33–34; Southern African liberation, 63–65; strategic minerals, 36–38; trade between, 2, 196–197, 212–216, 227–228; United States–Africa Leaders' Summit, 216–217; US Navy and, 2; wartime logistics, 11–12; white minority rule, 57–59, 64–65, 68, 170. *See also* Bush, George H. W.; Bush, George W.; Carter, Jimmy; Clinton, Bill; Eisenhower, Dwight D.; Ford, Gerald; Johnson, Lyndon B.; Kennedy, John F.; Nixon, Richard; Obama, Barack; Reagan, Ronald; Roosevelt, Franklin D.; Truman, Harry S.; Trump, Donald; *specific countries*

Africa Command (AFRICOM), 209, 243–244

Africa Contingency Operations Training and Assistance (ACOTA), 243

African Americans, 10, 137

African Asian Group, 50

African diplomats, Civil Rights Act and, 61–62

African Growth and Opportunity Act (AGOA), 197, 213, 227–228

African independence, vii–viii, 22, 32, 36–40; African embassies in Washington after, 61–62; in DRC, 42; electric power needs of, 213–214; in Northern Rhodesia and Malawi, 67; Portugal on, 90; in Portuguese

colonies, 100–103; Southern Africa liberation in, 63–64; UK and, 29–30, 81; UN and, 58, 61; US policy and, 54–55; white minority governments and, 63, 107

African National Congress (ANC), 133–134, 159–160, 168, 170

African nationalists, 21, 28, 36, 63–64, 66–69, 122

African Union (AU), 218, 246

African Union Mission in Somalia (AMISOM), 218

AFRICOM. *See* Africa Command

AGOA. *See* African Growth and Opportunity Act

AIAI. *See* al-Ittihad al-Islamia

Aideed, Mohamed Farah, 176–178

Air Force, US, 65

Albright, Madeleine, 183, 190

Algeria, 22–23, 33–34

Ali, Mohammed, 129–130

Alliance for the Restoration of Peace and Counter-Terrorism (ARPCT), 208

Alliance of Democratic Forces for the Liberation of Congo (AFDL), 187–188

American Colonization Society (ACS), 9, 145

Americo-Liberians, 10, 145

AMISOM. *See* African Union Mission in Somalia

ANC. *See* African National Congress

Angola, 25–26, 90–91, 100; Brezhnev Doctrine in, 137; Carter on, 136; communism and, 101–102; Cuba in, 102–105, 133–135, 139; Cuban-Soviet military initiative in, 104–105, 116; FNLA in, 64, 101–102, 104, 119–120, 134–135; Kissinger and, 101, 103–105, 137; Marxists in, 153–154; Mobutu Sese Seko and, 152–153, 189; MPLA in, 99, 101–103, 105, 134–135, 139; Namibia and, 133–134, 136; negotiations on, 154–156, 158–159; NSC on, 101; Reagan on, 137; Rwanda and, 192; dos Santos in, 154–155; Soviet Union in, 147–148, 152, 154–156, 158; UNITA in, 64, 101–105, 119–120, 134–135, 137–141, 153–158; US and, 104,

134–136, 139–140, 147–148, 152, 154–158; Windhoek talks on, 154–155

Angola Covert Paramilitary Program, of CIA, 103

Anti-Apartheid Act of 1986, 168, 170

Anticapitalism, 76–77

Anticolonialism, 2–3, 20–21, 58–59, 63–64

Apartheid regime, in South Africa, 34, 64–65, 90, 94–95, 134, 138, 167–170

AQIM. *See* al-Qaeda in the Maghreb

Arab Spring, 221–225

Arms Export Control Act of 1976, 104

Army, US, 5, 108

ARPCT. *See* Alliance for the Restoration of Peace and Counter-Terrorism

Arusha Accords, 180–182

Aspin, Les, 175

Atlantic Charter, 3–4, 7, 14, 21

AU. *See* African Union

Azores archipelago, 158–159

Baker, James, 94–95, 148, 153–155, 157–158, 167, 170–173

Balewa, Abubakar Tafawa, 81

Barclay, Edwin, 10

Barnard, John, 82

al-Bashir, Omar, 204, 206

Belgian Congo, 12–13, 41–44

Belgium, 13, 41–43, 47–48, 51–52, 73–78, 182

Benghazi, Libya, 222–225

Biafra, 81–84, 86–89

bin Laden, Osama, 195–196, 208

Bizimungu, Pasteur, 186

Black Hawk Down, 177–178, 183–185, 207

Blake, Robert, 77

Boko Haram, 219–221

Bolton, John, 229–230

Boren, David, 169

Botha, P. W., 128

Botha, Pik, 128, 169

Botswana, 166

Bourguiba, Habib, 21

Boutros-Ghali, Boutros, 182–183

Bowdler, William, 126

Brazzaville Protocol, 139

Brezhnev, Leonid, 117, 129, 137, 139

Brody, Reed, 188

Brzezinski, Zbigniew, 115–117, 128–129

Buchanan, Patrick, 138

Bureau of African Affairs, of US State Department, 41, 87, 97–98, 144, 150, 152, 161; on Botswana, 166; Nixon and, 91; RPF and, 180; on Somalia, 165; under Bush, G. H. W., 212–213

Bureau of Intelligence and Research (INR), 143

Burundi, 95–98, 109, 178

Bush, George H. W., 142, 146, 205; Africa policy of, 147; Bureau of African Affairs under, 212–213; Chissano and, 160–161; Gorbachev and, 147–148, 156; Habyarimana and, 179; on Iraq, 171, 174; on Liberia, 163; Middle East policy, 171–173; Mobutu Sese Seko and, 154, 187; in Mozambique peace process, 160–162; NIF and, 195; in Operation Restore Hope, 175; Reagan and, 160–161; on Rwanda, 179–181; on Somalia, 165–166; South Africa and, 167–168, 170; USAID under, 239

Bush, George W., 194, 196; AFRICOM and, 209; CBFP and, 202; on continental war in Congo, 202–203; CPA and, 205–207, 225; on debt relief, 201–202; evangelical Christians and, 203–205; foreign and national security policy priorities, 199; on HIV/AIDS in Africa, 199–200; ICU and, 207–208, 217–218; on Iraq, 225; MCC and, 200–201, 213; PEPFAR of, 200; President's Malaria Initiative of, 200; on Somalia, 207–209; on Sudanese civil war, 203–204

Byrd Amendment, 92

C-130 aircraft, 79–80

Callaghan, James, 106

Canup, William, 49–50, 52

Cape Verde, 90, 101

Carlson, Paul, 73

Carlucci, Frank, 52

Carnegie Endowment for International Peace, 98

Carrington, Peter, 123

Carter, Jimmy, 173; on Angola, 136; to Botha, P. W., 128; Brzezinski and, 115–117; EPLF and, 149; Ford and, 107, 111; on FRELIMO, 140; Gromyko and, 117; on Middle East, 130; Mobutu, J., and, 119–120; Moscow Summer Olympics boycott, 129–130; on Namibia, 128, 133; to Siad Barre, 117; on Somalia, 116; South Africa and, 133; on Southern Rhodesia, 113, 122–123, 133; UK and, 124; Vance and, 115, 120, 122, 125, 128; on white minority rule in Southern Africa, 120–124

Castro, Fidel, 102

Catholic Church, 140, 161

Cavaco Silva, Aníbal, 158–159

CBFP. *See* Congo Basin Forest Partnership

Central African Federation, 66

Central Intelligence Agency (CIA), 43, 75–76, 78–79, 103–104, 121, 208

Chad, 8, 144–145, 221

Chapin, Fred, 118

Chibok kidnapping, 220–221

China, 20–22, 104–105, 248–249

Chissano, Joaquim, 160–161

Christopher, Warren, 114

Chrome, Rhodesian, 91–92

Churchill, Winston, 3–4, 6, 13

CIA. *See* Central Intelligence Agency

Civil Rights Act of 1964, 61–62, 90

Clark Amendment, 104, 137–138

Clinton, Bill, 146, 175, 203, 223–224; AGOA of, 197, 213, 227; Black Hawk Down and, 177–178, 184–185, 207; on free trade, 196–197; Kabila, L. D., and, 190; Khartoum missile strike, 196; on Mobutu Sese Seko, 187, 189; Rwanda and, 181–182, 184–185; on Sudan, 204

CODESA. *See* Convention for a Democratic South Africa

Cold War, vii, 29–31, 40, 45, 65, 136, 142

Colonialism: anticolonialism and, 2–3, 20–21, 58–59, 63–64; "Fourteen Points" document on, 2–3; US, UN debating, 20–22. *See also* Africa, colonialism in

Colonial-racial problem, Algeria, 22–23

Communism, 27–29, 31–33, 37, 39–40, 47, 101–102, 117

Comprehensive Peace Agreement (CPA), 205–207, 225

Conditions and Trends in Tropical Africa (NIE-72), 37

"Conditions and Trends in Tropical Africa" (NIE-83), 36

Congo, 7; Adoula in, 51–52; Belgian Congo, 12–13, 41–44; Belgium and, 13, 41–43, 47–48, 51–52, 76–78; continental war in, 192–194, 202–203; crisis in, 48–54, 72–81; DRC, 12, 42, 44, 72, 74–75, 228–229; Eisenhower administration on, 41–44; genocide in, 98; Godley in, 75–77; Johnson administration on, 72–73; Kabila, L. D., in, 190–194; Kasavubu in, 42–43, 48–51, 72; Katanga mines in, 12–13, 49, 53; Katanga province of, 43, 47–54; Kennedy, J. F., administration policy on, 48–54; Kinshasa, 77–79; Léopoldville, 43, 48, 50–52, 75; Lumumba in, 42–44, 47–48, 51, 72, 74–75; McBride in, 78–81; military coup, by Mobutu, J., in, 74–75; Mobutu, J., in, 74–81; NATO on crisis in, 53; Nkrumah on, 50; Operation Dragon Rouge in, 73–74; Rwanda and, 190–191, 203; Simbas rebel group in, 72; Stanleyville, rebel takeover in, 72–74; Tutsis in, 190–191; UMHK in, 12–13, 48, 53, 76–78; UN and, 43–44, 47–54, 72; US and, 49–54. *See also* Zaire

Congo Basin Forest Partnership (CBFP), 202

Conte-Long law, 109

Convention for a Democratic South Africa (CODESA), 170–171

Cooper, James F., 10

Copper region, of Zambia, 71–72

Côte d'Ivoire, 10–11, 146, 162–164, 172

Counterterrorism, 243–244

CPA. *See* Comprehensive Peace Agreement

Crocker, Chester, 134–136, 138–140, 142–143, 154, 159, 171

Cuba, 102–105, 114, 116, 119–120, 133–137, 139
Cuban missile crisis, 59–60

Danforth, John, 204–205
Darfur, Sudan, 205–206
Davidow, Jeffrey, 161
Debt relief, 201–202
Decolonization, in Africa, 36–38, 57
Defense Department, US, 64–65, 119, 137–138
Democratic Republic of the Congo (DRC), 12, 42, 44, 72, 74–75, 228–229
Development aid, 56–57. *See also* US Agency for International Development
Devlin, Larry, 43, 74–75, 78
Dhlakama, Afonso, 161
Diouf, Abdou, 163, 173
Djibouti, 8, 118–119, 232
Dobrynin, Anatoly, 105
Doe, Samuel, 145–146, 162–164
DRC. *See* Democratic Republic of the Congo
Dulles, John Foster, 20, 31–32, 34, 37, 39–40

East Africa, 108–111, 173
Economic Community of West African States (ECOWAS), 163–164
ECOWAS Ceasefire Monitoring Group (ECOMOG), 163
Education, 40, 242
Egypt, 5, 34–35, 37, 222
Eisenhower, Dwight D.: Belgian Congo collapse and, 41–44; Dulles and, 31–32, 34, 37, 39–40; farewell address to UN, 45; Kennedy, J. F., and, 54, 235; Nixon and, 40, 43; OECD and, 57; on Soviets, in Congo, 43; Truman and, 30–31; US embassies in Africa established by, 39
Electric power, 213–215
Elizabethville, Katanga, 49–52
EPLF. *See* Eritrean People's Liberation Front
Eritrea, 5, 8, 23–25, 108, 110, 116–118, 151–152

Eritrean People's Liberation Front (EPLF), 114, 148–151
Essy, Amara, 172
Ethiopia, 5, 35, 44; Addis Ababa, 115–116, 150–151; communism in, 117; Conte-Long on, 109; the Derg in, 109–110; EPLF in, 148–151; Eritrea and, 24–25, 108, 110, 114, 116–118, 151–152; Ford and, 109–111; Haile Selassie in, 8–9, 24, 100, 108, 118; Jews in, 148–150, 152; Kifle in, 109–110; London conference on, 150–152; Marxists in, 109–110; Mengistu Haile Mariam in, 114–116, 118, 148–150; NSC on, 116; OAU signing in, 59; Ogaden region, 110, 113–115; Somalia and, 110–111, 114–119, 164; Soviet Union in, 114, 116–117, 147–149; Tesfaye Dinka in, 151, 172; TPLF in, 148–151; UK in, 113; US and, 8–9, 108–111, 114–116, 118, 147–152; US State Department and, 111, 150, 152
European Recovery Program. *See* Marshall Plan
Evangelical Christians, 203–205

Federal military government (FMG), of Nigeria, 86–87, 89
Feed the Future (FTF), 216
Flatin, Bruce, 179
FMG. *See* Federal military government
FNLA. *See* National Front for the Liberation of Angola
Ford, Gerald: Africa policy of, 99; Carter and, 107, 111; on Cuban-Soviet intervention in Angola, 104–105; Ethiopia and, 109–111; Kissinger and, 99–101, 104–105, 107, 109, 113, 124; Mozambique and, 100–101; Nixon and, 99, 111
Foreign aid, US, 56–57, 231, 235–238, 241–245
Foreign Service, US, vii–viii, 56, 103
"Fourteen Points" document, of Wilson, W., 2–3
France, 1–2, 9; Algeria and, 22–23, 34; Biafra and, 87–88; colonialism in Africa, 6–8, 21–23; Free France, 6–8; Morocco and, 12, 21–22; Nixon on,

34; safe zone, in Rwanda, 183–184; Tunisia and, 21–22; Vichy, 6–8, 12
Fraser, Donald, 98, 238
Free France, 6–8
FRELIMO. *See* Front for the Liberation of Mozambique
French Territory of the Afars and Issas (TFAI), 118
Front for the Liberation of Mozambique (FRELIMO), 64, 100, 140–141, 159–161
FTF. *See* Feed the Future
"The Future of Africa" policy statement, by US State Department, 28–29

Garang, John, 204–205, 225–226
de Gaulle, Charles, 6–7, 88
Gbadolite conference, 153
Gbenye, Christopher, 72–74
GCA. *See* Global Coalition for Africa
Geneva conference, 107–108
Genocide: in Burundi, 95–98, 109, 178; in Congo, 98; Kabila, L. D., insurgency and, 188; in Rwanda, 98, 182–185, 193; US failure to act on, 97–98
Germany, 5–9, 13, 16, 26, 30, 49–50, 95, 108
Ghana, 32, 34–35, 38, 50
Gizenga, Antoine, 44, 47–48, 51
Glasnost policy, of Gorbachev, 139
Global Coalition for Africa (GCA), viii
Godley, McMurtrie, 75–77
Gold Coast, 11, 29–30, 33–34
Goldberg, Arthur, 65
Goldwater, Barry, 62
Gorbachev, Mikhail, 139, 147–148, 156
Gowon, Yakubu, 81–82, 89
Gromyko, Andrei, 117
Guinea Bissau, 100–101

Habib, Philip, 115
Habré, Hissène, 144–145
Habyarimana, Juvénal, 179–182
Haig, Alexander, 134, 143–144
Haile Selassie, 8–9, 24, 100, 108, 118
Haley, Nikki, 228–229
Hammarskjöld, Dag, 48–49, 53
Harriman, Averell, 62–63
Harris, F. Allen, 167

Harrop, William, 79
Hausa-Fulani, 81, 83
Heavily Indebted Poor Countries (HIPC), 201–202
Herscowitz, Andrew, 214
HIPC. *See* Heavily Indebted Poor Countries
HIV/AIDS, 139, 199–200
Hoffacker, Lewis, 52
Holbrooke, Richard, 193–194
Houphouët-Boigny, Félix, 162, 164, 172
Howe, Jonathan, 176–177
Hoyt, Michael, 72–73, 96
Humphrey, Hubert, 80–81
Hutus, 95–97, 178–179, 181–188

Ibos, 81–83, 87, 89
ICRC. *See* International Committee of the Red Cross
ICU. *See* Islamic Courts Union
IFC. *See* International Finance Corporation
IMET. *See* International Military Education and Training
IMF. *See* International Monetary Fund
Inhofe, James, 204
INR. *See* Bureau of Intelligence and Research
International Committee of the Red Cross (ICRC), 88
International Court of Justice, 23–24
International Finance Corporation (IFC), 214
International Military Education and Training (IMET), 242
International Monetary Fund (IMF), 81
International Trusteeship System, in UN Charter, 16–17
Iran, 130–131
Iraq, 171–174, 206, 225
Ironsi, Johnson, 81
Isaias Afwerki, 149, 151–152
ISIL. *See* Islamic State in the Levant
ISIS. *See* Islamic State in Iraq and Syria
Islamic Courts Union (ICU), 207–208, 217–218
Islamic State, 231–232
Islamic State in Iraq and Syria (ISIS), 221
Islamic State in the Levant (ISIL), 219

Islamist extremism, 207–209, 232
Israel, 148–149, 152
Italy, 5, 8–9, 24, 108, 113
al-Ittihad al-Islamia (AIAI), 208

Janjaweed, 206
Janssens, Emile, 42
Japan, 16–17, 19
Jefferson, Thomas, 1–2
Jester, Perry N., 12
Jews (Ethiopian), 22–23, 148–150, 152
Johnson, Lyndon B.: on Biafra, 84; Civil Rights Act and, 61–62, 90; on Congo crisis, 72–73; crisis management by, 84; Harriman and, 62–63; on Korry Report, 237; McBride and, 78, 80; Mobutu, J., and, 79–80; on Nigeria, 82–84, 87; Nixon and, 85, 87; Rusk and, 70–71; to Smith, 68; Southern Rhodesia boycott, 70–71

Kabarebe, James, 191
Kabila, Joseph, 203, 229
Kabila, Laurent Desiré, 187–194
Kagame, Paul, 185–186, 191, 194, 203, 242
Kasavubu, Joseph, 42–43, 48–51, 72, 74–75
Katanga mines, 12–13, 49, 53
Katanga province, 43, 47–54, 119
Kennan, George, 27–28
Kennedy, Edward, 87, 96–97
Kennedy, John F., 47; Adoula and, 51–52; assassination of, 61; Congo policy of, 48–54; in Cuban missile crisis, 59–60; on development aid, 56–57; diplomatic approach of, 50, 52–53; Eisenhower and, 54, 235; Kenyan Airlift under, 211; Obote and, 59–60; Peace Corps and, 56, 240; Rusk and, 48–49, 52–53; Stevenson and, 58; to UN General Assembly, 58
Kenya, 33, 131, 192, 211, 218–219
Khartoum, Sudan, 148–149, 196, 203–206, 225–226
Kidan, Tesfaye Debre, 150
Kifle Wodajo, 109–111
Kinshasa, Congo, 77–79
Kissinger, Henry, 87, 89; Angola and, 101, 103–105, 137; on Burundi

genocide, 97–98; on Cuban-Soviet military initiative in Angola, 104–105, 116; Ford and, 99–101, 104–105, 107, 109, 113, 124; Kifle and, 109–111; Nixon and, 91–92, 97, 99; Nujoma and, 126; on Portugal, 99; South Africa and, 108; on Southern Rhodesia, 105–107
de Klerk, F. W., 167–170
Korean War, 24, 31, 108
Korry Report, 237–238
Kuwait, 130–131, 165, 171, 173, 206

Lancaster House Conference, 123–124
Laval, Pierre, 6
League of Nations, 8–9, 15–19, 21, 23, 64, 92–93
Léopoldville, Congo, 43, 48, 50–52, 75
Levin, Melvin H., 97
Lewis, Paul, 142
Liberia, 35; Bush, G. H. W., on, 163; Côte d'Ivoire and, 162–164; Doe and, 162–164; former slaves in, 9–10, 145; Roosevelt and, 10–11; Shultz in, 146; Taylor, C., in, 162–164; Tolbert, W. R., assassination in, 145; US and, 8–11, 162–163
Libya, 35, 143–145, 209, 222–225, 232
Lloyd, Selwyn, 32, 35
Lumumba, Patrice, 42–44, 47–48, 51, 72, 74–75
Lusaka, Zambia, 71

Malawi, 67
Mali, 224
Manafort, Paul, 153
Mandela, Nelson, 168–171, 188
Manhattan Project, 13
Marshall Plan, 21, 27, 29, 56
Marxists, 109–110, 113, 153–154, 160, 170
Mathews, Elbert G., 89
Mauritania, 12
Mboya, Tom, 211
McBride, Robert, 78–81
MCC. *See* Millennium Challenge Corporation
McDermott, Jim, 196–197
McGhee, George, 28–30
McHenry, Donald, 120–121, 124–125

McNamara, Robert, 65, 77–78
Melady, Thomas, 96
Meles Zenawai, 151–152
Mengistu Haile Mariam, 114–116, 118, 148–150
Middle East, 130–131, 171–173, 195
Military support, foreign aid and, 241–245
Millennium Challenge Corporation (MCC), 200–201, 213–214
Minneapolis, Minnesota, 219
Mitifu, Faida, 193
Mobutu, Joseph, 48, 50, 74–81, 119–120
Mobutu Sese Seko, 152–154, 185, 187–190
Mogadishu, Somalia, 164–165, 176, 207–208, 217–218
Moi, Daniel Arap, 161
Mombasa, Kenya, 131
Mondale, Walter, 121
Montreal Summer Olympics, 130
Morocco, 6, 12, 21–22, 34
Morris, Roger, 89
Moscow Summer Olympics, 129–130
Mozambican National Resistance (RENAMO), 141–142, 159–161
Mozambique, 25–26, 70, 90–91; Catholic Church in, 161; Ford and, 100–101; FRELIMO in, 64, 100, 140–141, 159–161; peace process, 159–162; Portugal and, 158–160; Reagan on, 140–142, 159; RENAMO in, 141–142, 159–161; South Africa and, 141–142, 159–160; Southern Rhodesia and, 105–106, 108, 141
MPLA. *See* Popular Movement for the Liberation of Angola
Mubarak, Hosni, 222
Mugabe, Robert, 105, 107, 122–124, 133, 161–162
Munongo, Godefroid, 52
Museveni, 179–181, 186
Muslims, 22–23, 194, 220–221
Muzorewa, Abel, 122–123

NAFTA. *See* North American Free Trade Agreement
Nagy, Tibor, 230
Namibia, 23–24, 29, 64, 120–121; Angola, Cuba and, 133–134, 136; Brazzaville Protocol on, 139; Carter on, 128, 133; negotiations on, 126–129, 138–140; Reagan on, 133; South Africa and, 125–129, 133, 138; SWAPO and, 125–127; UN and, 124–126, 134–135, 138–139; Vance on, 128; Western Contact Group and, 126–128. *See also* Southwest Africa
Namibian Contact Group, 125
National Front for the Liberation of Angola (FNLA), 64, 101–102, 104, 119–120, 134–135
National intelligence estimates (NIEs), 36–37
National Islamic Front (NIF), 194–195
National Patriotic Front of Liberia (NPFL), 163
National Security Council (NSC), 36, 38, 40, 57, 93, 116; on Angola, 101; on Ethiopia, 116; Kissinger and, 97; on Siad Barre, 117
NATO. *See* North Atlantic Treaty Organization
Navy, US, 2–3, 108, 119
Nazi Germany, 6–8, 13, 26, 108
Neoimperialism, 58–59, 74
Newsom, David, 87
NGO Transparency International, 201
Nguesso, Denis Sassou, 139
NIEs. *See* National intelligence estimates
NIF. *See* National Islamic Front
Niger, 221, 224, 232, 243
Nigeria, 32–33; Biafra crisis in, 81–84, 86–89; Boko Haram in, 219–221; cassava production in, 216; crude oil production of, 213; FMG of, 86–87, 89; de Gaulle on, 88; Hausa-Fulani in, 81, 83; Ibos in, 81–83, 87, 89; Johnson administration on, 82–84, 87; military coups in, 81–82; Nixon administration on, 87–88; State Department on, 82–83, 87–88; UK and, 81
Nixon, Richard, 211; Africa policy of, 85–86; Africa tours of, 34–36, 40, 85; on basic human needs, 238–239; Bureau of African Affairs to, 91; on Burundi genocide, 97; Eisenhower and, 40, 43; Ford and, 99, 111; Johnson and, 85, 87; Kissinger and,

91–92, 97, 99; on Nigeria, 87–88; on South Africa, 93–95; on Southern Africa, 89–95; on Southwest Africa, 94–95; on US consulate in Salisbury, 92; "U.S. Foreign Policy for the 1970s" report by, 86
Nkomati Accord, 159–160
Nkomo, Joshua, 69, 107, 120, 122–123
Nkrumah, Kwame, 29–30, 34, 50
North American Free Trade Agreement (NAFTA), 227
North Atlantic Treaty Organization (NATO), 21, 25–26, 28, 31, 41, 43, 53, 223–224
Northern Rhodesia, 12, 67
NPFL. *See* National Patriotic Front of Liberia
NSC. *See* National Security Council
NSC-32, 116
NSC-5719, 38
Nujoma, Sam, 126
Nyasaland, 67
Nyerere, Julius, 97

Oakley, Robert, 166, 176
OAU. *See* Organization of African Unity
Obama, Barack, 207–209, 232, 239–240; AMISOM under, 218; Arab Spring and, 221–225; Boko Haram and, 221; counterterrorism under, 243–244; FTF initiative of, 216; Kenyan father of, 211; Libya and, 222–223, 225; Power Africa initiative of, 213–215; as realist, 212; on Somalia, 217–218; South Sudan and, 226; on trade and investment in Africa, 212–216; United States–Africa Leaders' Summit of, 216–217; YALI of, 217
Obote, Milton, 59–60
OECD. *See* Organisation for Economic Co-operation and Development
Office of Strategic Services (OSS), 13
Ogaden region, of Ethiopia, 110, 113–115
Ojukwu, Odumegwu, 89
Operation Desert Storm, 165, 173
Operation Dragon Rouge, 73–74
Operation Restore Hope, 175, 177–178
OPIC. *See* Overseas Private Investment Corporation

Organisation for Economic Co-operation and Development (OECD), 57
Organization of African Unity (OAU), 59, 62–63, 68, 103, 107, 115–116, 130, 180–181, 245
OSS. *See* Office of Strategic Services
Overseas Private Investment Corporation (OPIC), 214, 231
Owen, David, 121–122

Pacific islands, Japanese, 17, 19
PAIGC. *See* Party for the Independence of Guinea and Cape Verde
Pakistan, 176
Palmer, Joseph, 83–84
Party for the Independence of Guinea and Cape Verde (PAIGC), 101
Peace Corps, 56, 240–241
PEPFAR. *See* President's Emergency Plan for AIDS Relief
Persian Gulf, 130
Pétain, Marshall Philippe, 6, 8
Plitt, Edward A., 21
Popular Movement for the Liberation of Angola (MPLA), 99, 101–103, 105, 134–135, 139
Portugal, 65; on African independence, 90; Angolan peace negotiations in, 155, 158–159; colonialism in Africa, 25–26, 57–58, 63–64, 90–91, 99–103, 158–162; Cuba and, 102; Mozambique and, 158–160; in Southern Africa, 90–91; US and, 25, 59, 66
Powell, Colin, 166, 202–203, 205
Power Africa, 213–215
President's Emergency Plan for AIDS Relief (PEPFAR), 200
President's Malaria Initiative, 200
Prosper Africa, 229–230
Public opinion on South Africa, in US, 136–138

Qaddafi, Muammar, 143–145, 209, 222–224, 232
al-Qaeda, 208, 219
al-Qaeda in the Maghreb (AQIM), 221

Racism, 59, 65, 93, 95

Rally for Congolese Democracy (RCD), 191

Rangel, Charles, 197

Rawson, David, 180–181

RCD. *See* Rally for Congolese Democracy

Reagan, Ronald, 19, 241; on Angola, 137; Buchanan and, 138; Bush, G. H. W., and, 160–161; Doe and, 146; Habré and, 144–145; Haig and, 143; on Mozambique, 140–142, 159; on Namibia, 133; on Qaddafi, 144–145; South Africa and, 136, 138, 167

the Red Terror, 109, 115

RENAMO. *See* Mozambican National Resistance

Rhodesia. *See* Northern Rhodesia; Southern Rhodesia

Rhodesian Front Party, 67

Rice, Susan, 185, 190

Richard, Ivor, 107

Roberto, Holden, 102

Roosevelt, Franklin D., 3, 6, 9–11, 13, 26

RPF. *See* Rwandan Patriotic Front

Rusk, Dean, 48–49, 52–55, 65, 70–71

Rwanda, 97; Albright on, 183; Angola and, 192; Arusha negotiations on, 180–181; Belgium and, 182; Burundi and, 95; Bush, G. H. W., on, 179–181; Clinton and, 181–182, 184–185; Congo and, 190–191, 203; French safe zone in, 183–184; genocide in, 98, 182–185, 193; Hutus and Tutsis in, 178–179, 181–184; against Mobutu Sese Seko, 187; OAU on, 180–181, 245; RPF in, 179–182, 184–186; Uganda and, 185–186, 191–192; US and, 189; Zaire and, 184–185, 189; Zaire refugee camps destroyed by, 186–187

Rwandan Patriotic Front (RPF), 179–182, 184–186

Rwigyema, Fred, 186

SADC. *See* Southern African Development Community

Sahel region, of Africa, 231–232, 243

Salisbury, Southern Rhodesia, 92

San Francisco conference, for establishment of UN, 15–17

Santos, Eduardo dos, 152–155, 157

São Tomé, 90, 101

Sarbanes, Paul, 169

Satterthwaite, Joseph, 41

Savimbi, Jonas, 152–158, 162

Schaufele, William, 126

Sears, Mason, 33–34

Self-government, 29–30, 32, 63

Senegal, 7, 12, 173, 214–215

Sengier, Edgar, 13

al-Shabaab, 208, 217–219

Shekau, Abubakar, 220

Shevardnazde, Eduard, 156

Shultz, George, 134, 146

Siad Barre, Mohamed, 110–111, 113–114, 117, 164, 218

Sierra Leone, 10–11

Simbas, 72, 74

Simon, Paul, 169

Sithole, Ndabaningi, 69, 122

Six Day War, 85

Smith, Ian, 67–69, 106–107, 121–122

Somalia, 130; Aideed in, 176–178; Black Hawk Down in, 177–178, 207; Bureau of African Affairs on, 165; Bush, G. H. W., on, 165–166; Bush, G. W., and, 207–209; Carter on, 116; Ethiopia and, 110–111, 114–119, 164; Islamist extremism in, 207–209; as Marxist socialist, 113; Mogadishu, 164–165, 176, 207–208, 217–218; Obama on, 217–218; Operation Restore Hope in, 175, 177–178; refugees from, 218–219; al-Shabaab in, 208, 217–218; Soviet Union and, 110–111, 113–115; Sudan and, 208; UNOSOM in, 175–176; US and, 111, 115–116, 118–119; US State Department on, 165–166

South Africa, 5, 9, 17, 19, 23–24, 29, 33; African nationalist movement against, 63–64; ANC in, 133–134, 159–160, 168, 170; Angola, Cuba and, 134–135, 139; apartheid regime in, 34, 64–65, 90, 94–95, 134, 138, 167–170; Bush, G. H. W., and, 167–168, 170; Carter and, 133; CODESA on, 170–171; economic sanctions against, 138; Kissinger and, 108; de Klerk in, 167–170; Mandela in, 168–171; Mozambique and, 141–142,

159–160; on Mugabe, 133; Namibia
and, 125–129, 133, 138; Nixon on,
93–95; Reagan and, 136, 138, 167;
Southern Rhodesia and, 121;
Southwest Africa and, 92–95, 106,
121, 124–129; UK arms sales to, 94;
UN on, 64, 89, 92–94, 121; UNITA
and, 105; US on, 59, 93–94, 136–
138, 170; white minority rule in, 57–
58, 97–98
South African Embassy, 136
South Sudan, 207, 225–226, 228
Southern Africa, 57–59, 63–65, 89–95,
120–124
Southern African Development
Community (SADC), 192
Southern Rhodesia, 34; African
nationalists in, 66–69, 122; Carter on,
113, 122–123, 133; CIA on, 121;
crisis, of November 1965, 65–72;
Declaration of Independence, 70–71;
Geneva conference on, 107–108;
Johnson on, 70–71; Kissinger on,
105–107; Mozambique and, 105–106,
108, 141; OAU on, 107; Salisbury,
92; Smith in, 67–69, 106–107, 121;
South Africa and, 121; Southwest
Africa and, 120; UK, US and, 68–69,
91–92, 141; UK and, 57–59, 65–70,
91–92, 106, 141; Umtali oil refinery
in, 70; UN sanctions against, 91; US
boycott of, 70–72; US intelligence
community on, 69–70; white exodus
from, 121–122; white minority rule
in, 57–59, 63–70, 89, 107–108;
Wilson, H., on, 67–69; Zambia and,
70–71
Southwest Africa, 23–24, 29, 57, 64–65,
92–95, 106, 120–121, 124–129. *See
also* Namibia
Southwest Africa People's Organization
(SWAPO), 105, 108, 125–127, 133
Soviet Union, 20–22, 26–32, 37–40;
Afghanistan invasion, 129–131; in
Angola, 147–148, 152, 154–156, 158;
Brzezinski on, 116–117; China and,
104–105; as chrome source, 91; in
Congo, 43; Cuba and, 103–105, 114,
116, 119–120, 136; in Cuban missile
crisis, 60; in Ethiopia, 114, 116–117,
147–149; Gorbachev in, 139, 147;

Mobutu, J., against, 119–120; Siad
Barre and, 110, 117; Somalia and,
110–111, 113–115; US–USSR
détente and, 104–105, 111, 116–118.
See also United States (US), Soviet
Union and
Spaak, Paul-Henri, 52
Spinola, Antonio de, 100
SPLM. *See* Sudan People's Liberation
Movement
Stanleyville, Congo, 72–74
Stassen, Harold, 16
State Department, US, 4, 22, 27–29, 33,
39, 131; on African airport access,
55; in Ali's Africa tour, 129–130; on
Angola, 156–157; on Biafra, 87; on
Burundi, 96–98; against Byrd
Amendment, 92; in Congo crisis, 54;
on Cuba, in Angola, 102; EPLF and,
149–150; Ethiopia and, 111, 150,
152; Kenyan Airlift of, 211; on
Mobutu, J., coup, 75; on Nigeria, 82–
83, 87–88; Nixon on, 35–36; to
Obote, 59–60; Policy Review
Committee, 114–115; on Somalia,
165–166; on South Africa, 170; strict
neutrality policy, 88–89; to USAID,
71. *See also* Bureau of African
Affairs, of US State Department
Stevenson, Adlai, 58
Sudan, 35; Bush, G. W., on civil war in,
203–204; Clinton on, 204; Darfur,
205–206; Khartoum, 148–149, 196,
203–206, 225–226; Muslims in, 194;
Somalia and, 208; South Sudan, 207,
225–226, 228; terrorism, in US, 195–
196
Sudan Peace Act of 2002, 204
Sudan People's Liberation
Movement (SPLM), 148, 204–205,
225–226
Sullivan, John, 244–245
SWAPO. *See* Southwest Africa People's
Organization

Tanzania, 178, 180
Taylor, Charles, 162–164
Taylor, Lawrence W., 7
Terrorism, 192, 194–196, 202, 208, 219–
221, 231–232, 243–244
Tesfaye Dinka, 151, 172

TFAI. *See* French Territory of the Afars and Issas

Thatcher, Margaret, 123

Tigre People's Liberation Front (TPLF), 148–151

Timberlake, Claire H., 8

Tingi Tingi massacre, 188–190

Tolbert, A. P., 162

Tolbert, William R., Jr., 145, 162

Touré, Sekou, 62

TPLF. *See* Tigre People's Liberation Front

Trade, between Africa and US, 2, 196–197, 212–216, 227–228

Truman, Harry S., 15–16, 21, 23–31, 56

Trump, Donald, 208–209, 227–233

Tshombe, Moïse, 43, 47, 49–53, 72, 79–80, 119

Tunisia, 5, 21–22, 34, 222

Tunney, John, 97

al-Turabi, Hassan, 194–195

Turnhalle Constitutional Conference, 125–126

Tutsis, 95–97, 178–179, 181–184, 186, 190–191

UDI. *See* Unilateral Declaration of Independence

Uganda, 59, 179–181, 185–186, 191–192

UK. *See* United Kingdom

UMHK. *See* Union Minière de Haut Katanga

Umkhonto we Sizwe, 134

UN. *See* United Nations

UN High Commission for Refugees (UNHCR), 179, 185

UN Transitional Advisory Group (UNTAG), 126

UNAMIR. *See* United Nations Assistance Mission for Rwanda

UNHCR. *See* UN High Commission for Refugees

Unilateral Declaration of Independence (UDI), 65–66

Union Carbide Corporation, 91–92

Union Minière de Haut Katanga (UMHK), 12–13, 48, 53, 76–78

United Front for the Total Liberation of Angola (UNITA): in Angola, 64, 101–105, 119–120, 134–135, 137–141, 153–158; Baker on, 154–155; Bush, G. H. W. and, 154; Marxists and, 153–154; Savimbi in, 153–158

United Kingdom (UK), 9, 18–20; African independence and, 29–30, 81; Carter and, 124; Conservative party government, 123–124; Dulles on, 32; Eritrea and, 24–25; in Ethiopia, 113; Nigeria and, 81; South Africa and, 94; Southern Rhodesia and, 57–59, 65–70, 91–92, 106, 141; on Umtali oil refinery, 70; US and, 2–4, 58–59, 68–69, 91–92, 94, 122–123, 141; Wilson, H., and, 67–69

United Nations (UN), 13–14; African independence and, 58, 61; Black Hawk Down and, 177–178; colonial system debate in, 20–22; Commission on Human Rights, 188; Congo and, 43–44, 47–54, 72; Cuba in, 102; Eisenhower farewell address to, 45; on Eritrea and Ethiopia, 118; General Assembly, 17–19, 20–23, 29, 31, 58, 65, 125; Global Fund, 200; on Iraq, 172; on Katangan secession, 53–54; Namibia and, 124–126, 134–135, 138–139; peacekeepers, in Congo, 43–44, 47–48, 72; San Francisco conference for establishment of, 15–17; Security Council, 17, 41, 43–44, 68, 73–74, 92–93, 125, 172, 177, 182–185, 188, 193, 218, 222–223; on South Africa, 64, 89, 92–94, 121; Southern Rhodesia sanctions, 91; on Southwest Africa, 92–93; Trusteeship Council, 16–20, 23, 34, 65. *See also* United States (US), UN and

United Nations Assistance Mission for Rwanda (UNAMIR), 181–182

United Nations Operation in Somalia (UNOSOM), 175–176

United States (US), 1; Agency for International Development, 56; Air Force, 65; on Angola, 104, 134–136, 139–140, 147–148, 152, 154–158; Anti-Apartheid Act, 168, 170; anticolonialism in, 2–3, 20–21; Arms Export Control Act, 104; Army, 5,

108; on Atlantic Charter, 3–4; Belgium and, 73–74; Congo and, 49–54; Congress, economic sanctions against South Africa, 138; consulate in Elizabethville, 49–52; Defense Department, 64–65, 119, 137–138; East Africa interests, 108–111; economic boycott of Southern Rhodesia, 70–72; embassies, in Africa, 39; embassy, in Léopoldville, 43, 48, 50–52, 75; embassy, in Lusaka, 71; Ethiopia and, 8–9, 108–111, 114–116, 118, 147–152; foreign aid, 56–57, 235–238, 241–245; Foreign Service, vii–viii, 56, 103; freed slaves of, 9–10, 145; Kabila, L. D., and, 189–190; on Katanga province, of Congo, 49; in Korean War, 24; Liberia and, 8–11, 162–163; military facilities, in Kenya, 131; Navy, 2–3, 108, 119; OSS, 13; policy in Africa (*See Africa, US and*; *specific topics*); Portugal and, 25, 59, 66; public political opinion on, 136–138; Rwanda and, 189; Somalia and, 111, 115–116, 118–119; South Africa policy, 93; on Southern Rhodesia, 66, 68–71; Sudan-based terrorism in, 195–196; UK and, 2–4, 58–59, 68–69, 91–92, 94, 122–123, 141; uranium and, 12–13; USAID, 71; Vichy France and, 6; on War of Eritrean Independence, 118; Webster-Ashburton Treaty of 1842, with UK, 2; Zambia exports and, 71. *See also* Africa, US and; Bureau of African Affairs, of US State Department; State Department, US; *specific US presidents*

United States (US), Soviet Union and, 114–115, 129–130; on Angola, 147–148, 152, 154–156, 158; Cold War, vii, 29–31, 40, 45, 65, 136, 142; détente between, 104–105, 111, 116–118; on Ethiopia, 147–149

United States (US), UN and: colonial system debate, 20–22; Congo and, 49–53; CPA, 205, 207; Portugal, UK and, 58–59; Rusk on, 48–49, 52–53; Rwandan genocide, 183–185;

Somalia, 165–166; South Africa and, 64; Southern Rhodesia sanctions, 91; Trusteeship Council, 18

United States-Africa Leaders' Summit, 216–217

UNOSOM. *See* United Nations Operation in Somalia

UNTAG. *See* UN Transitional Advisory Group

Uranium, 12–13

US. *See* United States

US Agency for International Development (USAID), 71, 77, 212–214, 216–217, 235–237, 239

"U.S. Foreign Policy for the 1970s" report, by Nixon, 86

"U.S. Interests in Southern Africa" paper, by NSC, 93

US International Development Finance Corporation (USIDFC), 231

US Trade and Development Agency (USTDA), 214

USAID. *See* US Agency for International Development

USIDFC. *See* US International Development Finance Corporation

USTDA. *See* US Trade and Development Agency

Vance, Cyrus Roberts, 115, 120, 122–123, 125–126, 128

Vandenberg, Arthur, 16

Vichy France, 6–8, 12

Vietnam War, 73, 85, 104

Vorster, B. J., 106, 121, 126

War of Eritrean Independence, 117–118

Washington, D.C., African embassies in, 61–62

Watson, Thomas, 129

Webster-Ashburton Treaty of 1842, 2

Weinstein, Warren, 212–213

Welensky, Roy, 66

Wells, Sumner, 7

West African airports, in World War II, 11–12

Western Contact Group, 126–128

White minority rule: African independence and, 63, 107; apartheid regime, in South Africa, 34, 64–65,

90, 94–95, 134, 138, 167–170; in South Africa, 57–58, 97–98; in Southern Africa, 57–59, 63–65, 120–124; in Southern Rhodesia, 57–59, 63–70, 89, 107–108; US and, 57–59, 64–65, 68, 170
Williams, G. Mennen, 54, 57–58, 67
Williams, Haydn, 55
Wilson, Harold, 67–69, 91
Wilson, Woodrow, 2–3
World Bank, 201, 213–214
World Trade Center bombings, 195
World war, African, 192–193
World War II, 2–14, 16, 24–27, 55–56

YALI. *See* Young African Leaders Initiative
Yalta Conference, 13–14, 26
Yoruba, 81
Young, Andrew, 120–121, 124–125, 128
Young African Leaders Initiative (YALI), 217
Yusuf, Mohammed, 220

Zaire, 71, 77–80, 101–102, 104, 120, 172; Hutus in, 185–188; Kabila, L. D., insurgency in, 187–189; Katanga province of, 119; Mobutu Sese Seko in, 152–154, 185, 187; refugee camps in, 185–187; Rwanda and, 184–185, 189
Zambia, 12, 67, 69–72
ZANU. *See* Zimbabwe African National Union
ZANU-PF. *See* Zimbabwe African National Union–Patriotic Front
ZAPU. *See* Zimbabwe African Patriotic Union
Zimbabwe, 69, 122, 161
Zimbabwe African National Union (ZANU), 69, 105, 107
Zimbabwe African National Union–Patriotic Front (ZANU-PF), 107, 122
Zimbabwe African Patriotic Union (ZAPU), 69, 107, 122
Zimbabwe-Rhodesia, 123–124, 133

About the Book

Herman Cohen draws on both the documentary record and his years of on-the-ground experience to provide a uniquely comprehensive survey and interpretation of nearly eight decades of US policy toward Africa.

Tracing how this policy has evolved across successive administrations since 1942 (beginning with President Franklin D. Roosevelt's third term in office), Cohen illuminates the debates that have taken place at the highest levels of government; shows how policy toward Africa has been affected over the years by US relations with Europe, the Soviet Union, the Middle East, and most recently China; and points to the increasing reliance of Western economic interests on Africa's natural resources. His deeply informed narrative reveals the roles not only of circumstance and ideology, but also of personalities, in the formulation and implementation of US foreign policy.

Herman J. Cohen was a member of the US Foreign Service for thirty-eight years, posted to embassies in France, the Democratic Republic of the Congo, Uganda, Zambia, and Zimbabwe. He was US ambassador to Senegal and Gambia and served as assistant secretary of state for Africa under President George H. W. Bush. Subsequently, he was senior adviser in the Africa region at the World Bank. He is now president of Cohen and Woods, an international consulting firm.

Related ADST Series Titles

Claudia E. Anyaso, ed., *Fifty Years of U.S. Africa Policy: Reflections of Assistant Secretaries for African Affairs and U.S. Embassy Officials*

Prudence Bushnell, *Terrorism, Betrayal, and Resilience: My Story of the 1998 US Embassy Bombings*

Herman J. Cohen, *Intervening in Africa: Superpower Peacemaking in a Troubled Continent*

———, *The Mind of the African Strongman: Conversations with Dictators, Statesmen, and Father Figures*

Wilson Dizard Sr., *Inventing Public Diplomacy: The Story of the United States Information Agency*

Harriet L. Elam-Thomas, *Diversifying Diplomacy: My Journey from Roxbury to Senegal*

Christopher Goldthwait, *Ambassador to a Small World: Letters from Chad*

Brandon Grove, *Behind Embassy Walls: The Life and Times of an American Diplomat*

Judith M. Heimann, *Paying Calls in Shangri-La: Scenes from a Woman's Life in American Diplomacy*

Dennis C. Jett, *American Ambassadors: The Past, Present, and Future of America's Diplomats*

Jane C. Loeffler, *The Architecture of Diplomacy: Building America's Embassies*

David D. Newsom, *Witness to a Changing World*

Richard B. Parker, *Memoirs of a Foreign Service Arabist*

David Rawson, *Prelude to Genocide: Arusha, Rwanda, and the Failure of Diplomacy*

Raymond F. Smith, *The Craft of Political Analysis for Diplomats*

James W. Spain, *In Those Days: A Diplomat Remembers*

Jean Wilkowski, *Abroad for Her Country: Tales of a Pioneer Woman Ambassador in the U.S. Foreign Service*

For a complete list of series titles, visit http://adst.org/publications.